THE FREEDOM FORMULA

THE FREEDOM FORMULA

DANIEL PAYNE

Copyright © 2025 by Daniel Payne
All rights reserved. No part of this book may be reproduced in any manner whatsoever without written permission except in the case of brief quotations embodied in critical articles and reviews.
First Printing, 2025

CONTENTS

Dedication   vi

1 Introduction: The Invisible Cage   1
2 The Hidden Prison of Over-Management   7
3 The Psychology Behind the Need to Manage   21
4 The True Cost of Managing Everyone Else   38
5 Reclaiming Your Personal Boundaries   53
6 The Art of Strategic Disengagement   70
7 Emotional Detachment with Love   90
8 Rediscovering Your Own Life Vision   110
9 The Time and Energy Reallocation Plan   131
10 Building Your Own Success Systems   152
11 The New Relationship Operating System   175
12 Communication That Empowers Others   199
13 Navigating Resistance and Pushback   225
14 The Daily Practice of Freedom   256
15 Advanced Freedom Strategies   286
16 Living Your Freedom Formula   306

To everyone who has ever felt lost in the maze of other people's needs—may you find your way back to yourself. And to those brave enough to love others by trusting them with their own lives—you are the quiet revolutionaries healing our world, one relationship at a time.

CHAPTER 1

Introduction: The Invisible Cage

There's a particular kind of exhaustion that settles into your bones when you've spent years managing everyone else's life but your own. It's the bone-deep weariness that comes from carrying emotional loads that were never yours to bear, solving problems that weren't yours to solve, and living a life that feels more like a series of crisis interventions than actual living.

If you picked up this book, chances are you know this exhaustion intimately. You might be the person everyone turns to when their world falls apart. The one who gets the panicked phone calls at midnight, who's expected to have all the answers, who somehow became responsible for keeping everyone else's life on track. You might be the parent who can't stop micromanaging their adult children, the manager who hovers over every detail of their team's work, or the friend who's become the unofficial therapist for your entire social circle.

You probably think this makes you caring, responsible, maybe even indispensable. And in many ways, it does. But here's what no one tells you about being the person who manages everyone else's life: while you're busy orchestrating everyone else's happiness and success, your own life quietly slips away, unlived and unexplored.

The Manager's Paradox

I learned this lesson the hard way through my own journey and through working with thousands of people who found themselves trapped in what I call "the management cage." This invisible prison is built from the best of intentions—love, care, responsibility, the desire to help—but it confines us just as surely as iron bars.

The paradox of being everyone's manager is that the more you try to control outcomes for others, the more out of control your own life becomes. The more you focus on fixing everyone else's problems, the more your own dreams and desires fade into the background. The more indispensable you make yourself to others, the more you disappear from your own story.

Sarah's story perfectly illustrates this paradox. When I first met her, she was forty-three years old and hadn't taken a vacation in six years. Not because she couldn't afford it, but because her family "needed" her too much. Her teenage daughter called her multiple times a day for help with everything from homework to friend drama. Her elderly mother expected daily check-ins and frequent problem-solving sessions about her health, finances, and social life. Her husband had somehow become incapable of making decisions about anything more complex than what to have for lunch without consulting her first.

Sarah had become the family's Chief Operating Officer, and like many COOs of dysfunctional organizations, she was working herself to death while everyone else coasted. She came to me not because she wanted to abandon her family, but because she was starting to realize that she had no idea who she was outside of her role as their manager. She couldn't remember the last time she'd had a thought that wasn't about someone else's needs. She'd stopped reading books she enjoyed, given up hobbies that brought her joy, and hadn't pursued any of her own goals in so long that she wasn't sure she had any anymore.

"I feel like I'm disappearing," she told me in our first session. "But every time I try to step back, something falls apart, and I have to jump back in. I don't know how to stop without feeling like I'm abandoning everyone I love."

Sarah's dilemma is the central tension of the management trap: How do you reclaim your own life without feeling like you're betraying everyone who depends on you? How do you stop managing others without stopping caring about them? How do you build boundaries without building walls?

The Cost of Caring Too Much

The management trap affects different people in different ways, but the underlying pattern is always the same: good, caring, responsible people gradually sacrifice their own lives on the altar of other people's needs, comfort, and growth. They become so skilled at anticipating and preventing other people's pain that they forget to pay attention to their own.

This isn't about being a martyr or seeking recognition. Most people caught in the management trap don't even realize what's happening until they're deep in the cycle. It starts innocently enough—helping a friend through a crisis, stepping up when a family member struggles, taking on extra responsibilities at work to support a colleague. These are admirable impulses that reflect the best of human nature.

But somewhere along the way, helping becomes fixing, supporting becomes controlling, and caring becomes carrying. The people in your life stop developing their own problem-solving muscles because you've become their personal problem-solving service. Your identity becomes so intertwined with being needed that you unconsciously sabotage any attempts they make toward independence.

The cost of this pattern extends far beyond your own missed opportunities and unfulfilled dreams, though those costs are significant. When you manage other people's lives, you rob them of the chance to develop resilience, confidence, and self-reliance. You prevent them from experiencing the natural consequences of their choices, which are often the most powerful teachers. You create a dynamic where love becomes conditional on need, where your value in the relationship depends on your usefulness rather than your inherent worth.

Perhaps most tragically, you model for the people you love that this is what caring looks like—that love means sacrificing yourself for others, that being responsible means being responsible for everything and everyone. You teach them that their problems are too big for them to handle, that they're not capable of managing their own lives, that they need someone else to think for them, worry for them, and solve for them.

The Promise of Freedom

This book is not about becoming selfish, uncaring, or irresponsible. It's not about abandoning the people you love or stop contributing to their wellbeing. It's about learning to love and support others in ways that empower rather than enable, that strengthen rather than weaken, that encourage growth rather than dependency.

The freedom formula I'll share with you throughout these pages is deceptively simple: redirect the energy you've been spending managing other people's lives toward building and living your own. But simple doesn't mean easy. Breaking free from the management trap requires courage, patience, and a willingness to tolerate some discomfort—both your own and others'—in service of long-term freedom and authentic relationships.

When you stop managing everyone else's life, several remarkable things happen. First, you discover that most people are far more capable than you've been giving them credit for. When you step back and create space for others to handle their own challenges, they often rise to the occasion in ways that surprise everyone, including themselves.

Second, you begin to remember who you are underneath all the roles you've been playing. You reconnect with interests, dreams, and aspects of your personality that got buried under years of focusing on everyone else's needs. You start to have opinions that aren't about other people's problems and preferences that aren't shaped by other people's limitations.

Third, your relationships improve. I know this seems counterintuitive—how can relationships get better when you're paying less attention to them? But relationships built on mutual independence and respect are infinitely stronger than those built on dependency and management. When people know you love them enough to let them handle their own lives, when they understand that your support comes from choice rather than obligation, the connection deepens in ways that constant management never allows.

Finally, you discover that your greatest contribution to the people you love isn't solving their problems for them—it's showing them what it looks like to live a full, authentic, purpose-driven life. When you reclaim your own story and start living with intention and joy, you give everyone around you permission to do the same.

How to Use This Book

This book is structured as a journey from recognition to transformation to mastery. We'll start by helping you understand exactly how you got trapped in the management cycle and what it's costing you. Then we'll build the foundation skills you need to step back without stepping away—boundaries, disengagement strategies, and emotional detachment techniques.

From there, we'll focus on the positive work of reclaiming your own life: rediscovering your vision, reallocating your time and energy, and building systems for your own success. We'll then explore how to maintain loving, supportive relationships without falling back into management mode, and finally, we'll cover the advanced strategies for making this transformation a permanent part of who you are.

Each chapter builds on the previous one, so I encourage you to read them in order, at least the first time through. The frameworks and exercises are designed to work together, creating a comprehensive system for breaking free from the management trap and building a life of authentic freedom and purpose.

This work isn't just about changing your behavior—it's about fundamentally shifting your understanding of what it means to love, support, and care for others. It's about discovering that the greatest gift you can give the people in your life isn't your constant management and intervention, but your own flourishing, authentic self.

The path to freedom isn't always comfortable, but it's always worth it. Your life is waiting for you to claim it, to live it, to make it your own. The people you love will be better for it, and so will you.

Welcome to your freedom formula.

CHAPTER 2

The Hidden Prison of Over-Management

The alarm clock screamed at 5:30 AM, just as it had every morning for the past three years. But Jennifer wasn't sleeping anyway. She'd been awake since 4:15, mentally rehearsing the conversation she needed to have with her twenty-five-year-old son about his job interview, crafting the perfect email to her team about the project that was falling behind, and worrying about whether her mother had remembered to take her evening medication.

By the time her feet hit the floor, Jennifer had already solved four problems that weren't technically hers to solve, made three decisions for other people, and added six new items to her mental to-do list that would benefit everyone except herself. She didn't recognize this pattern as unusual because it had become her normal. What she didn't realize was that she was living in a prison of her own construction—one built from the best intentions but confining her just as surely as concrete walls.

Jennifer's story illustrates what I've come to call the hidden prison of over-management: a psychological and emotional cage that traps well-meaning, caring people in a cycle of constant vigilance, intervention, and responsibility for other people's lives. Unlike a physical prison, this one comes with praise rather than punishment. Society celebrates the over-manager as dedicated, caring, and responsible. Family members depend on them. Colleagues admire their reliability. Friends seek their wisdom and intervention.

But inside this prison of perpetual responsibility, the over-manager slowly loses touch with their own life, their own dreams, and their own sense of self. They become so skilled at reading other people's needs that they forget how to recognize their own. They become so practiced at solving other people's problems that they stop believing they have the right to focus on their own goals and challenges.

The Exhaustion Epidemic

The first sign that you're living in the hidden prison of over-management is a particular kind of exhaustion that goes far deeper than physical tiredness. This is the exhaustion of carrying emotional and mental loads that were never meant for one person to bear. It's the fatigue that comes from being perpetually "on"—constantly scanning for problems to solve, needs to meet, and crises to prevent.

Dr. Rachel Martinez, a family therapist I've worked with for over a decade, describes this as "hypervigilant caregiving." She explains, "When someone becomes the designated problem-solver in their family or workplace, their nervous system never fully relaxes. They're always in a state of low-level activation, ready to spring into action at the first sign of distress from someone they care about."

This hypervigilant state is extraordinarily draining because it requires the over-manager to hold not just their own emotional and mental experience, but to track, anticipate, and respond to everyone else's as well. Imagine trying to watch twelve different television screens at once, each showing a different drama that you're somehow responsible for directing. This is the mental reality of the chronic over-manager.

Lisa, a marketing executive and mother of three, described her experience this way: "I realized I was mentally carrying the emotional weather forecast for seven different people every day. I knew my husband's stress level about work, my teenage daughter's anxiety about social situations, my son's frustration with his college choices, my mother's loneliness, my best friend's marriage troubles, and my direct reports' various professional challenges. I was monitoring all of these emotional climates constantly, trying to predict storms and prevent disasters. No wonder I felt like I was drowning."

The exhaustion of over-management isn't just about the time and energy spent on other people's problems. It's also about the constant low-level anxiety that comes from feeling responsible for outcomes you can't actually control. When you've appointed yourself as the manager of other people's lives, their failures become your failures, their pain becomes your emergency, and their choices become your responsibility.

This creates what psychologists call "learned helplessness" in reverse. Instead of learning that you can't control outcomes and therefore giving up, the over-manager becomes convinced that they can and must control outcomes, leading to an escalating cycle of effort and intervention that becomes increasingly frantic and less effective over time.

Common Manifestations of the Management Prison

The hidden prison of over-management manifests differently in different contexts, but the underlying pattern remains consistent: taking responsibility for things that aren't yours to manage, trying to control outcomes that aren't yours to control, and sacrificing your own growth and wellbeing in service of managing others.

In parenting, over-management often looks like helicopter parenting on steroids. It's the mother who still does her adult child's laundry not because they can't do it themselves, but because she's convinced they won't do it "right." It's the father who calls his daughter's college professors to discuss her grades, or the parent who completes their teenager's college applications because they're "just helping."

These parents genuinely believe they're showing love through their management, but they're actually communicating a devastating message: "I don't believe you're capable of handling your own life." They're so focused on protecting their children from failure, disappointment, and natural consequences that they rob them of the very experiences that build resilience, confidence, and competence.

Maria, a successful attorney and mother of two college-age children, shared her wake-up call: "I realized I was still making doctor's appointments for my twenty-year-old son. Not because he was incapable, but because I was convinced that if I didn't manage it, something terrible would happen to his health. When I finally asked him why he never scheduled his own appointments, he said, 'Because you always do it, and I figured you didn't trust me to do it right.' That's when I understood that my 'help' was actually handicapping him."

In the workplace, over-management manifests as micromanagement, but with a twist of emotional investment that makes it even more problematic. The over-managing boss doesn't just want to control work processes; they feel personally responsible for their team members' professional development, job satisfaction, and even personal wellbeing. They're the manager who stays late to fix their employee's mistakes instead of allowing natural consequences to teach the lesson, or who takes on additional work rather than risk their team experiencing the discomfort of being stretched.

David, a senior director at a technology company, described his pattern: "I told myself I was being a good leader by protecting my team from upper management pressure, by buffering them from difficult clients, by making sure they never felt overwhelmed. But what I was really doing was creating a team of people who couldn't function without me. They stopped taking initiative because they knew I would handle anything challenging. They stopped developing problem-solving skills because I was always there to solve the problems for them."

In friendships and romantic relationships, over-management often disguises itself as being supportive, caring, or emotionally available. It's the friend who becomes the unpaid therapist for their entire social circle, absorbing everyone's problems and dispensing advice whether it's requested or not. It's the romantic partner who can't bear to see their loved one struggle, so they constantly intervene to smooth the path, eliminate obstacles, and prevent their partner from experiencing the natural ups and downs of life.

Jennifer, whose morning routine we explored earlier, realized that her twenty-year marriage had become a series of management transactions. "I scheduled his doctor's appointments, managed his relationship with his difficult mother, reminded him about important dates, and even chose his clothes for important meetings. I thought I was being a good wife, but I was actually treating him like he was incompetent. Worse, over time, he started believing it too."

The Illusion of Control Versus Actual Influence

At the heart of the over-management prison lies a fundamental misunderstanding about the difference between control and influence. Over-managers operate under the illusion that they can control outcomes in other people's lives through their vigilance, intervention, and management. This illusion is seductive because sometimes it appears to work. The child whose homework you complete gets good grades. The employee whose work you fix doesn't get criticized. The friend whose problems you solve feels grateful and supported.

But this apparent success masks a deeper truth: you cannot actually control other people's choices, growth, or life outcomes. You can influence them, certainly. You can provide information, support, encouragement, and resources. But the moment you cross the line from influence to control, you enter territory that isn't really yours to inhabit.

The distinction between control and influence is crucial because it determines whether your actions strengthen or weaken the people you care about. Influence respects the other person's autonomy and capacity for growth. It offers support while maintaining clear boundaries about who is responsible for what. Control, on the other hand, assumes that the other person isn't capable of managing their own life and that your intervention is necessary for their wellbeing.

Dr. Susan Chen, a researcher who studies family dynamics, has found that people who receive high levels of management from well-meaning family members often develop what she calls "learned dependency." She explains, "When someone consistently steps in to solve your problems, prevent your mistakes, and manage your challenges, you gradually lose confidence in your own ability to handle life's difficulties. You start to believe that you need someone else to think for you, worry for you, and make decisions for you."

This learned dependency creates a vicious cycle. The more you manage someone else's life, the more dependent they become on your management. The more dependent they become, the more convinced you are that they need your management. What started as helping becomes enabling, and what started as love becomes a prison for both parties.

The tragedy of this dynamic is that it often destroys the very thing it's trying to preserve. Parents who over-manage their children in the name of love often end up with adult children who resent their involvement and feel incompetent to handle their own lives. Managers who over-manage their teams in the name of support often end up with employees who lack initiative and avoid responsibility. Friends who over-manage their relationships in the name of caring often end up isolated and exhausted, wondering why everyone seems to take advantage of their generosity.

Sarah's Story: From Crisis Manager to Personal Freedom

Sarah's transformation illustrates both the depth of the over-management trap and the possibility of breaking free. When I first met Sarah, she was trapped in what she called "crisis management mode." Her life had become a series of emergency responses to other people's problems, and she had no space or energy left for her own growth, interests, or dreams.

Sarah's pattern had started innocently enough. As the oldest of four children in a chaotic household, she had learned early that stepping up to handle problems earned praise and reduced family stress. She became the child who mediated her parents' fights, who helped her younger siblings with homework, who anticipated needs and prevented crises before they occurred.

This pattern followed her into adulthood. She chose a career in human resources partly because it allowed her to continue her role as the problem-solver and helper. She married a man who appreciated her take-charge attitude and gradually came to depend on her to manage most aspects of their shared life. When they had children, Sarah naturally became the primary manager of not just childcare logistics, but of her children's emotional wellbeing, academic success, and social development.

By the time Sarah reached her forties, she was managing the lives of approximately nine people on a daily basis: her husband, her three children, her elderly parents, her mother-in-law, and two siblings who regularly called her for advice and crisis intervention. She had become the family's emotional headquarters, the person everyone called when they needed something handled, worried about, or solved.

"I didn't even realize what was happening," Sarah told me. "I just gradually became the person who took care of everything and everyone. People would say things like 'Sarah's so organized' or 'Sarah always knows what to do,' and I felt proud of that. But somewhere along the way, I stopped having my own life. I was living everyone else's life, just not my own."

Sarah's wake-up call came during what should have been a celebration. Her youngest child had just graduated from high school, and she had been looking forward to having more time for herself. But instead of feeling free, she felt completely lost. "I realized I had no idea who I was when I wasn't managing someone else's crisis," she said. "I didn't know what I wanted to do with my time, what my interests were, or what would make me happy. I had been so busy being everything to everyone else that I had completely lost track of myself."

The turning point came when Sarah's daughter called her from college, sobbing because she had received a C on an important paper. Sarah's immediate impulse was to call the professor, to find out what had gone wrong, to figure out how to fix it. But something made her pause. Instead of springing into action, she asked her daughter, "What do you think you want to do about this?"

The question surprised both of them. Sarah's daughter was so accustomed to her mother taking charge of problems that she had never been asked to think through a solution herself. But after a few minutes of conversation, she came up with a plan: she would email the professor to ask for feedback, revise the paper using that feedback, and use the experience to improve her writing for future assignments.

"It was such a simple thing," Sarah reflected, "but it was revolutionary for both of us. My daughter solved her own problem, and she felt proud and capable afterward. And I realized that by always stepping in to fix things, I had been robbing her of the chance to develop her own problem-solving skills and confidence."

This experience became the catalyst for Sarah's transformation. She began to systematically examine all the ways she was managing other people's lives and started experimenting with stepping back. The process wasn't easy—both Sarah and her family members experienced discomfort as they adjusted to new roles and responsibilities. But gradually, something remarkable happened.

Sarah's husband started taking initiative in areas he had previously left entirely to her. Her children became more resourceful and confident in handling their own challenges. Her elderly parents, rather than becoming helpless when Sarah stepped back from constant management, actually became more engaged and proactive in managing their own care.

Most importantly, Sarah began to rediscover herself. She remembered her love of photography, which she had abandoned years earlier. She started taking classes, joining photography groups, and eventually began selling her work. She developed friendships that weren't based on her role as helper and advisor, but on shared interests and mutual support.

"The most surprising thing," Sarah said, "was how much better my relationships became when I stopped managing everyone. When my children knew I trusted them to handle their own lives, they started sharing more with me—not because they needed me to fix things, but because they wanted my perspective and support. When my husband knew I wasn't going to take over every household task, he started taking more ownership and actually became more engaged in our family life."

The Energy Leak Audit

One of the most powerful tools for recognizing the extent of your over-management patterns is what I call the Energy Leak Audit. This process helps you identify all the ways your energy is flowing toward managing other people's lives instead of building your own.

For one week, carry a small notebook or use your phone to track every time you find yourself thinking about, worrying about, or taking action on someone else's problem or responsibility. Don't judge these instances or try to change them yet—simply notice and record them.

Include mental energy as well as physical energy. Note when you're lying awake at night worried about your adult child's job situation, when you're distracted at work because you're thinking about your mother's health, when you're researching solutions to your friend's relationship problems, or when you're feeling anxious about your spouse's work stress.

At the end of the week, review your notes and categorize your energy leaks. How much mental and emotional energy are you spending on your children's problems versus their joys and successes? How much time are you devoting to solving other people's challenges versus pursuing your own goals? How often are you reacting to other people's crises versus creating proactive momentum in your own life?

Most people who complete this audit are shocked by what they discover. Janet, a college professor and mother of two, found that she was spending approximately four hours a day either actively managing other people's problems or mentally rehearsing solutions to their challenges. "I was more focused on my twenty-three-year-old son's career development than my own," she realized. "I knew more about his job interviews, networking opportunities, and professional goals than I knew about my own research interests or career aspirations."

The Energy Leak Audit reveals patterns that are often invisible to us because they've become so habitual. We don't realize we're constantly monitoring other people's emotional states, anticipating their needs, or holding space for their problems until we start paying attention. The audit helps you see the full scope of your over-management patterns and understand why you might be feeling drained, resentful, or disconnected from your own life.

The Control Versus Influence Matrix

Understanding the difference between control and influence is crucial for breaking free from the over-management prison, but it can be challenging to distinguish between them in real-world situations. The Control Versus Influence Matrix provides a framework for evaluating your actions and determining whether you're operating from a place of healthy influence or problematic control.

The matrix has four quadrants, each representing a different combination of high or low control attempts and high or low actual influence. The goal is to operate primarily from the high influence, low control quadrant—where you have a genuine positive impact on others while respecting their autonomy and responsibility for their own lives.

High Control, Low Influence represents the most problematic quadrant. This is where you're constantly trying to manage and control outcomes in other people's lives, but your efforts actually have little positive impact or may even be counterproductive. This includes behaviors like doing your adult child's laundry because you don't trust them to do it properly, calling your employee's clients to fix problems they should handle themselves, or giving unsolicited advice to friends about their relationships.

High Control, High Influence might seem positive because you're having an impact, but it's ultimately problematic because it creates dependency and resentment. This quadrant includes behaviors like consistently solving problems for others (so they never develop their own problem-solving skills), making decisions for capable adults, or using your competence to take over tasks that others should be learning to handle themselves.

Low Control, Low Influence represents disengagement or abdication of appropriate responsibility. This isn't the goal—you don't want to stop caring about the people in your life or withdraw your support entirely. However, this quadrant can be a temporary stopping point as you learn to distinguish between appropriate and inappropriate involvement.

Low Control, High Influence is the sweet spot. This is where you have a genuine positive impact on others while respecting their autonomy and encouraging their growth. This includes behaviors like asking thoughtful questions that help others think through their own solutions, offering support and resources while letting others decide how to use them, sharing your perspective when asked while acknowledging that others must make their own decisions, and modeling healthy behavior rather than trying to control others' choices.

Moving from the control quadrants to the influence quadrant requires a fundamental shift in your understanding of what it means to help and support others. Instead of trying to prevent people from experiencing challenges, you help them develop the skills and resilience to handle challenges effectively. Instead of solving problems for them, you support them in solving their own problems. Instead of making decisions for them, you help them gather information and think through options so they can make better decisions themselves.

The Management Addiction Scale

Recognizing over-management patterns can be challenging because they often develop gradually and are reinforced by positive feedback from others. The Management Addiction Scale is a self-assessment tool that helps you evaluate the extent to which you've become trapped in the over-management prison.

Consider how frequently you experience each of the following patterns. Do you find yourself feeling responsible for other people's emotions, working harder to solve their problems than they are, or feeling anxious when you can't fix something for someone you care about? Do you frequently give advice that isn't requested, take on tasks that others could handle themselves, or feel guilty when you focus on your own needs instead of others' needs?

The scale also explores the emotional components of over-management. Do you feel more valuable when people need your help? Do you worry that people won't love you if you stop managing their lives? Do you feel guilty or selfish when you set boundaries around what you will and won't do for others?

Physical and mental symptoms are also important indicators. Do you frequently feel exhausted despite not having done anything particularly strenuous? Do you have trouble sleeping because you're worried about other people's problems? Do you find it difficult to relax because you're always mentally managing someone else's situation?

The assessment also examines the impact on your own life and goals. Have you postponed your own dreams or goals to focus on helping others achieve theirs? Do you know more about other people's interests and aspirations than you do about your own? Do you feel like you've lost touch with who you are outside of your helping and managing roles?

High scores on this assessment don't mean you're a bad person or that caring about others is wrong. They simply indicate that you've crossed the line from healthy support into problematic over-management. The good news is that recognizing these patterns is the first step toward changing them.

Breaking Free from the Hidden Prison

Understanding that you're trapped in the hidden prison of over-management can initially feel overwhelming. You might wonder how you'll maintain your relationships if you stop managing everyone's lives, or worry that people will see you as selfish if you start focusing on your own growth and goals.

These concerns are natural and valid, but they're based on false premises about what it means to love and support others. Breaking free from over-management doesn't mean becoming uncaring or uninvolved. It means learning to care in ways that strengthen rather than weaken the people you love, that encourage their growth rather than stunting it, and that create genuine interdependence rather than unhealthy dependency.

The process begins with recognition—developing awareness of your over-management patterns and understanding their costs, both to you and to the people you're trying to help. This awareness creates space for choice. Once you can see the pattern, you can begin to interrupt it and choose different responses.

The journey from the hidden prison of over-management to authentic freedom requires courage, patience, and self-compassion. It means tolerating the discomfort of watching others struggle without immediately jumping in to fix things. It means dealing with guilt and anxiety as you shift from managing others to managing your own life. It means having faith that the people you love are more capable than your management has allowed them to demonstrate.

But the rewards of this journey are extraordinary. When you step out of the prison of over-management, you discover not only your own freedom but the capacity to offer others something far more valuable than your management: your authentic self, your own growth and vitality, and the powerful modeling of what it looks like to live a life of purpose and joy.

The hidden prison of over-management might feel safe because it's familiar, but it's ultimately a cage that confines everyone involved. The key to that cage is in your hands, and the door is waiting to be opened. Your life—your real, authentic, purposeful life—is waiting for you on the other side.

CHAPTER 3

The Psychology Behind the Need to Manage

Rebecca was eight years old when she learned that her emotional state could determine whether her family had a good day or a bad day. It was a Tuesday morning, and she had woken up feeling excited about a class field trip. But when she bounded into the kitchen for breakfast, she found her mother sitting at the table with tears streaming down her face and her father standing at the counter with his jaw clenched in frustration.

"What's wrong?" Rebecca asked, her excitement immediately replaced by a familiar knot of anxiety in her stomach.

"Nothing, sweetheart," her mother said, quickly wiping her eyes. "Mommy's just having a hard morning."

But Rebecca had learned to read between the lines. Her parents had been fighting again, probably about money or her father's drinking, and now the whole house felt heavy with unexpressed anger and sadness. She watched her mother try to pull herself together to make breakfast, noticed her father's silence as he grabbed his coffee and headed for the door, and felt the weight of responsibility settle on her young shoulders.

Without fully understanding what she was doing, Rebecca shifted into caretaker mode. She hugged her mother extra tight, told her a silly joke that made her smile, and spent the morning being exceptionally well-behaved and helpful. By the time she left for school, the tension in the house had eased slightly, and her mother seemed more stable.

"You're such a good girl," her mother said, giving her a grateful hug. "I don't know what I'd do without you."

Those words planted a seed that would shape Rebecca's entire approach to relationships for the next thirty years. She learned that her value lay in her ability to manage other people's emotional states, that love was earned through caretaking, and that she was responsible not just for her own feelings but for everyone else's as well.

Rebecca's story illustrates one of the most common origins of the over-management pattern: childhood programming that teaches us we're responsible for other people's emotional wellbeing. But this is just one of several psychological roots that can lead to a lifetime of managing everyone else's life instead of living your own. Understanding these roots is crucial because you can't truly break free from a pattern until you understand why it developed in the first place.

Childhood Programming: The Origin Stories of Over-Management

The need to manage others almost always begins in childhood, when we develop our core beliefs about love, responsibility, and our role in other people's lives. These beliefs are rarely formed through explicit teaching. Instead, they're absorbed through hundreds of small interactions that teach us what behaviors earn love, approval, and safety in our family system.

Children are natural observers and adapters. They instinctively learn what makes the adults in their lives happy, calm, or upset, and they adjust their behavior accordingly. This is a normal and healthy part of development—children need to understand the emotional landscape of their family in order to navigate it successfully. But in some family systems, children learn that they're not just responsible for adapting to the emotional climate, but for managing and controlling it.

This happens in several different ways. In families where one or both parents struggle with emotional regulation, children often become emotion managers by default. They learn to monitor their parents' moods, anticipate their needs, and intervene to prevent emotional storms. These children become hypervigilant to signs of distress in others and develop an inflated sense of responsibility for fixing whatever is wrong.

Michael remembers walking on eggshells around his father, who had unpredictable angry outbursts. "I became an expert at reading his mood from the way he walked in the door," Michael recalls. "If he seemed stressed, I would immediately start thinking about what I could do to help him feel better. I'd offer to get him a drink, I'd make sure my little sister was quiet, I'd even do extra chores without being asked. I thought it was my job to keep him calm."

In families dealing with addiction, mental illness, or other chronic stressors, children often step into premature caretaking roles. They become the family stabilizers, the ones who hold everything together when the adults can't. These children learn that their own needs are secondary to managing the family crisis, and they develop an identity built around being helpful, responsible, and indispensable.

Another common origin story involves children who are praised and valued primarily for their helpfulness and emotional maturity. These are the children who are told they're "wise beyond their years," who are treated as confidants for adult problems, who are given responsibilities that should belong to adults. While this praise feels good in the moment, it teaches children that their worth is conditional on their ability to take care of others.

Lisa was the oldest of five children in a chaotic household where her mother was overwhelmed and her father was frequently absent for work. "I became like a second mother to my younger siblings," she remembers. "I helped with homework, mediated fights, and even attended parent-teacher conferences when my mom couldn't make it. Everyone always told me how mature and responsible I was, and I was proud of that. But I also learned that my value in the family came from what I could do for others, not from who I was as a person."

Parentification—the process by which children are forced into adult roles prematurely—creates a deep psychological pattern that can persist throughout life. Children who are parentified learn that love and approval come through caretaking, that they're responsible for outcomes they can't actually control, and that their own needs are less important than everyone else's.

But over-management patterns don't only develop in obviously dysfunctional families. They can also emerge in families that appear healthy but have subtle dynamics that teach children to over-function. This might include families where conflict is avoided at all costs, where children are expected to regulate their parents' anxiety by being perfect, or where love is expressed primarily through doing things for others rather than through emotional intimacy.

The key insight is that children who become over-managers aren't responding to explicit requests to take care of everyone else. They're responding to implicit family rules about how love works, what makes someone valuable, and who is responsible for maintaining emotional equilibrium. These rules are rarely spoken aloud, but they're communicated through countless daily interactions that shape a child's understanding of their role in relationships.

Fear-Based Motivations: What We're Really Trying to Control

While childhood programming plants the seeds of over-management, fear is what keeps the pattern alive in adult relationships. Understanding the specific fears that drive your need to manage others is crucial because these fears often operate below the level of conscious awareness, making choices for you before you even realize you have a choice.

The most fundamental fear underlying over-management is the fear of loss. When you believe that your value in relationships depends on your usefulness, any reduction in your management activities feels like a threat to your connection with others. This fear whispers dangerous lies: "If you stop fixing their problems, they won't need you anymore. If you're not constantly helpful, they'll find someone else who is. If you focus on yourself instead of them, they'll think you're selfish and withdraw their love."

This fear of abandonment drives people to make themselves indispensable through their management and caretaking. They unconsciously create situations where others depend on their intervention, problem-solving, and emotional regulation because dependency feels like insurance against abandonment. The more someone needs you, the logic goes, the less likely they are to leave you.

But this strategy backfires in several ways. First, relationships built on dependency rather than genuine connection are inherently unstable and resentful. Second, the constant effort required to maintain your indispensable status is exhausting and unsustainable. Third, people eventually rebel against being managed, no matter how well-intentioned the management might be.

Another core fear is the fear of other people's pain or failure. Overmanagers often have difficulty tolerating distress in others, especially people they love. They jump in to fix, solve, and prevent not because others can't handle their own challenges, but because witnessing struggle feels unbearable.

This intolerance for others' discomfort often stems from childhood experiences where someone's pain felt dangerous or overwhelming. Children who grew up with depressed, anxious, or emotionally volatile parents often develop an oversensitivity to signs of distress in others. They learned early that someone else's emotional pain could destabilize their entire world, so they became experts at preventing, managing, and soothing distress before it could spiral out of control.

Janet, a social worker and mother of three, recognized this pattern in herself: "I realized I couldn't stand to see my children struggle with anything. If my daughter was upset about a friendship issue, I immediately wanted to call the other child's mother to fix it. If my son was having trouble with homework, I would essentially do it for him rather than let him figure it out. I told myself I was being supportive, but really I was just trying to eliminate their discomfort because their distress made me so anxious."

The fear of being judged as uncaring or irresponsible also drives many over-management patterns. In a culture that often equates love with doing, many people worry that stepping back from constant intervention will be seen as selfish, lazy, or uncaring. This is particularly challenging for women, who are often socialized to believe that their worth is measured by their ability to anticipate and meet others' needs.

This fear of judgment creates a vicious cycle. The more you manage others to prove your caring, the more others come to expect and depend on your management. The more they depend on your management, the more guilty and irresponsible you feel when you consider stepping back. The more guilty you feel, the more you manage to alleviate the guilt.

Perhaps the deepest fear underlying over-management is the fear of your own powerlessness. When you focus on managing others, you avoid confronting the areas of your own life where you feel helpless, stuck, or uncertain. It's often easier to solve someone else's career problems than to face your own professional dissatisfaction. It's more comfortable to manage your spouse's health issues than to address your own. It's less scary to worry about your adult child's finances than to examine your own relationship with money.

Over-management becomes a sophisticated form of avoidance—a way of staying busy with other people's lives so you don't have to face the challenging work of living your own. This avoidance is often unconscious, but it serves a protective function. As long as you're focused on fixing everyone else, you don't have to acknowledge the places where you feel powerless to create change in your own life.

The Helper's High and Codependency Patterns

The over-management pattern is often reinforced by genuine biochemical rewards that make it difficult to recognize as problematic. When you help someone else, your brain releases endorphins, dopamine, and oxytocin—the same chemicals associated with other pleasurable experiences. This "helper's high" creates a positive feedback loop that can become addictive.

The problem arises when helping becomes the primary way you experience meaning, connection, and self-worth. When your brain learns to associate your value with the neurochemical reward of helping others, you unconsciously seek out opportunities to fix, solve, and manage. You begin to need other people to have problems so you can feel good about yourself.

This creates what psychologists call "codependency"—a relationship dynamic where your emotional wellbeing becomes entirely dependent on your ability to manage someone else's life. In codependent relationships, both parties lose their individual identity and become locked in a dance where one person over-functions while the other under-functions.

The over-functioning partner (the codependent) takes responsibility for most decisions, emotions, and outcomes in the relationship. They monitor their partner's moods, anticipate their needs, and work harder to solve their partner's problems than their partner does. The under-functioning partner gradually gives up more and more responsibility, learning that someone else will handle whatever they don't.

This pattern can develop in any type of relationship—romantic partnerships, parent-child relationships, friendships, or professional relationships. The key characteristic is that one person's identity becomes organized around managing the other person's life, while the other person's identity becomes organized around being managed.

Dr. Melody Beattie, who pioneered much of the research on codependency, describes it as "a condition characterized by preoccupation and extreme dependence on another person or relationship." But codependency isn't really about the other person—it's about using the other person's problems as a way to avoid dealing with your own life and challenges.

The insidious nature of codependent over-management is that it feels like love. The codependent person genuinely believes they're showing care and support through their constant intervention and management. They point to all the ways they've helped, all the problems they've solved, all the crises they've prevented, as evidence of their love and dedication.

But true love respects the other person's autonomy and capacity for growth. True love supports without taking over, cares without controlling, and helps without creating dependency. Codependent management, no matter how well-intentioned, ultimately infantilizes the other person and prevents them from developing their own strength, resilience, and problem-solving abilities.

The helper's high also makes it difficult to recognize when helping has crossed the line into harmful enabling. The good feeling you get from solving someone's problem can blind you to the fact that your solution prevented them from learning to solve it themselves. The gratitude you receive for your intervention can mask the reality that your intervention created more dependency rather than more capability.

Breaking free from the helper's high requires developing other sources of meaning, connection, and self-worth that don't depend on other people having problems for you to solve. It means learning to tolerate the discomfort of not being needed, not being the hero, not being the one with all the answers. It means finding ways to feel valuable that don't require anyone else to be struggling or dependent.

Cultural and Gender Conditioning Around Caretaking

The tendency toward over-management isn't just a personal psychological pattern—it's often reinforced by cultural messages about what it means to be a good person, particularly for women. Many cultures teach that caring for others is not just admirable but obligatory, that selflessness is the highest virtue, and that focusing on your own needs and goals is inherently selfish.

These cultural messages are particularly strong around gender roles. Women are often socialized from birth to be attuned to others' needs, to prioritize relationships over individual achievement, and to measure their worth by their ability to support and nurture others. They're taught that a good mother anticipates and meets her children's every need, that a good wife manages her husband's comfort and success, and that a good friend is always available to listen, advise, and help.

This conditioning goes far beyond explicit teaching. It's embedded in the stories we tell about heroic women (who sacrifice everything for others), in the way we praise girls for being helpful and boys for being independent, and in the subtle messages that suggest women's natural role is to manage the emotional and practical lives of everyone around them.

Men, while less likely to be explicitly trained as caretakers, can develop over-management patterns in different ways. They might be conditioned to believe that their worth lies in their ability to solve problems and provide for others. They might feel pressure to be the family protector, the one who prevents bad things from happening, the one who has all the answers. This can lead to patterns of over-management that focus more on practical problem-solving and less on emotional caretaking, but the underlying dynamic is the same.

The cultural glorification of self-sacrifice makes it particularly difficult to recognize over-management as problematic. When society consistently praises people who "put others first," who are "always there for everyone," and who "never think of themselves," it becomes easy to mistake over-management for virtue.

Religious and spiritual traditions can sometimes reinforce these patterns by teaching that selflessness is a spiritual ideal and that focusing on your own growth and happiness is somehow less evolved or enlightened. While these traditions often contain profound wisdom about the interconnected nature of life, they can be misinterpreted in ways that support unhealthy patterns of over-functioning and self-sacrifice.

The challenge is learning to distinguish between healthy interdependence and unhealthy codependence, between genuine service and compulsive caretaking, between appropriate responsibility and inappropriate over-functioning. This requires developing a more nuanced understanding of what it means to care for others in ways that actually serve their highest good rather than just making you feel needed and valuable.

The Anxiety-Control Cycle: How Fear Drives Over-Management

At the heart of most over-management patterns lies a fundamental misunderstanding about the relationship between control and anxiety. Most over-managers believe that if they can just control enough variables, anticipate enough problems, and manage enough outcomes, they can eliminate anxiety and create safety for themselves and the people they love.

This belief creates what I call the anxiety-control cycle: anxiety about potential problems leads to increased efforts to control outcomes, which temporarily reduces anxiety but ultimately creates more problems to be anxious about, which leads to even more intense efforts to control, and so on.

The cycle typically begins with hypervigilance—a state of constant alertness to potential problems, threats, or needs. The over-manager's nervous system is always scanning for signs that someone they care about might be struggling, that something might go wrong, that intervention might be needed. This hypervigilant state is exhausting, but it feels necessary because the over-manager believes that constant monitoring is the only way to prevent disaster.

When the hypervigilant monitoring identifies a potential problem, anxiety spikes, and the over-manager feels compelled to take action.

This might involve giving advice, making a phone call, solving a problem, or otherwise intervening in the situation. The intervention temporarily reduces anxiety because it creates the illusion that the problem has been handled or prevented.

But this temporary relief comes at a cost. First, the intervention often prevents the other person from developing their own problem-solving skills, which means they're more likely to need intervention in the future. Second, the over-manager's nervous system learns that the only way to manage anxiety is through control and intervention, which strengthens the compulsive nature of the pattern. Third, the intervention often creates new problems or complications that require additional management.

The anxiety-control cycle becomes self-perpetuating because each intervention confirms the over-manager's belief that their vigilance and control are necessary. When problems are prevented or solved through intervention, the over-manager concludes that the intervention was essential, not recognizing that many of those problems would have been solved naturally or that the intervention may have prevented important learning and growth.

Sarah, whose story we explored in the previous chapter, described her anxiety-control cycle this way: "I was constantly worried about my teenage son's grades, so I checked his assignments online every day and reminded him about due dates. When he did well on a test, I felt relieved and told myself that my monitoring was working. When he struggled with an assignment, I felt anxious and increased my involvement. What I didn't realize was that my constant checking was actually making him less responsible for his own academic success, not more."

Breaking the anxiety-control cycle requires learning to tolerate anxiety without immediately trying to control it away. This means developing the capacity to feel worried about someone you love without immediately jumping in to fix whatever you're worried about. It means learning to distinguish between problems that actually require your intervention and problems that only require your attention and support.

The paradox of the anxiety-control cycle is that the more you try to control outcomes in other people's lives, the more out of control your own life becomes. The more you focus on preventing others from experiencing difficulty, the more difficulty you create for yourself. The more you try to manage everyone else's anxiety, the more anxious you become.

Learning to interrupt this cycle is one of the most important skills you can develop in breaking free from the over-management trap. It requires developing what psychologists call "distress tolerance"—the ability to experience uncomfortable emotions without immediately acting to make them go away. It means learning to sit with uncertainty, to accept that you can't control most outcomes, and to trust that most people are more capable of handling their own lives than your anxiety wants you to believe.

The Fear Inventory Worksheet

One of the most powerful tools for understanding your personal over-management patterns is conducting a thorough fear inventory. This process involves identifying the specific fears that drive your need to manage others and examining how those fears might be influencing your behavior in ways you haven't fully recognized.

Begin by choosing one relationship where you tend to over-manage. This might be a relationship with your adult child, your spouse, a friend, or a colleague. Once you've identified the relationship, spend some time reflecting on what you're most afraid would happen if you stopped managing aspects of this person's life.

Write down every fear that comes to mind, no matter how irrational or unlikely it might seem. Include fears about what might happen to the other person, fears about what might happen to your relationship, and fears about how you might feel or be perceived. Don't edit or judge these fears—simply allow yourself to acknowledge them fully.

Common fears that emerge during this process include the fear that the other person will make terrible decisions without your guidance, that they'll experience pain or failure that you could have prevented, that they'll stop loving or needing you if you're not constantly helpful, that others will judge you as uncaring or irresponsible, and that you'll feel guilty or anxious if you're not actively involved in solving their problems.

Once you've identified your fears, examine each one more closely. Ask yourself: Is this fear based on evidence or assumption? Has this terrible outcome actually happened when you've stepped back in the past, or are you imagining worst-case scenarios? What would you tell a friend who expressed this same fear about their relationship?

Many people discover that their fears are based more on anxiety than on reality. They're afraid their adult child will become homeless if they stop giving financial advice, but their adult child has never actually been homeless and has successfully managed money in other areas of their life. They're afraid their spouse will feel unloved if they stop managing his schedule, but their spouse has never actually expressed feeling unloved when they've been less involved.

The fear inventory also helps you recognize how your fears might be creating the very outcomes you're trying to prevent. If you're afraid your teenager won't develop responsibility without constant supervision, your constant supervision prevents them from developing responsibility. If you're afraid your friend will make bad decisions without your advice, your constant advice-giving prevents them from developing their own decision-making skills.

This doesn't mean your fears are completely unfounded or that stepping back from over-management is risk-free. There may be some temporary difficulty or adjustment as people learn to handle more responsibility for their own lives. But the fear inventory helps you distinguish between realistic concerns that might require some planning or gradual change, and catastrophic fears that are keeping you trapped in patterns that aren't serving anyone.

The Responsibility Reality Check

Another crucial tool for understanding the psychology behind overmanagement is what I call the Responsibility Reality Check. This exercise helps you distinguish between responsibilities that genuinely belong to you and responsibilities that you've assumed but that actually belong to someone else.

Create three columns on a piece of paper. In the first column, list all the responsibilities you currently carry related to other people's lives. Include both practical responsibilities (like managing someone's schedule or handling their paperwork) and emotional responsibilities (like monitoring their mood or worrying about their problems).

In the second column, write whose responsibility each item actually belongs to from an objective perspective. If you were advising a friend who was carrying these same responsibilities, whose job would you say each one really is?

In the third column, note how you would feel if you stopped carrying each responsibility. Would you feel guilty, anxious, relieved, scared? What would you imagine others would think or feel?

This exercise often reveals significant discrepancies between the responsibilities people carry and the responsibilities that actually belong to them. Parents discover they're managing college applications for their eighteen-year-old children. Spouses realize they're handling their partner's relationship with their own parents. Friends recognize they're taking more responsibility for their friend's career decisions than their friend is.

The Responsibility Reality Check isn't about abruptly dropping all responsibilities that don't technically belong to you. Some responsibilities might need to be transitioned gradually, and some might be appropriate to maintain by mutual agreement. The goal is to create awareness about what you're carrying and to make conscious choices about what you want to continue carrying rather than unconsciously assuming responsibility for things that aren't really yours to manage.

This exercise also helps you recognize the difference between taking appropriate responsibility for your own actions and choices, and taking inappropriate responsibility for other people's actions and choices. You're responsible for your own words, behavior, emotions, and decisions. You're not responsible for how other people respond to your words and behavior, for managing their emotions, or for ensuring they make good decisions.

Understanding this distinction is crucial because over-managers often have an inflated sense of responsibility that extends far beyond what they can actually control. They feel responsible for their adult child's happiness, their spouse's career success, their friend's relationship problems, or their colleague's job performance. This inflated responsibility creates enormous pressure and often leads to resentment when their efforts to control these outcomes inevitably fail.

The responsibility reality check helps you right-size your sense of responsibility and recognize that releasing inappropriate responsibilities isn't selfish—it's actually a gift to the people you love. When you stop taking responsibility for things that belong to them, you give them the opportunity to develop their own competence, confidence, and sense of agency.

Transforming Fear into Freedom

Understanding the psychology behind your need to manage others is the first step toward transformation, but understanding alone isn't enough. The fears, conditioning, and patterns that drive over-management are deeply ingrained and often feel like essential parts of your identity. Changing them requires not just intellectual understanding but emotional courage and practical skills.

The good news is that the same psychological mechanisms that created your over-management patterns can be redirected toward creating healthy, empowering relationships and a fulfilling personal life. The energy you've been using to monitor, worry about, and manage others can be channeled toward your own growth, goals, and dreams. The caring and attention you've been giving to everyone else's problems can be turned toward creating solutions in your own life.

The fears that drive over-management often contain important information about your own unmet needs and unlived life. The fear of not being needed might be pointing toward a need to develop your own sense of worth and purpose independent of others. The fear of others' pain might be highlighting your own unprocessed pain that needs attention and healing. The fear of being judged as selfish might be revealing your own need to develop a healthier relationship with self-care and personal boundaries.

Transforming these fears doesn't mean eliminating them entirely—some level of concern for the people you love is natural and healthy. But it does mean learning to hold these fears more lightly, to question their assumptions, and to make choices based on what truly serves everyone's highest good rather than what temporarily reduces your anxiety.

The journey from fear-based management to love-based influence requires developing new skills, new perspectives, and new sources of meaning and connection. It means learning to trust in other people's capacity for growth, to tolerate uncertainty about outcomes you can't control, and to find your own sense of purpose and fulfillment that doesn't depend on being needed by others.

This transformation is not just possible—it's essential if you want to break free from the hidden prison of over-management and step into authentic freedom. The psychology that created your management patterns is not your destiny. With understanding, courage, and the right tools, you can rewrite the programming, transform the fears, and create relationships based on mutual respect, genuine support, and healthy independence.

The people you love don't need your management—they need your trust in their capability, your support of their growth, and your modeling of what it looks like to live an authentic, purposeful life. And you don't need to be needed in order to be loved. You need to be yourself, to pursue your own growth and dreams, and to offer the gift of your authentic presence rather than your constant intervention.

Understanding why you developed the need to manage others is the foundation for learning how to love them in healthier ways while reclaiming your own life in the process.

CHAPTER 4

The True Cost of Managing Everyone Else

At fifty-two, Margaret had achieved what many would consider a successful life. She was a respected physician, the mother of three accomplished adult children, and the wife of a prominent attorney. Her friends often commented on how "together" she seemed, how she always had everything under control, how lucky her family was to have someone so capable managing their lives.

But behind the facade of competence and control, Margaret was dying inside. She couldn't remember the last time she had felt genuinely excited about anything in her own life. She had no hobbies, no personal goals, no dreams that weren't somehow connected to other people's needs and aspirations. She had become so skilled at anticipating and managing everyone else's problems that she had completely lost touch with her own desires, preferences, and sense of purpose.

The wake-up call came on a Tuesday afternoon when her youngest daughter called to thank her for handling a complex insurance issue that had been causing stress. "I don't know what I'd do without you, Mom," her daughter said. "You're like our family's personal assistant, but better because you actually care about us."

Margaret hung up the phone and stared at her reflection in her office window. Personal assistant. After decades of medical training, years of building her practice, and a lifetime of caring for others, she had become her family's personal assistant. The realization hit her like a physical blow: she had traded her own life for the illusion of being indispensable to everyone else.

That night, Margaret began to calculate the true cost of her over-management patterns. What she discovered shocked her. She had been so focused on preventing costs for others—their stress, their mistakes, their struggles—that she had never counted the costs to herself. And those costs were staggering.

Personal Costs: The Price of Living Everyone Else's Life

The most devastating cost of chronic over-management is the gradual erosion of your own identity and life force. When you spend your days focused on other people's problems, goals, and needs, your own inner world begins to atrophy. You lose touch with what brings you joy, what challenges excite you, what dreams call to you, because you've trained yourself to pay attention only to what other people need from you.

Margaret's experience illustrates this perfectly. As a young woman, she had been passionate about medical research, specifically studying autoimmune diseases. She had planned to split her time between clinical practice and research, with dreams of making significant contributions to treatment protocols. But somewhere along the way, her research interests had been sacrificed to the demands of managing her growing family's needs and her husband's career requirements.

"I kept telling myself I would get back to research later," Margaret reflected. "When the children were older, when my husband's practice was more established, when things calmed down. But things never calmed down because I kept taking on more and more management responsibilities. By the time I looked up, fifteen years had passed, and I realized I knew more about my children's career goals than I did about my own."

This loss of personal direction is one of the most tragic costs of over-management because it happens so gradually that you often don't notice until it's become pervasive. You start by putting your dreams on the back burner temporarily to handle a family crisis. Then you postpone a personal goal to support someone else's important project. Then you sacrifice your own interests to maintain harmony in your relationships. Each individual choice seems reasonable and caring, but the cumulative effect is the disappearance of your own authentic life.

The chronic stress of over-management also takes a severe toll on physical and mental health. When you're constantly monitoring other people's emotional states, solving their problems, and carrying responsibility for outcomes you can't actually control, your nervous system never gets to rest. You exist in a state of perpetual low-level activation, always ready to spring into crisis management mode.

This chronic stress manifests in numerous ways: insomnia caused by lying awake worrying about other people's problems, digestive issues related to constantly suppressed anxiety, headaches from the tension of trying to control things beyond your influence, and a general sense of physical depletion that no amount of rest seems to cure.

Dr. Elena Rodriguez, who studies the health impacts of chronic caregiving, explains: "When someone is constantly managing other people's lives, their cortisol levels remain elevated in ways that are damaging to nearly every system in the body. We see increased rates of autoimmune disorders, cardiovascular problems, and mental health issues in people who chronically over-function in their relationships."

The emotional costs are equally severe. Over-managers often struggle with depression that seems to have no obvious cause. They've achieved many of their goals, their families are doing well, their careers are successful, yet they feel empty and disconnected from their own lives. This depression often goes unrecognized because from the outside, everything appears to be going well.

Jennifer, a successful marketing executive and mother of three, described this experience: "I felt guilty for being depressed because my life looked so good on paper. My kids were thriving, my marriage was stable, my career was advancing. But I felt like I was watching someone else's life rather than living my own. I couldn't figure out why I felt so empty when everyone around me seemed happy and grateful for all my help."

This emptiness is often accompanied by a profound sense of resentment that over-managers feel guilty about acknowledging. They resent the constant demands on their time and energy, the assumption that they'll handle whatever needs handling, the lack of appreciation for the extent of their sacrifice. But because their over-management patterns are often praised and rewarded, they feel selfish for wanting recognition or relief.

The resentment is particularly painful because it conflicts with the over-manager's self-image as a caring, selfless person. They believe they should feel fulfilled by helping others, should find meaning in their service, and should be happy that they're making everyone else's life easier. When instead they feel bitter and depleted, they often conclude that something is wrong with them rather than recognizing that something is wrong with the pattern.

Relationship Costs: How Management Destroys What It Means to Protect

While over-managers typically begin their patterns with the intention of strengthening relationships and helping the people they love, chronic management ultimately damages the very relationships it's meant to protect. The costs to relationships are often hidden because they develop slowly and because the managed person may initially appreciate the help and support. But over time, management creates dynamics that undermine genuine intimacy, respect, and mutual growth.

One of the most significant relationship costs is the development of unhealthy dependency. When you consistently solve problems for someone else, make decisions for them, or shield them from natural consequences, you inadvertently communicate that you don't believe they're capable of handling their own life. Over time, they begin to believe this message and stop developing their own problem-solving muscles, decision-making skills, and emotional resilience.

Tom realized this had happened in his relationship with his adult son when the young man called him in panic because his apartment's hot water heater had broken. "He was twenty-six years old and didn't know how to call a plumber," Tom recalled. "He was waiting for me to handle it for him because I had always handled everything for him. In trying to protect him from stress and difficulty, I had created a young man who couldn't function independently."

This dependency often breeds resentment on both sides. The managed person begins to feel infantilized and controlled, even when they initially welcomed the help. They may start to rebel against the management or feel frustrated by their own lack of competence. Meanwhile, the manager feels increasingly burdened by the dependency they've created and resentful that their "help" isn't appreciated.

The resentment is often mutual but rarely discussed openly. The managed person feels smothered and controlled but guilty about complaining since the manager is "only trying to help." The manager feels unappreciated and taken for granted but guilty about wanting recognition since they're "supposed to be selfless." This creates a dynamic where both people feel frustrated but neither feels free to address the real issue.

Over-management also prevents the development of genuine intimacy because it creates a fundamental inequality in the relationship. When one person is consistently in the role of helper, problem-solver, and manager, while the other is consistently in the role of being helped, managed, and rescued, the relationship becomes more like a parent-child dynamic than a relationship between equals.

This inequality makes authentic sharing and vulnerability difficult. The manager often feels they can't share their own struggles because they're supposed to be the strong one, the one with answers, the one who handles everything. The managed person often feels they can't offer support or assistance to the manager because the relationship has been structured around their needs being met rather than around mutual support and care.

Sarah, whose transformation we've followed throughout these chapters, described how over-management had affected her marriage: "I realized that my husband and I hadn't had a real conversation in years. Our interactions were all about logistics, problem-solving, and me managing various aspects of our life together. He had stopped sharing his thoughts and feelings with me because he knew I would immediately try to fix whatever he was experiencing rather than just listening and connecting with him."

Perhaps most tragically, over-management often prevents the managed person from developing their full potential. When someone knows that their problems will be solved for them, their decisions will be made for them, and their path will be smoothed for them, they have little incentive to stretch, grow, and develop their own capabilities. They remain perpetually dependent and underdeveloped because the management prevents them from encountering the challenges that would foster their growth.

This stunted growth doesn't just affect practical skills—it affects emotional and psychological development as well. People who are consistently managed often struggle with low self-confidence, poor decision-making abilities, and a limited sense of their own efficacy. They may appear successful in areas where they receive management, but they often feel insecure and incompetent in areas where they must function independently.

Professional Costs: When Management Becomes Micromanagement

The over-management patterns that develop in personal relationships often extend into professional settings, where they can have devastating effects on career advancement, team dynamics, and overall job satisfaction. Managers who over-function personally often struggle with delegation, empowerment, and creating sustainable systems at work.

Linda, a senior director at a consulting firm, recognized that her personal over-management patterns were sabotaging her professional effectiveness. "I was working sixty-hour weeks not because the work required it, but because I couldn't stop myself from taking over tasks that my team members should have been handling," she explained. "I would redo their presentations, handle client calls that they could have managed, and basically function as a highly paid individual contributor rather than a strategic leader."

This over-functioning in professional settings creates several serious problems. First, it prevents team members from developing their own skills and capabilities. When a manager consistently takes over challenging tasks or fixes team members' mistakes, the team never learns to handle complexity or develop problem-solving abilities. This creates a team that can only function at the level their manager provides for them, rather than a team that can think, innovate, and perform independently.

Second, over-managing managers often become bottlenecks in their organizations. Because they insert themselves into every decision and process, work can't move forward without their involvement. This limits the organization's capacity to grow and creates dangerous single points of failure. If the over-managing manager is unavailable, sick, or leaves the organization, critical functions may grind to a halt.

The personal costs to the over-managing professional are also severe. They often work longer hours than necessary, feel constantly overwhelmed by their workload, and struggle to focus on the strategic, high-level work that would actually advance their careers. They become trapped in operational details and crisis management, never having time to step back and think about bigger picture issues or long-term planning.

Marcus, a department head at a software company, described his realization: "I was proud of being the person who could handle any crisis, solve any problem, and work harder than anyone else on my team. But when I got passed over for a promotion for the second time, my boss told me it was because I was too focused on doing the work instead of leading others to do the work. I had been so busy proving I could handle everything that I had never demonstrated I could develop others to handle things without me."

Over-management in professional settings also often leads to team resentment and disengagement. Team members who are consistently managed and controlled often lose motivation and initiative. They may comply with directives but stop bringing creative ideas or taking ownership of outcomes. The manager ends up with a team that waits to be told what to do rather than a team that thinks proactively and takes initiative.

The career advancement implications are significant. Organizations increasingly value leaders who can develop others, create sustainable systems, and operate strategically rather than tactically. Managers who are trapped in over-management patterns often struggle to demonstrate these capabilities because they're too busy doing the work themselves to focus on developing others or thinking strategically.

The Ripple Effect: How Over-Management Hurts Those We're Trying to Help

Perhaps the most heartbreaking cost of over-management is the way it ultimately harms the very people we're trying to help. While the intention behind management is typically protection, support, and love, the long-term effects often include decreased self-confidence, impaired problem-solving abilities, and a sense of learned helplessness that can persist throughout life.

Children who are over-managed often struggle with anxiety and self-doubt in adulthood. They've received the message that the world is too dangerous or complex for them to navigate independently, that they need someone else to think for them, worry for them, and solve problems for them. This programming can create adults who are paralyzed by decision-making, who constantly seek external validation and approval, and who struggle with basic life skills that they never had the opportunity to develop.

Dr. Peter Gray, who studies the effects of overprotective parenting, has found that children who are excessively managed show increased rates of anxiety, depression, and learned helplessness in young adulthood. "When we prevent children from encountering age-appropriate challenges and solving their own problems," he explains, "we rob them of the experiences they need to develop resilience, confidence, and competence. We think we're protecting them, but we're actually handicapping them."

The effects aren't limited to childhood over-management. Adults who are consistently managed in their relationships often develop similar patterns of dependency and self-doubt. They may become risk-averse, avoiding challenges or opportunities that would require them to function independently. They may struggle with decision-making because they've become accustomed to having someone else think through options and consequences for them.

Emily realized this had happened in her friendship with her best friend, who had been managing various aspects of Emily's life for over a decade. "I gradually stopped trusting my own judgment about everything from career decisions to relationship choices," Emily recalled. "I would run every decision by her and basically let her talk me through every choice I made. When she moved across the country and wasn't available for daily consultation, I felt completely lost. I realized I had no confidence in my own ability to make good decisions because I had been outsourcing that responsibility for so long."

The ripple effects extend beyond the immediate relationship to affect how managed people relate to others. Children who are over-managed often grow up to either over-manage others or to seek out relationships where they can be managed. They may perpetuate the pattern by becoming over-managers themselves, or they may continue the pattern by remaining in the role of being managed throughout their adult relationships.

Adult children of over-managing parents often struggle with taking appropriate responsibility in their own families and professional lives. They may swing between being overly dependent and overly controlling, never having learned what healthy, balanced responsibility looks like. They may struggle to teach their own children independence because they never learned it themselves, or they may go to the opposite extreme and under-parent in reaction to having been over-parented.

The tragedy of these ripple effects is that they're often invisible to the over-manager, who sees only the immediate results of their intervention. They see that their help prevented a crisis, solved a problem, or eliminated stress for someone they love. They don't see the long-term developmental costs, the gradual erosion of confidence, or the way their help is preventing the person from becoming who they're capable of becoming.

Financial Implications of the Management Trap

While the emotional and relational costs of over-management are often the most visible, there are also significant financial costs that are frequently overlooked. These costs affect both the over-manager and the people they manage, creating patterns of financial dependency and inefficiency that can persist for decades.

For the over-manager, the financial costs often begin with the opportunity costs of not pursuing their own career advancement and personal goals. Time and energy spent managing other people's lives is time and energy not spent on activities that could increase earning potential, develop new skills, or create additional income streams.

Margaret, the physician we met at the beginning of this chapter, calculated that her over-management patterns had cost her approximately $500,000 in lost income over fifteen years. "I had turned down research opportunities, speaking engagements, and leadership positions because

I was too busy managing my family's various needs and crises," she realized. "I chose the path that allowed me to be available for everyone else's emergencies, but it was also the path that limited my own professional growth and earning potential."

Over-managers often make career choices based on what allows them to maintain their management role rather than what would best serve their own development and advancement. They may choose jobs with flexible schedules that allow them to handle family crises, turn down travel opportunities that would advance their careers, or avoid leadership positions that would require them to focus on work rather than on managing others.

The financial costs also include the direct expenses of over-management: paying for services or products that others should be handling themselves, covering costs that others should be responsible for, and absorbing financial consequences of other people's decisions. Parents might pay for their adult children's car repairs, insurance, or even basic living expenses well into their twenties or thirties. Spouses might handle all the financial planning and bill-paying for partners who are capable of managing their own finances.

These direct costs are often justified as temporary help or necessary support, but they frequently become permanent patterns that prevent the managed person from developing financial responsibility and independence. The over-manager absorbs financial stress and responsibility that doesn't belong to them while preventing others from learning to manage their own financial lives.

Robert, a successful business owner, realized he had been financially enabling his three adult children for over a decade. "I was paying for everything from their cell phone bills to their vacation expenses because I didn't want them to struggle financially," he explained. "But I realized that my 'generosity' was actually preventing them from learning to live within their means and make responsible financial decisions. I was subsidizing their irresponsibility instead of helping them develop financial competence."

The financial implications extend beyond direct costs to include the stress-related expenses that often accompany chronic over-management. Over-managers frequently spend money on stress relief, health care for stress-related conditions, and various forms of self-care that become necessary to cope with the exhaustion of managing everyone else's life.

They may also make expensive decisions designed to reduce their management burden, such as hiring services to handle tasks that family members should be managing themselves, or purchasing products designed to solve problems that could be addressed through better boundaries and clearer expectations.

The Life Impact Assessment

Understanding the true cost of over-management requires taking an honest inventory of how your management patterns are affecting every area of your life. The Life Impact Assessment is a comprehensive tool for evaluating these costs and creating motivation for change.

Begin by examining the personal costs in detail. What dreams have you deferred or abandoned in order to focus on managing others? What aspects of your health have suffered due to chronic stress and lack of self-care? What interests, hobbies, or personal goals have been pushed aside to make room for other people's needs and crises?

Consider not just what you've given up, but what you've never even attempted because you were too busy managing everyone else. What career opportunities have you declined? What relationships have you not pursued? What experiences have you missed because you were handling other people's problems instead of creating your own adventures?

Next, examine the relationship costs honestly. How has your over-management affected the quality of your connections with others? Are your relationships based on genuine mutual respect and support, or have they become transactional relationships where you provide services in exchange for feeling needed? Do the people you manage come to you for authentic connection and conversation, or primarily when they need something handled or solved?

Look at the professional costs as well. How has your tendency to over-manage affected your career advancement? Are you stuck in operational roles when you could be advancing to strategic roles? Are you working harder than necessary because you can't delegate effectively? Are you missing opportunities for growth and development because you're too focused on managing others?

Finally, consider the financial costs comprehensively. Add up not just the direct costs of your over-management, but the opportunity costs, stress-related expenses, and long-term financial implications of your patterns. What would your life look like financially if you redirected the time, energy, and resources you currently spend managing others toward your own financial growth and security?

The Life Impact Assessment isn't meant to create guilt or self-blame. Over-management patterns develop for understandable reasons and are maintained by the best of intentions. The assessment is meant to create clarity about what your patterns are actually costing you and to provide motivation for making changes that will serve everyone better in the long run.

The Relationship Health Scorecard

Just as the Life Impact Assessment helps you understand personal costs, the Relationship Health Scorecard helps you evaluate how your over-management patterns are affecting the quality and sustainability of your relationships. This tool examines whether your relationships are characterized by mutual growth and respect or by dependency and control.

For each important relationship in your life, consider several key indicators of relationship health. Does this relationship involve mutual support, where both people offer and receive help, or is the support primarily flowing in one direction? Do both people in the relationship take responsibility for their own problems and decisions, or has one person become dependent on the other for problem-solving and decision-making?

Examine the level of respect in the relationship. Do you treat this person as capable and competent, or do you treat them as needing your management and oversight? Do they treat you as a whole person with your own needs and goals, or primarily as a resource for meeting their needs?

Consider the growth dynamics in the relationship. Are both people encouraged to stretch, learn, and develop their capabilities, or does the relationship structure prevent one or both people from growing? Does the relationship support both people becoming their best selves, or does it require one person to remain small or dependent in order to function?

Look at the communication patterns as well. Do you and this person have genuine conversations about thoughts, feelings, and experiences, or do your interactions focus primarily on logistics, problem-solving, and managing various issues? Can both people be vulnerable and authentic with each other, or has the relationship become structured around roles and functions rather than authentic connection?

The Relationship Health Scorecard often reveals that relationships that feel loving and supportive on the surface are actually characterized by unhealthy dependency and control. This doesn't mean the relationships are doomed or that the people involved don't care about each other. It means the relationships would benefit from restructuring in ways that support mutual growth, respect, and authentic connection.

Counting the True Cost

The true cost of managing everyone else's life is far greater than most over-managers realize. It includes not just the obvious costs of time and energy, but the hidden costs of dreams deferred, health compromised, relationships damaged, and potential unrealized. It includes both what you've lost and what you've never had the chance to gain.

Perhaps most significantly, the cost includes the gradual erosion of your authentic self and the life you were meant to live. When you spend your days focused on everyone else's needs, problems, and goals, you lose touch with your own sense of purpose, passion, and possibility. You become a supporting character in everyone else's story instead of the protagonist of your own.

But understanding these costs isn't meant to create despair—it's meant to create clarity and motivation for change. Every cost you've paid for over-management is recoverable. Every dream you've deferred can be reclaimed. Every relationship damaged by unhealthy patterns can be healed and restructured. Every aspect of yourself that has been neglected can be rediscovered and developed.

The same energy you've been using to manage everyone else's life can be redirected toward creating the life you truly want to live. The same caring and attention you've been giving to other people's problems can be focused on solving challenges in your own life. The same commitment you've shown to other people's growth and success can be applied to your own development and achievement.

Recognizing the true cost of over-management is the first step toward freedom. Once you understand what your patterns are really costing you and the people you love, you can begin the work of building something better: relationships based on mutual respect and support, a life built around your own authentic goals and dreams, and the deep satisfaction that comes from loving others in ways that truly serve their highest good while honoring your own.

CHAPTER 5

Reclaiming Your Personal Boundaries

The text message arrived at 11:30 PM on a Tuesday: "Mom, I know you're probably sleeping, but I'm having a panic attack about my presentation tomorrow. Can you call me?"

For the hundredth time in recent months, Janet felt the familiar surge of adrenaline that came with her adult daughter's crisis calls. Her first instinct was to reach for her phone immediately, to drop everything and rescue Emma from her anxiety, to spend the next hour talking her through breathing exercises and helping her rehearse her presentation.

But this time, something made Janet pause. Maybe it was the exhaustion from being woken up three times the previous week by similar "emergency" calls. Maybe it was the conversation she'd had with her therapist about enabling versus supporting. Or maybe it was simply the growing awareness that these midnight rescue missions weren't actually helping Emma develop the skills she needed to manage her own anxiety.

Instead of immediately calling back, Janet took a deep breath and typed a response: "I love you and I believe in your ability to handle this. Let's talk tomorrow after your presentation." Then she turned off her phone and went back to sleep.

The next morning, Emma texted: "Thanks for not rescuing me last night. I figured out how to calm myself down, and the presentation went great. I'm proud of myself for handling it on my own."

This small act of boundary-setting marked the beginning of Janet's transformation from chronic rescuer to supportive parent. It was the first time in years that she had chosen her own wellbeing over someone else's immediate comfort, and the first time she had trusted her daughter's capability over her own need to fix and manage.

But that moment of boundary-setting didn't happen overnight. It was the result of months of learning to distinguish between healthy limits and harmful walls, between appropriate support and enabling rescue, between loving someone and managing their life. Janet had to learn what boundaries actually were, why they felt so foreign and frightening, and how to implement them in ways that strengthened rather than damaged her relationships.

Understanding Boundaries: More Than Just Saying No

Most people think of boundaries as rules about what they will and won't do, or as ways of saying no to requests and demands from others. While these elements are part of healthy boundaries, this understanding is incomplete and often leads to boundary attempts that feel rigid, punitive, or disconnected from love and care.

Healthy boundaries are actually much more nuanced and sophisticated. They're not walls that keep people out or weapons that punish others for their needs and behaviors. Instead, boundaries are the invisible infrastructure that allows relationships to function with mutual respect, appropriate responsibility, and genuine intimacy. They're the framework that makes it possible to love others deeply while maintaining your own sense of self, autonomy, and wellbeing.

Dr. Henry Cloud, whose research on boundaries has influenced thousands of therapists and coaches, describes boundaries as "property lines of the soul." Just as property lines define where your responsibility for your yard ends and your neighbor's responsibility for their yard begins, personal boundaries define where your responsibility for your life ends and others' responsibility for their lives begins.

This property line metaphor is particularly helpful for over-managers because it highlights the distinction between what belongs to you and what belongs to others. You're responsible for maintaining your own property—your emotions, decisions, behaviors, and life outcomes. You're not responsible for maintaining other people's property, even if their yard looks messy or seems to need attention.

The confusion about boundaries often stems from conflating boundaries with barriers. Barriers are designed to keep people out, to prevent connection, and to protect through isolation. Boundaries, on the other hand, are designed to make real connection possible by creating a framework within which both people can be authentic, responsible, and respectful.

Think of boundaries like the walls of a house. The walls don't exist to keep people out of your life entirely—they exist to create a space where you can be yourself, where you can invite people in when you choose, and where you can maintain your own sense of home and safety. A house without walls would be uninhabitable, but a house that was completely sealed off would be a prison rather than a home.

Healthy boundaries serve several crucial functions in relationships. They preserve your energy and resources so you can offer genuine support rather than resentful compliance. They protect your emotional wellbeing so you can engage with others from a place of wholeness rather than depletion. They maintain clarity about responsibility so both people can grow and develop rather than becoming stuck in dysfunctional patterns.

Perhaps most importantly, boundaries create the safety and structure that makes genuine intimacy possible. When both people in a relationship know where the limits are, when both understand what they can expect from each other and what they're responsible for themselves, they can relax into an authentic connection without the anxiety that comes from unclear expectations and blurred responsibilities.

The Boundary Spectrum: Physical, Emotional, Time, and Energy Boundaries

Boundaries exist across multiple dimensions of human experience, and over-managers often need to strengthen their boundary skills in all of these areas. Understanding the different types of boundaries helps you recognize where your particular challenges lie and develop more comprehensive boundary strategies.

Physical boundaries involve your body, your personal space, and your physical environment. These might seem like the most straightforward boundaries, but over-managers often struggle with physical boundaries in subtle ways. You might allow people to go through your personal belongings without permission, use your home as a hotel or storage facility, or expect you to be available for physical help whenever they need it.

Maria, a small business owner and mother of two, realized that her physical boundaries had been completely eroded when she found herself cleaning her adult son's apartment every weekend because "it stressed her out to see it messy." She was spending her only free time maintaining someone else's living space while her own home and self-care needs were neglected.

Physical boundaries also include your right to physical comfort and safety. Over-managers sometimes sacrifice their own physical needs to accommodate others—staying up all night to help someone with a crisis, skipping meals to handle someone else's emergency, or putting their own health needs on hold to manage someone else's problems.

Emotional boundaries are perhaps the most challenging for over-managers to understand and implement. These boundaries involve taking responsibility for your own emotional experience while not taking responsibility for others' emotional experiences. Emotional boundaries mean you can feel concerned about someone without feeling responsible for fixing their feelings, you can offer support without absorbing their anxiety or pain, and you can care about someone's problems without making their problems your emergency.

The difficulty with emotional boundaries is that they require you to tolerate others' discomfort without immediately moving to alleviate it. For people who have been trained to monitor and manage others' emotional states, sitting with someone's distress without jumping in to fix it can feel almost physically painful.

Jennifer, whose story we've followed throughout these chapters, described learning to maintain emotional boundaries with her teenage daughter: "When she was upset about friend drama, my automatic response was to feel her pain as if it were my own and immediately start brainstorming solutions. Learning to maintain emotional boundaries meant I could acknowledge her feelings, offer empathy and support, but not take on her emotional experience as my own emergency to solve."

Time boundaries involve protecting your schedule and commitments in ways that honor your own priorities and responsibilities. Over-managers often have very poor time boundaries, making themselves available for others' needs at the expense of their own plans, goals, and obligations. They say yes to requests without considering the impact on their own time and energy, and they often feel guilty about having commitments that prevent them from being immediately available to help others.

Establishing time boundaries means learning to evaluate requests against your own priorities and commitments, rather than automatically saying yes because someone needs something. It means protecting time for your own goals, relationships, and self-care, and treating these commitments as seriously as you treat commitments to help others.

Energy boundaries are perhaps the most sophisticated and important for breaking free from over-management patterns. These boundaries involve being intentional about how you invest your mental and emotional energy, rather than automatically directing it toward whatever seems most urgent or whoever seems most needy.

Energy boundaries mean recognizing that your mental and emotional resources are finite and valuable, and that how you invest them determines the quality of your own life as well as your ability to genuinely support others. When you constantly direct your energy toward monitoring, worrying about, and managing other people's lives, you have little energy left for your own growth, creativity, and fulfillment.

David, a senior manager who had struggled with over-functioning at work, described learning about energy boundaries: "I realized I was spending 80% of my mental energy thinking about my team members' problems, performance issues, and career development, but only 20% thinking about strategic planning, my own professional development, and the bigger picture initiatives that were actually my responsibility. No wonder I felt like I was spinning my wheels and not advancing in my own career."

Common Boundary Violations and How to Spot Them

Boundary violations often happen gradually and subtly, making them difficult to recognize until they've become entrenched patterns. Learning to spot boundary violations as they're happening is crucial for maintaining healthy relationships and preventing the resentment and exhaustion that come from chronic boundary erosion.

One of the most common boundary violations for over-managers is the assumption of automatic availability. This happens when others expect you to be immediately responsive to their needs, requests, and crises without regard for your own schedule, priorities, or wellbeing. The violation isn't necessarily in their asking—it's in the expectation that you should always say yes and the guilt or pressure that follows if you don't.

This automatic availability assumption often develops because over-managers have trained others to expect immediate responsiveness. When you consistently drop everything to handle others' problems, you inadvertently teach them that their needs should take priority over your own plans and commitments. The boundary violation becomes entrenched when others begin to feel entitled to your immediate attention and become upset or manipulative when you're not available.

Another common violation is the delegation of emotional regulation. This happens when someone expects you to manage their emotional state, to prevent their upset, or to fix their feelings when they're distressed. The person may not explicitly ask you to regulate their emotions, but they communicate through their behavior that they expect you to monitor their emotional temperature and intervene when necessary.

Sarah noticed this pattern in her relationship with her husband: "Whenever he was stressed about work, he would become irritable and short-tempered at home. I gradually took on the responsibility of managing his stress levels by monitoring his mood, asking careful questions about his day, and basically walking on eggshells to avoid adding to his stress. He never asked me to do this, but his behavior made it clear that he expected me to help him manage his emotional state."

Responsibility transfer is another frequent boundary violation that can be particularly subtle. This happens when someone consistently brings their problems to you not for advice or support, but with the implicit or explicit expectation that you'll solve the problem for them. They may present the problem as if they're just seeking perspective, but their response to your input reveals that they're actually expecting you to take action.

This violation often involves the language of helplessness: "I don't know what to do," "I can't handle this," "You're so much better at this than I am." While these statements might be expressions of genuine overwhelm, they become boundary violations when they're used to transfer responsibility for problem-solving from the person who owns the problem to the person they're asking for help.

Time and energy hijacking is a boundary violation that happens when someone consistently pulls you into lengthy conversations, problem-solving sessions, or emotional processing without regard for your own schedule or energy levels. The person may justify this by saying they "really need to talk" or that it's "an emergency," but the pattern reveals a lack of respect for your time and energy as valuable resources.

This violation is particularly challenging because it often involves people you care about who are genuinely struggling. The boundary violation isn't in their need for support—it's in their expectation that you should provide unlimited time and energy for their needs without consideration for the impact on your own wellbeing and responsibilities.

Decision abdication is a more sophisticated boundary violation that happens when someone consistently defers important decisions to you, even when those decisions are clearly within their domain of responsibility. This might involve asking you to choose their career path, decide how they should handle relationship conflicts, or determine how they should spend their money.

While this might initially feel flattering—after all, they're seeking your wisdom and input—it becomes a boundary violation when it prevents the person from developing their own decision-making skills and places the burden of responsibility for their life choices on your shoulders.

The Guilt Factor: Why Boundaries Feel Selfish

For over-managers, implementing boundaries often triggers intense feelings of guilt, selfishness, and fear of damaging relationships. Understanding why boundaries feel so threatening is crucial for developing the emotional resilience necessary to maintain them consistently.

The guilt around boundaries often stems from fundamental misunderstandings about what love looks like and what responsibilities we have toward others. Many over-managers have been conditioned to believe that love means sacrificing yourself for others, that caring means being available whenever someone needs you, and that good people always put others' needs before their own.

These beliefs make boundaries feel like betrayals of love rather than expressions of it. When you've been taught that your value lies in your usefulness to others, protecting your own time, energy, and wellbeing can feel selfish and wrong. The guilt is often accompanied by fears that others will see you as uncaring, that they'll withdraw their love, or that something terrible will happen if you're not constantly available to help.

Rebecca, a therapist who struggled with boundaries in her personal life, described this internal conflict: "Intellectually, I knew that boundaries were healthy and necessary. I taught my clients about boundaries every day. But when it came to my own family, setting boundaries felt like I was abandoning them or being a bad daughter, sister, and friend. I felt guilty for wanting time for myself, for not being immediately available for every crisis, for focusing on my own goals instead of constantly helping others with theirs."

The guilt is often reinforced by others' reactions to your boundary-setting attempts. People who have become accustomed to your over-functioning may respond to boundaries with hurt, anger, or manipulation. They may accuse you of being selfish, remind you of all the ways they've helped you in the past, or suggest that you don't really care about them if you're not willing to help with their current need.

These reactions can be particularly challenging because they often contain kernels of truth mixed with manipulation. The person may genuinely feel hurt by your boundary, and they may genuinely need support. But their reaction may also be designed to guilt you back into your old patterns of over-functioning.

Understanding the difference between healthy guilt and manipulative guilt is crucial for maintaining boundaries. Healthy guilt arises when you've actually done something wrong or hurtful to someone. Manipulative guilt arises when someone wants you to feel responsible for their feelings, needs, or life circumstances in ways that aren't actually your responsibility.

The fear that boundaries will damage relationships is often based on the assumption that relationships can only function when one person over-functions and the other under-functions. But this assumption is false. Healthy relationships are actually strengthened by clear boundaries because boundaries create the safety and structure that allow both people to be authentic, responsible, and genuinely supportive of each other.

Many over-managers discover that their fears about boundaries damaging relationships are unfounded. When they begin setting healthy limits, many of their relationships actually improve. People who initially resist the boundaries often come to respect them and function better within the new structure. And relationships that can't survive healthy boundaries often weren't healthy relationships to begin with.

Boundary Setting Scripts for Different Relationships

Learning to set boundaries effectively requires developing language and scripts that communicate your limits clearly and kindly while remaining firm about what you will and won't do. Different relationships and situations require different approaches, but certain principles apply across all boundary-setting communications.

Effective boundary-setting language is clear, specific, and focused on your own choices rather than the other person's behavior. Instead of saying "You always call me at inappropriate times," you might say "I'm not available to take phone calls after 9 PM." Instead of "You're too dependent on me," you might say "I won't be able to help you with this particular issue, but I have confidence in your ability to handle it."

The key is to communicate what you will and won't do without justifying your boundary or trying to convince the other person that your boundary is reasonable. Boundaries aren't up for negotiation or debate—they're simply statements about how you've chosen to manage your own time, energy, and resources.

In parent-child relationships, boundary-setting often involves transitioning from managing your child's life to supporting their independence. This might sound like: "I'm not going to call your professor about your grade, but I'm happy to listen if you want to talk through how you plan to address it." Or "I won't be doing your laundry anymore, but I'm glad to help you learn how to use the washing machine."

The key with adult children is to communicate your confidence in their capability while offering appropriate support. You're moving from doing things for them to believing in their ability to do things for themselves.

In romantic partnerships, boundaries often involve clarifying responsibilities and expectations. This might sound like: "I'm not going to manage your relationship with your mother anymore, but I support you in handling it however you think is best." Or "I won't be making decisions about our social calendar by myself anymore. Let's figure out a system where we both contribute to planning."

Partnership boundaries are often about moving from over-functioning to equal participation, from managing your partner's responsibilities to trusting them to handle their own areas of responsibility.

In friendships, boundaries often involve limiting your role as unpaid therapist or problem-solver. This might sound like: "I care about you and I can see you're struggling, but I'm not in a position to give advice about this situation. Have you considered talking to a counselor?" Or "I have about fifteen minutes to talk right now. Can we catch up quickly, or would you prefer to schedule a longer conversation for another time?"

Friendship boundaries are often about maintaining mutual support rather than one-sided caregiving, and about protecting your time and emotional energy while still being a caring friend.

In professional settings, boundaries might involve delegating appropriately and not taking on responsibilities that belong to others. This could sound like: "This project is a great learning opportunity for you to handle independently. I'm available for questions, but I won't be reviewing every step of your work." Or "I won't be staying late to fix errors that could have been prevented with more careful attention to detail."

Professional boundaries are often about developing others' capabilities rather than doing their work for them, and about focusing your time on the responsibilities that truly require your level of expertise and authority.

The Boundary Blueprint Method

Implementing boundaries successfully requires more than just good intentions and scripts—it requires a systematic approach that helps you identify where boundaries are needed, plan how to implement them, and maintain them consistently over time. The Boundary Blueprint Method provides a framework for this process.

The first step involves conducting a boundary audit to identify where your current boundaries are insufficient or nonexistent. This means examining all your important relationships and noting where you feel resentful, depleted, or taken advantage of. These negative feelings are often signals that boundaries need to be established or strengthened.

Look for patterns where you consistently say yes when you'd prefer to say no, where you take on responsibilities that belong to others, where you feel obligated to manage other people's emotions or problems, or where you sacrifice your own priorities to accommodate others' requests or needs.

The audit should also identify your boundary strengths—areas where you already maintain healthy limits effectively. Understanding what makes boundaries work in some areas can help you apply those same principles to areas where boundaries are lacking.

Once you've identified where boundaries are needed, the next step is to design specific boundaries that address the particular issues in each relationship. This involves deciding what you will and won't do, what you will and won't be available for, and what you will and won't take responsibility for.

Effective boundary design considers both your own needs and well-being and the other person's capacity for growth and responsibility. The goal isn't to punish or control the other person, but to create a structure that allows both of you to function in healthier ways.

The implementation phase involves communicating your boundaries clearly and then consistently following through on them. This is often the most challenging phase because it requires tolerating others' discomfort with your boundaries and resisting the urge to rescue them from the natural consequences of their choices.

Consistent follow-through is crucial because boundaries that aren't maintained consistently aren't really boundaries at all—they're just suggestions or threats. If you set a boundary but then abandon it when someone pushes back or seems upset, you teach them that your boundaries aren't real and that persistence in violating them will eventually succeed.

The maintenance phase involves ongoing vigilance about boundary erosion and regular adjustments as relationships and circumstances change. Boundaries aren't set-and-forget structures—they require ongoing attention and fine-tuning to remain effective.

This might involve strengthening boundaries that are being consistently violated, adjusting boundaries that are too rigid for the relationship, or developing new boundaries as new situations arise.

The STOP Technique

One of the most practical tools for implementing boundaries in real-time is the STOP technique, which provides a framework for pausing before automatically saying yes to requests or taking on responsibilities that may not be yours to handle.

STOP stands for Stop, Think, Options, and Proceed. When someone makes a request or presents a problem that triggers your automatic helping response, the first step is to literally stop before responding. This might mean saying "Let me think about that and get back to you" or "I need a moment to consider how I can best support you with this."

The stopping phase is crucial because it interrupts the automatic pattern of immediately saying yes or jumping into problem-solving mode. It creates space for conscious choice rather than unconscious reaction.

The thinking phase involves considering several key questions: Is this request or problem actually something that requires my involvement?

Does this fall within my appropriate areas of responsibility? Do I have the time, energy, and resources to help with this without neglecting my own priorities and commitments? Will my help actually serve this person's growth and development, or will it prevent them from developing their own capabilities?

The thinking phase also involves checking in with your own emotional state and motivations. Are you feeling pressured to help because of guilt or fear? Are you wanting to help because it makes you feel needed or important? Are you considering saying yes because you're genuinely in a position to offer appropriate support?

The options phase involves considering different ways you might respond to the request or situation. This might include offering the specific help requested, offering a different type of support, referring the person to other resources, or declining to help while expressing confidence in their ability to handle the situation themselves.

The goal of considering options is to move beyond the binary choice of either jumping in to fix everything or completely withdrawing support. Most situations offer multiple possibilities for how you might respond, and considering these options helps you choose responses that truly serve everyone involved.

The proceed phase involves implementing your chosen response with clarity and kindness. This might mean offering specific, limited help with clear boundaries around your involvement. It might mean expressing empathy and confidence in the person's ability to handle the situation themselves. It might mean providing resources or suggestions while making it clear that the responsibility for action remains with them.

The key to the proceed phase is communicating your decision clearly and then maintaining it consistently, even if the other person pushes back or expresses disappointment with your choice.

The Boundary Violation Recovery Protocol

Even with the best intentions and clearest boundaries, violations will sometimes occur. People may push past your limits, you may find yourself reverting to old patterns under pressure, or circumstances may arise that make maintaining your boundaries more challenging than usual. Having a protocol for recovering from boundary violations helps you get back on track quickly without abandoning your boundary-setting efforts entirely.

The first step in boundary violation recovery is recognizing that a violation has occurred. This might seem obvious, but over-managers often minimize or rationalize boundary violations, convincing themselves that "this situation is different" or that their boundary wasn't really that important. Learning to honestly acknowledge when boundaries have been crossed is crucial for maintaining them over time.

The second step involves taking responsibility for your part in the violation without taking responsibility for the other person's behavior. You might have contributed to the violation by not communicating your boundary clearly, by not following through on consequences you had established, or by sending mixed messages about what you would and wouldn't accept. Taking responsibility for your own choices helps you make different choices going forward.

However, taking responsibility for your part doesn't mean taking responsibility for the other person's choice to violate your boundary. Other people are responsible for their own behavior, and you can't control their choices, only your own responses to those choices.

The third step involves recommitting to your boundary and, if necessary, communicating it again more clearly. This might mean having a direct conversation about what happened and what you expect going forward. It might mean implementing stronger consequences for future violations. It might mean adjusting your boundary to make it more realistic or enforceable.

The key is to treat boundary violations as information about what adjustments need to be made rather than as evidence that boundaries don't work or that you should abandon your boundary-setting efforts.

Building Your Defense System

Learning to set and maintain boundaries is ultimately about building a defense system that protects your wellbeing, preserves your energy for what matters most to you, and creates the structure that allows your relationships to flourish. This defense system isn't about keeping people out of your life—it's about creating the conditions that allow you to engage with others from a place of choice rather than obligation, strength rather than depletion, and authentic care rather than resentful compliance.

Building this defense system takes time, practice, and patience with yourself as you learn new skills and adjust to new ways of relating to others. There will be setbacks, violations, and moments when maintaining boundaries feels more difficult than reverting to old patterns. But with consistent effort and commitment to your own wellbeing, boundaries become easier to maintain and more natural to implement.

The ultimate goal of boundary work isn't to become a person who doesn't care about others or who is unwilling to help. The goal is to become a person who can choose how to care and how to help from a place of wholeness and strength rather than from a place of compulsion and depletion. When you have strong boundaries, your support of others becomes more valuable because it comes from choice rather than obligation, and your relationships become stronger because they're based on mutual respect rather than one-sided management.

Your boundaries are not selfish—they're the foundation that makes genuine love and support possible. They're the framework that allows you to show up as your best self in your relationships while maintaining your own sense of identity, purpose, and wellbeing. Reclaiming your personal boundaries is one of the most loving things you can do, both for yourself and for the people you care about most.

CHAPTER 6

The Art of Strategic Disengagement

The email arrived on a Monday morning at 6:47 AM: "Mom, I'm completely overwhelmed with work and my apartment is a disaster. Can you come over this weekend and help me organize everything? I just can't handle it all by myself."

Reading these words from her twenty-eight-year-old daughter, Patricia felt the familiar surge of anxiety and urgency that had driven her parenting for nearly three decades. Her immediate impulse was to clear her weekend schedule, drive across town, and spend two days organizing her daughter's life. After all, Emma sounded genuinely distressed, and Patricia knew she could solve the problem quickly and efficiently.

But this time, Patricia paused. Over the past several months, she had been learning about the difference between supporting and enabling, between helping and taking over. She realized that Emma's "overwhelming" situations had become increasingly frequent, and her requests for help had become increasingly broad in scope. What had started as occasional assistance during genuine crises had evolved into regular weekend rescue missions that seemed to prevent Emma from developing her own organizational and stress-management skills.

Instead of immediately offering to fix everything, Patricia typed a different kind of response: "It sounds like you're dealing with a lot right now. I have confidence that you can figure out a manageable approach.

Would you like to brainstorm some strategies over the phone, or would you prefer to tackle it on your own and tell me how it goes?"

This response represented a profound shift in Patricia's approach to parenting her adult child. She was learning the art of strategic disengagement—the skill of stepping back from management and control while maintaining love, connection, and appropriate support. She was discovering that disengagement didn't mean abandonment, and that sometimes the most loving thing you can do is trust someone to handle their own challenges.

Strategic disengagement is one of the most nuanced and challenging aspects of breaking free from over-management patterns. It requires developing the wisdom to know when to step in and when to step back, the courage to tolerate others' discomfort without immediately rushing to fix it, and the faith to trust that people are more capable than your anxiety wants you to believe.

Disengagement Versus Abandonment: The Crucial Difference

The fear that stops most over-managers from stepping back is the belief that disengagement equals abandonment. This fear is understandable given how our culture often conflates love with doing, care with managing, and support with taking over. But the distinction between strategic disengagement and abandonment is crucial because one strengthens relationships while the other damages them.

Abandonment involves withdrawing emotional connection, support, and care from someone when they need it most. It means becoming unavailable, unresponsive, and uninvested in their wellbeing. Abandonment is about protecting yourself from others' needs and problems by refusing to engage with them at all.

Strategic disengagement, on the other hand, involves stepping back from management and control while maintaining emotional connection and appropriate support. It means being available for encouragement, perspective, and companionship while refusing to take over responsibilities that belong to the other person. Disengagement is about empowering others to handle their own lives while remaining connected and caring.

The difference lies not in the level of care you feel, but in how you express that care. Abandonment says, "Your problems are not my concern." Strategic disengagement says, "Your problems are your responsibility, but you are my concern, and I believe in your ability to handle them."

Dr. Brené Brown, whose research on shame and vulnerability has influenced millions, describes this distinction beautifully: "We can love people fiercely and still refuse to pick up what's not ours to carry. In fact, loving someone fiercely often requires refusing to carry their load because carrying it prevents them from developing their own strength."

This distinction becomes clearer when you consider the long-term outcomes of each approach. Abandonment often leads to damaged relationships, increased anxiety and insecurity in the abandoned person, and mutual resentment. Strategic disengagement, while initially uncomfortable for both parties, typically leads to stronger relationships, increased confidence and competence in the other person, and mutual respect.

The challenge is that disengagement often feels like abandonment to both the person stepping back and the person being stepped back from. When you've been in the role of manager and rescuer, withdrawing from that role can trigger fears about whether you still matter, whether the relationship will survive, and whether the other person will be able to cope without your management.

Similarly, the person who has become accustomed to your management may interpret your disengagement as a withdrawal of love and support. They may feel confused, hurt, or angry when you stop providing the level of management they've come to expect. Their distress can trigger your own anxiety and guilt, making it tempting to abandon the disengagement and return to old patterns.

Understanding this emotional landscape is crucial for maintaining disengagement during the difficult transition period. Both parties need time to adjust to new roles and expectations, and both may experience discomfort as they learn to relate in healthier ways.

Marcus, a father who had been heavily involved in managing his adult son's finances, described his experience with strategic disengagement: "When I stopped monitoring his bank account and offering unsolicited financial advice, he accused me of not caring about him anymore. It was heartbreaking because stepping back was actually an expression of my care—I wanted him to develop financial confidence and independence. But it took several months for him to understand that my disengagement came from love, not from lack of caring."

The Graduated Withdrawal Approach

Effective disengagement rarely happens all at once. Abrupt withdrawal from management roles can create unnecessary drama, confusion, and resistance. Instead, strategic disengagement is most successful when it's implemented gradually, allowing all parties to adjust to new expectations and responsibilities over time.

The graduated withdrawal approach involves systematically reducing your level of management and intervention while increasing your level of trust and empowerment. This process requires careful planning, clear communication, and patience with the adjustment period that inevitably follows changes in relationship dynamics.

The first step in graduated withdrawal is identifying which areas of management you want to step back from and in what order. It's usually most effective to start with areas where your management is least critical or where the other person has shown some capacity for independent functioning. This allows everyone to build confidence with smaller changes before tackling more significant areas of disengagement.

For example, if you've been managing multiple aspects of your teenager's life—homework, social calendar, room cleanliness, and college planning—you might choose to step back from room cleanliness first, since this has the least impact on their future success and allows them to experience natural consequences without serious long-term effects.

The second step involves clearly communicating your intention to step back and the timeline for the transition. This communication should emphasize your confidence in the other person's abilities and your continued availability for appropriate support, while being clear about what you will no longer be managing.

This might sound like: "I've realized that I've been too involved in managing your schedule, and I want to step back so you can develop your own organizational skills. Over the next month, I'm going to transition this responsibility to you. I'm happy to help you set up systems or answer questions, but I won't be tracking your appointments or reminding you about commitments anymore."

The third step involves implementing the withdrawal gradually while providing scaffolding and support for the person's developing independence. This might involve teaching skills they'll need to manage the responsibility themselves, helping them set up systems that support their success, or simply being available for consultation when they request it.

The scaffolding phase is crucial because it provides support without taking over. You're not abandoning the person to figure everything out alone, but you're also not continuing to manage for them. You're providing the tools and resources they need to manage for themselves.

Jennifer, whose journey we've followed throughout this book, used the graduated withdrawal approach with her adult daughter's career concerns. "Instead of continuing to research job opportunities for her, networking on her behalf, and editing her résumé, I gradually stepped back from each of these areas. First, I stopped doing the research but helped her develop her own research strategies. Then I stopped networking for her but introduced her to contacts who could help her build her own network. Finally, I stopped editing her résumé but helped her find professional resources for that kind of support."

The fourth step involves maintaining the disengagement consistently while offering encouragement and emotional support. This is often the most challenging phase because the other person may struggle with their new responsibilities, make mistakes, or experience frustration as they develop new skills. The temptation to jump back in and "help" can be overwhelming.

However, maintaining the disengagement during this adjustment period is crucial for the long-term success of the process. Jumping back in whenever someone struggles sends the message that you don't really trust their capability and that the disengagement isn't permanent. It can undermine the entire process and make future disengagement attempts more difficult.

The final step involves celebrating progress and adjusting the level of support as needed. As the other person develops competence and confidence in managing their own responsibilities, you can continue to step back while acknowledging their growth and success. You may also need to fine-tune the level of support you provide, offering more help in some areas or less involvement in others based on how the transition is progressing.

Managing the Guilt and Fear That Arise During Disengagement

Strategic disengagement almost inevitably triggers intense emotions in the person stepping back. Guilt, fear, anxiety, and doubt are normal responses to changing long-established patterns of relationship, especially when those patterns have been reinforced by praise, gratitude, and a sense of being needed and valuable.

The guilt often centers around the fear that you're being selfish, uncaring, or irresponsible by stepping back from management roles. This guilt is particularly intense for people who have been socialized to believe that love equals sacrifice, that good people always put others first, and that caring means being available to fix and manage whatever goes wrong in others' lives.

Understanding the source of this guilt can help you work through it more effectively. Much of the guilt stems from internalized messages about what it means to be a good parent, partner, friend, or colleague. These messages often equate worth with usefulness and love with management. Challenging these messages requires developing a more nuanced understanding of what true support and care actually look like.

Patricia, whose story opened this chapter, described her guilt about stepping back from managing her daughter's life: "I felt like I was failing as a mother. I had been taught that good mothers always help their children, always make their lives easier, always sacrifice their own needs for their children's comfort. Stepping back felt selfish and wrong, even though intellectually I knew it was healthier for both of us."

The fear that accompanies disengagement often focuses on potential negative outcomes: What if something goes wrong? What if they can't handle it? What if they fail and it's my fault for not helping? What if they get hurt because I wasn't there to prevent it? These fears can be so intense that they override rational thinking and make disengagement feel dangerous and irresponsible.

Working through these fears requires distinguishing between realistic concerns and catastrophic thinking. Some level of struggle, difficulty, and even failure is a normal and necessary part of human development. Most people are far more capable of handling challenges than the over-manager's anxiety would suggest. And preventing someone from experiencing manageable difficulties often prevents them from developing the skills and confidence they need to handle larger challenges later.

It's also important to remember that your management and intervention can't actually prevent all negative outcomes. Life involves risk, struggle, and sometimes failure regardless of how much someone tries to control and manage outcomes. The illusion of control that drives over-management is exactly that—an illusion.

The anxiety that arises during disengagement often manifests as hypervigilance about the other person's wellbeing and functioning. You may find yourself constantly wondering how they're managing, looking for signs of struggle or distress, and fighting the urge to check in or offer help. This anxiety is a normal part of the adjustment process, but it requires conscious management to prevent it from driving you back into old patterns.

Developing strategies for managing disengagement anxiety is crucial for maintaining your commitment to stepping back. This might involve setting specific times for checking in rather than constantly monitoring, finding other activities to occupy your mind and energy, or working with a therapist or coach to process the emotions that arise during the transition.

The doubt that accompanies disengagement often questions whether you're making the right choice, whether your approach is too harsh or too lenient, whether you should modify your boundaries or maintain them. This doubt is normal and can even be helpful if it leads to thoughtful adjustments in your approach. However, chronic doubt can undermine your confidence and make it difficult to maintain consistent boundaries.

Working through doubt requires trusting the process even when the outcomes aren't immediately clear. Disengagement is an investment in long-term growth and health rather than a strategy for short-term comfort. The benefits often aren't visible immediately, and there may be a period of adjustment where things feel worse before they get better.

Handling Pushback from Those Accustomed to Your Management

When you begin to disengage from management roles, it's almost inevitable that you'll encounter resistance from people who have become accustomed to your involvement in their lives. This pushback can take many forms—anger, hurt, guilt-trips, increased neediness, or attempts to pull you back into old patterns through crisis or manipulation.

Understanding that pushback is a normal response to changing relationship dynamics can help you prepare for it and respond effectively. When someone has become accustomed to having their problems solved for them, their decisions made for them, or their emotional states managed for them, your withdrawal from these roles naturally creates discomfort and anxiety. Their pushback is often an attempt to restore the familiar dynamic rather than adjust to new expectations.

The pushback often begins with expressions of hurt or confusion: "Why won't you help me anymore?" "Don't you care about me?" "You've changed and I don't understand why." These responses can be particularly difficult to handle because they often contain genuine emotion and may trigger your own guilt and doubt about your disengagement process.

It's important to distinguish between the emotional content of these responses and the underlying request for you to resume your management role. The person may genuinely feel hurt or confused, and those feelings deserve acknowledgment and empathy. However, their feelings don't necessarily mean that your disengagement is wrong or that you should abandon your boundaries.

Responding effectively to expressions of hurt requires acknowledging their feelings while maintaining your commitment to healthier relationship patterns. This might sound like: "I can see that you're hurt and confused by the changes I'm making. I care about you very much, which is exactly why I'm stepping back from managing parts of your life that you're capable of handling yourself. I believe in your ability to handle these challenges, and I'm still here to support you in appropriate ways."

The pushback often escalates to more intense forms of pressure when initial expressions of hurt don't restore the old dynamic. This might include increased crisis calls, dramatic presentations of helplessness, or attempts to involve other family members or friends in pressuring you to resume your management role.

Crisis escalation is a particularly challenging form of pushback because it triggers your instinct to help and can make disengagement feel cruel or dangerous. The person may present increasingly dramatic problems, emphasize their inability to cope, or suggest that something terrible will happen if you don't intervene.

Responding to crisis escalation requires maintaining perspective about what constitutes a genuine emergency versus what constitutes an attempt to manipulate you back into management mode. True emergencies that require immediate intervention are relatively rare. Most situations that are presented as crises are actually problems that the person could handle themselves with appropriate effort and resources.

Tom, a father who had been learning to disengage from managing his adult son's finances, described this dynamic: "When I stopped giving him money every time he had a financial crisis, the 'emergencies' became more frequent and more dramatic. Suddenly everything was urgent and catastrophic. It took me a while to realize that many of these crises were manufactured to pull me back into my old role of financial rescuer."

Guilt-tripping is another common form of pushback that can be particularly effective at undermining disengagement efforts. This might involve reminders of all the ways the person has helped you in the past, comparisons to how other people's family members or friends would handle the situation, or suggestions that your disengagement reveals a lack of love or commitment to the relationship.

Responding to guilt-trips requires maintaining clarity about your motivations and values. Disengagement that comes from a desire to support someone's growth and independence is fundamentally different from disengagement that comes from selfishness or lack of caring. Reminding yourself of your true motivations can help you maintain your boundaries even when others question your intentions.

The most sophisticated form of pushback often involves attempts to triangulate other people into the situation. The person may complain to other family members, friends, or colleagues about your "sudden selfishness" or "lack of caring," hoping that these others will pressure you to resume your management role.

Dealing with triangulation requires maintaining your boundaries even when others express concern or criticism about your approach. This might involve having direct conversations with the people who have been triangulated, explaining your perspective and requesting that they not get involved in your relationship decisions. It might also involve simply accepting that some people won't understand your approach and maintaining your boundaries regardless of their opinions.

Creating Space for Others to Grow and Solve Their Own Problems

The ultimate goal of strategic disengagement is not to withdraw your care and support, but to create the space that others need to develop their own capabilities, confidence, and independence. This space is crucial for growth because it allows people to encounter challenges, develop problem-solving skills, and experience the satisfaction that comes from handling their own lives successfully.

Creating this space requires resisting the urge to jump in at the first sign of struggle or discomfort. Growth often involves a degree of challenge, frustration, and even temporary failure. When you consistently prevent others from experiencing these natural parts of the learning process, you inadvertently prevent them from developing resilience and competence.

The space for growth includes both practical space—allowing others to handle their own logistics, decisions, and problems—and emotional space—allowing others to experience their own feelings without immediately trying to fix or manage those feelings.

Practical space means stepping back from tasks and responsibilities that others can reasonably handle themselves, even if they might not handle them exactly as you would. This might involve allowing your teenager to manage their own homework schedule, even if their approach seems less organized than yours. It might mean letting your spouse handle their own relationship with their difficult family members, even if you could smooth things over more diplomatically.

The key to providing practical space is distinguishing between situations where your involvement is truly necessary and situations where your involvement is simply more efficient or less stressful in the short term. While it might be faster for you to handle certain tasks yourself, this efficiency comes at the cost of preventing others from developing their own capabilities.

Emotional space means allowing others to experience their own emotional responses to life events without immediately moving to comfort, fix, or manage those emotions. This doesn't mean being cold or uncaring—it means trusting that others can handle their own emotional experiences and that working through difficult emotions is often necessary for growth and development.

Creating emotional space might involve listening to someone's distress without immediately offering solutions, acknowledging someone's disappointment without trying to make them feel better, or simply being present with someone's struggle without trying to eliminate it.

Sarah, whose transformation we've followed throughout this book, described learning to create emotional space for her teenage daughter: "When she was upset about not making the varsity team, my automatic response was to try to make her feel better by pointing out all her other accomplishments or suggesting ways she could improve for next year. Learning to create emotional space meant just sitting with her disappointment, acknowledging how much it hurt, and trusting that she could work through these feelings herself. It was much harder for me than trying to fix her feelings, but it was much better for her development."

The space for growth also includes the space to fail without immediate rescue. Failure is often one of the most powerful teachers, providing feedback about what doesn't work and motivation to try different approaches. When you consistently prevent others from experiencing the natural consequences of their choices, you rob them of this valuable learning opportunity.

This doesn't mean hoping that others will fail or refusing to provide appropriate support during genuine difficulties. It means allowing natural consequences to occur when those consequences provide valuable learning opportunities and aren't genuinely harmful.

David learned this lesson when his adult daughter was fired from her job for chronic lateness. His initial impulse was to call his contacts in her industry to help her find another position immediately. Instead, he provided emotional support while allowing her to experience the full consequences of her employment difficulties. "It was hard to watch her struggle," he recalled, "but that experience taught her lessons about responsibility and professionalism that my lectures never could have taught."

Creating space for growth requires faith in others' capabilities even when they don't yet believe in those capabilities themselves. This faith communicates a powerful message: "I believe you can handle this, even if you're not sure you can." This message can be life-changing for people who have been receiving the opposite message through consistent management and rescue.

The Disengagement Ladder

Successfully implementing strategic disengagement requires a systematic approach that allows you to step back gradually while maintaining appropriate support and connection. The Disengagement Ladder provides a framework for this process, helping you determine where to start, how to proceed, and when to adjust your approach.

The bottom rung of the ladder represents full management, where you're handling most decisions, solving most problems, and taking responsibility for most outcomes in the other person's life. This level of involvement might be appropriate for young children or people in genuine crisis, but it becomes problematic when it continues beyond the point where such intensive management is necessary.

The second rung represents guided management, where you're still heavily involved but beginning to include the other person in decision-making and problem-solving processes. This might involve asking for their input before making decisions that affect them, walking them through your problem-solving process so they can learn it, or giving them choices between pre-selected options.

The third rung represents collaborative support, where you and the other person share responsibility for decisions and problem-solving, with you providing expertise, resources, and guidance while they take increasing ownership of the process and outcomes. This level might involve brainstorming solutions together, sharing research responsibilities, or dividing tasks based on each person's strengths and capabilities.

The fourth rung represents consultative support, where the other person takes primary responsibility for their own life while you provide advice, perspective, and resources when requested. This level might involve being available for conversation and counsel while expecting them to make their own decisions and handle their own implementation.

The fifth rung represents emotional support, where you provide love, encouragement, and companionship while expecting the other person to handle their own practical responsibilities independently. This level might involve celebrating their successes, comforting them during difficulties, and maintaining emotional connection without getting involved in managing their choices or solving their problems.

The top rung represents healthy independence, where both people function autonomously while maintaining mutual care and appropriate interdependence. This doesn't mean emotional distance or lack of support—it means that both people take responsibility for their own lives while choosing to share experiences, provide mutual support, and maintain a loving connection.

Moving up the ladder typically involves spending time at each level, allowing both parties to adjust to new expectations and develop new skills before progressing to the next level. The pace of movement depends on various factors including the other person's age and capabilities, the complexity of the situations involved, and the history of the relationship.

Some relationships may require moving up the ladder more slowly, particularly if the management patterns have been entrenched for many years or if the other person has significant challenges that require ongoing support. Other relationships may progress more quickly, especially if the other person is eager for increased independence and demonstrates readiness to handle more responsibility.

The key is to calibrate your movement up the ladder based on the other person's developing capabilities rather than your own comfort level. Your anxiety about stepping back shouldn't keep you at lower levels of the ladder longer than necessary, but your desire for independence shouldn't push you to move up the ladder faster than the other person can reasonably adjust.

The Natural Consequences Framework

One of the most powerful tools for supporting others' growth while disengaging from management is learning to allow natural consequences to occur instead of constantly intervening to prevent or minimize them. Natural consequences are the automatic results of people's choices and behaviors, and they often provide more effective teaching than any lecture, advice, or management could provide.

The Natural Consequences Framework helps you distinguish between consequences that are appropriate to allow and situations where intervention is necessary. Not all consequences are appropriate to allow—some are genuinely harmful, dangerous, or disproportionate to the choice that created them. The framework helps you make wise decisions about when to step back and when to step in.

Natural consequences that are appropriate to allow typically have several characteristics: they're directly related to the choice or behavior that created them, they're not permanently harmful or dangerous, they provide clear feedback about what doesn't work, and they're manageable for the person experiencing them given their age, capabilities, and resources.

For example, if your teenager consistently forgets their lunch, the natural consequence of being hungry during the day provides clear feedback about the importance of remembering lunch. This consequence is directly related to their choice, not permanently harmful, and manageable for someone their age. Allowing this consequence to occur is likely to be more effective than constantly rescuing them by bringing forgotten lunches to school.

Consequences that may require intervention typically involve genuine danger, permanent harm, legal consequences that could affect their future, or situations where the person lacks the resources or capabilities to handle the outcome effectively. The goal isn't to allow people to experience serious harm, but to allow them to experience manageable difficulties that provide valuable learning opportunities.

The framework also considers the distinction between natural consequences and artificial consequences. Natural consequences occur automatically as a result of choices and behaviors, while artificial consequences are imposed by others as a form of punishment or control. Natural consequences are generally more effective for learning because they're directly connected to the choice that created them and don't involve power struggles or resentment about unfair treatment.

Margaret, the physician whose story we explored in earlier chapters, used the Natural Consequences Framework when her adult son was struggling with chronic lateness to work. Instead of continuing to wake him up each morning and drive him to work when he missed his usual transportation, she stepped back and allowed him to experience the natural consequences of his choices.

"The first few times he was late, I felt terrible and wanted to intervene," Margaret recalled. "But I realized that the natural consequences of his lateness—having to explain to his boss, losing pay for missed time, having to arrange alternative transportation—were much better teachers than my morning wake-up calls and rescue rides ever were. Within a few weeks, he had developed his own systems for getting to work on time."

Implementing the Natural Consequences Framework requires developing tolerance for others' discomfort and your own anxiety about their struggles. This tolerance is crucial because the automatic impulse to rescue often kicks in before natural consequences have had time to work their teaching magic.

It also requires clear communication about your decision to step back and allow consequences to occur. This communication should emphasize your confidence in the other person's ability to handle the situation and learn from it, rather than presenting the consequences as punishment or abandonment.

The Support Versus Enable Decision Tree

One of the most challenging aspects of strategic disengagement is learning to distinguish between support that empowers growth and "support" that actually enables dependency. The Support Versus Enable Decision Tree provides a framework for making these distinctions and choosing responses that truly serve the other person's development and wellbeing.

The decision tree begins with a fundamental question: Will my involvement in this situation increase or decrease the other person's capability and confidence over time? Support increases capability and confidence by providing resources, encouragement, and scaffolding that help people develop their own skills. Enabling decreases capability and confidence by doing things for people that they could reasonably do for themselves.

The second branch of the decision tree asks: Am I responding to a genuine request for help, or am I taking over because I'm uncomfortable with their struggle? Support typically responds to clear requests for specific assistance, while enabling often involves jumping in based on your own anxiety rather than their actual needs.

The third branch considers: Does my involvement teach skills and promote independence, or does it create dependency and prevent learning? Support involves teaching, modeling, and gradually transferring responsibility, while enabling involves doing things for others without helping them develop the ability to do these things themselves.

The fourth branch examines: Am I helping them handle their own responsibilities, or am I taking over responsibilities that belong to them? Support respects boundaries around responsibility and helps people function better within their own roles, while enabling involves crossing those boundaries and taking on responsibilities that belong to others.

The final branch asks: Does my involvement come from my strength and choice, or from my anxiety and compulsion? Support comes from a place of groundedness and intentional choice about how to help, while enabling comes from anxiety-driven compulsion to fix, rescue, and control outcomes.

Using this decision tree helps you evaluate specific situations and choose responses that truly support growth rather than enabling dependency. It also helps you recognize patterns in your own helping behavior and adjust your approach when you realize you've been enabling rather than supporting.

Jennifer used this decision tree when her adult daughter asked for help with a work presentation. Instead of automatically offering to research the topic and create slides as she had done in the past, Jennifer worked through the decision tree. She realized that doing the research and creating slides would decrease her daughter's capability, wasn't responding to a specific request for that level of help, wouldn't teach useful skills, involved taking over her daughter's work responsibilities, and came from her own anxiety about her daughter's success rather than from a genuine desire to support her growth.

Instead, Jennifer offered to brainstorm ideas with her daughter, review her slides once she had created them, or help her practice her presentation. These offers addressed her daughter's actual request for support while maintaining appropriate boundaries around responsibility and promoting skill development rather than dependency.

Learning to Trust the Process

Strategic disengagement requires developing faith in processes that aren't under your control—the process of other people's growth and development, the process of natural consequences providing feedback and motivation, and the process of relationships adjusting to healthier dynamics over time. This trust is often the most challenging aspect of disengagement because it requires letting go of the illusion that your management and intervention are necessary for others' wellbeing and success.

Learning to trust the process means accepting that growth often involves struggle, that competence develops through practice rather than through being protected from challenges, and that the most valuable lessons often come through experience rather than through advice or management.

This trust doesn't mean becoming passive or uninvolved. It means shifting from a position of control to a position of support, from managing outcomes to trusting processes, from preventing difficulties to having faith in others' ability to navigate difficulties successfully.

Developing this trust often requires examining your own beliefs about other people's capabilities and resilience. Many over-managers operate from unconscious beliefs that others are fragile, incompetent, or unable to handle life's normal challenges. These beliefs drive the compulsion to manage and control, but they're often inaccurate assessments of others' actual capabilities.

The process of strategic disengagement offers an opportunity to discover that most people are far more capable and resilient than your management patterns have allowed them to demonstrate. When you step back and create space for others to handle their own challenges, you often discover strengths and capabilities that your management had been covering up.

Patricia, whose story opened this chapter, described her growing trust in her daughter's capabilities: "As I stepped back from constantly solving her problems, I watched her develop problem-solving skills I didn't even know she had. She became more creative, more resourceful, and more confident. I realized that my 'help' had been preventing her from discovering her own strength and competence."

Trust in the process also means accepting that the timeline for others' growth and development may be different from what you would prefer. People learn and develop at their own pace, and attempting to control or accelerate this process often backfires by creating pressure and resistance.

This patience with others' developmental timelines is particularly challenging for over-managers who are accustomed to solving problems quickly and efficiently. Learning to step back and allow others to develop their own solutions at their own pace requires a fundamental shift in orientation from efficiency to empowerment, from quick fixes to sustainable growth.

The art of strategic disengagement is ultimately about learning to love others in ways that honor their autonomy, respect their capability, and support their growth into their fullest potential. It's about discovering that stepping back from management can be the most loving thing you can do, creating space for others to develop their own strength while freeing yourself to focus on your own growth and development.

This process isn't always comfortable, and it doesn't always produce immediate results. But over time, strategic disengagement creates the conditions for healthier relationships, greater mutual respect, and authentic connection based on choice rather than dependency. It transforms you from someone who manages others' lives into someone who trusts, supports, and empowers others to live their own lives with confidence and competence.

CHAPTER 7

Emotional Detachment with Love

The phone call came at 7:30 on a Thursday evening, just as Rachel was settling down with a cup of tea and a book she'd been trying to read for weeks. Her sister's voice was thick with tears and familiar desperation.

"Rachel, I can't take it anymore. Mark and I had another huge fight, and I think our marriage is really over this time. I'm so scared and I don't know what to do. I keep thinking about what will happen to the kids, how I'll manage financially, whether I'll ever find someone else who could love me..."

For twenty years, Rachel had been her sister's emotional lifeline during every relationship crisis, career setback, and life transition. She had absorbed Anna's anxiety as if it were her own, stayed awake at night worrying about Anna's problems, and carried her sister's emotional burdens until her own shoulders ached with the weight of living two lives instead of one.

As she listened to the familiar litany of fears and worst-case scenarios, Rachel felt the automatic tightening in her chest that always accompanied Anna's distress calls. Her nervous system was preparing to take on another emotional emergency that wasn't hers to carry. But this time, something was different.

Instead of immediately diving into problem-solving mode, instead of absorbing Anna's panic and making it her own, Rachel took a breath and consciously created space between her sister's emotional state and her own. She could hear Anna's pain, she could feel compassion for her struggle, but she wasn't drowning in it. She wasn't carrying it as if it belonged to her.

"Anna," Rachel said gently, "I can hear how much pain you're in right now, and I care about you deeply. This sounds incredibly difficult and scary. What do you think would be most helpful for you right now?"

This response marked a profound shift in Rachel's approach to emotional support. She was learning the art of emotional detachment with love—the ability to care deeply about someone while not absorbing their emotional experience as your own, to offer genuine support without taking responsibility for managing their feelings, and to maintain your own emotional equilibrium while being present for someone else's struggle.

Emotional detachment with love is perhaps the most sophisticated skill required for breaking free from over-management patterns. It requires developing the capacity to distinguish between empathy and emotional fusion, between caring and carrying, between being supportive and being consumed by others' emotional experiences.

Distinguishing Between Empathy and Emotional Fusion

The foundation of emotional detachment with love lies in understanding the crucial difference between healthy empathy and unhealthy emotional fusion. Both involve feeling connected to others' emotional experiences, but they have vastly different effects on your wellbeing and your ability to provide genuine support.

Empathy is the ability to understand and share another person's feelings while maintaining awareness that these feelings belong to them, not to you. When you're operating from empathy, you can recognize and respond to others' emotions without losing your own emotional center. You feel with them, but you don't become them emotionally.

Emotional fusion, on the other hand, involves absorbing others' emotions so completely that you lose the boundary between their emotional experience and your own. When you're emotionally fused with someone, their anxiety becomes your anxiety, their depression becomes your depression, their excitement becomes your excitement. You're no longer feeling with them—you're feeling as them.

Dr. Murray Bowen, who developed family systems theory, describes emotional fusion as a state where "individuals have poorly differentiated emotional and intellectual functioning." In fused relationships, people lose their individual emotional identity and become reactive to each other's emotional states in ways that are automatic and often destructive.

The problem with emotional fusion is that it actually decreases your ability to be helpful to the other person. When you're drowning in someone else's emotional experience, you can't offer the calm presence, clear thinking, and stable support that would actually be most beneficial. Instead, you add your own reactivity to their distress, often escalating rather than soothing the emotional intensity.

Emotional fusion also creates codependent dynamics where both people become dependent on each other for emotional regulation. The distressed person learns to rely on your absorption of their emotions rather than developing their own emotional regulation skills, while you become addicted to the intensity and drama of constantly managing emotional crises.

Sarah, whose journey we've followed throughout this book, described her experience with emotional fusion in her marriage: "Whenever my husband was stressed about work, I would become as anxious as he was, sometimes even more so. I would lie awake at night worrying about his projects, feeling his deadlines as if they were my own. I thought I was being a supportive wife, but really I was just adding my anxiety to his stress. It didn't help him cope better—it just meant that both of us were overwhelmed instead of one of us being able to offer stability and perspective."

Healthy empathy allows you to understand and respond to others' emotions from a place of stability and choice rather than automatic reactivity. When you're operating from empathy rather than fusion, you can offer genuine comfort, practical support, and emotional presence without losing yourself in the other person's experience.

The shift from fusion to empathy requires developing what psychologists call "emotional differentiation"—the ability to maintain your own emotional identity while remaining connected to others. This doesn't mean becoming cold or uncaring. It means caring in a way that actually serves the other person's wellbeing rather than just relieving your own discomfort with their distress.

Jennifer, whose story has appeared throughout these chapters, described learning this distinction: "I realized that when my daughter was upset, I was feeling her emotions more intensely than she was. I was catastrophizing about her problems, losing sleep over her struggles, and basically hijacking her emotional experience. When I learned to feel empathy without fusion, I could actually listen to her more clearly, offer better support, and help her develop her own emotional regulation skills."

The practice of maintaining empathy without fusion requires conscious awareness of whose emotions you're experiencing at any given moment. It requires asking yourself: "Is this feeling coming from my own experience, or am I absorbing it from someone else?" This awareness allows you to respond consciously rather than react automatically to others' emotional states.

The Observer Self: Developing Emotional Objectivity

One of the most powerful tools for achieving emotional detachment with love is developing what spiritual and psychological traditions call the "observer self"—the part of your consciousness that can witness your own emotional experiences and reactions without being completely identified with them.

The observer self is the aspect of your awareness that can step back from immediate emotional reactions and see them with some objectivity and perspective. It's the part of you that can notice when you're becoming emotionally activated, when you're absorbing someone else's emotions, or when you're reacting from old patterns rather than responding from conscious choice.

Developing your observer self doesn't mean suppressing emotions or becoming detached in a cold, uncaring way. It means creating enough internal space to experience emotions without being completely overwhelmed by them, to witness your reactions without being controlled by them, and to choose your responses rather than being driven by automatic patterns.

This observer capacity is crucial for emotional detachment with love because it allows you to maintain perspective during emotionally intense situations. Instead of being swept away by the immediate emotional content of a situation, you can step back, assess what's actually happening, and choose how to respond in ways that truly serve everyone involved.

Dr. Daniel Siegel, a psychiatrist who studies mindfulness and emotional regulation, describes this capacity as "mindsight"—the ability to see the internal world of yourself and others with clarity and compassion. He explains that developing mindsight allows people to "step back from the emotional intensity of the moment and see patterns, make choices, and respond rather than simply react."

The observer self develops through practices that create space between your immediate emotional reactions and your responses to those reactions. This might involve meditation, mindfulness practices, journaling, therapy, or simply pausing before responding to emotionally charged situations.

One of the most effective ways to develop the observer self is through what psychologists call "emotional labeling"—the practice of naming and describing your emotional experiences as they arise. Instead of just experiencing anxiety, you notice "I'm feeling anxiety right now." Instead of just being angry, you observe "I'm having angry thoughts and feelings." This labeling creates just enough distance to prevent complete identification with the emotion.

Marcus, a father who had struggled with emotional fusion with his teenage son, described developing his observer self: "I started noticing when my son's stress about school would trigger my own anxiety about his future. Instead of immediately jumping into problem-solving mode, I would pause and think, 'I'm feeling anxious right now, but this anxiety belongs to my old fears about academic performance, not to the current reality of my son's situation.' That little bit of space allowed me to respond much more helpfully."

The observer self also helps you distinguish between your own authentic emotional responses and emotions you're absorbing from others. When you can step back and observe your emotional state objectively, you can ask yourself: "Is this emotion arising from my own experience, or am I picking it up from someone else?" This distinction is crucial for maintaining emotional boundaries and responding appropriately to different situations.

Developing emotional objectivity doesn't mean becoming emotionally flat or disconnected. It means being able to experience emotions fully while maintaining enough perspective to make conscious choices about how to respond to those emotions. You can feel deeply without being overwhelmed, care intensely without being consumed, and support others without losing yourself in their experiences.

The practice of emotional objectivity requires patience and self-compassion as you learn to witness your own patterns and reactions without judgment. It's natural to become emotionally activated, especially in relationships that matter to you. The goal isn't to eliminate emotional reactions but to develop the capacity to observe them, understand them, and choose your responses consciously.

Techniques for Unhooking from Others' Emotional States

Learning to unhook from others' emotional states requires developing specific techniques that help you maintain your own emotional center even when people around you are experiencing intense emotions. These techniques aren't about becoming indifferent or uncaring—they're about caring in ways that actually serve others while protecting your own emotional wellbeing.

One of the most fundamental unhooking techniques is conscious breathing. When you're in the presence of someone who is emotionally dysregulated, your nervous system automatically begins to mirror their activation. Conscious breathing helps you maintain your own nervous system regulation even when others around you are activated.

This might involve taking slow, deep breaths while listening to someone's distress, focusing on lengthening your exhales to activate your parasympathetic nervous system, or simply maintaining awareness of your breath as an anchor to your own experience rather than getting swept away by others' emotional intensity.

Physical grounding techniques can also help you maintain emotional boundaries in challenging situations. This might involve feeling your feet on the floor, noticing the weight of your body in your chair, or consciously relaxing tension in your shoulders and jaw. These physical practices help you stay connected to your own experience rather than becoming absorbed in others' emotional states.

The practice of emotional boundary visualization can be particularly helpful for people who are highly sensitive to others' emotions. This involves imagining a protective boundary around yourself—perhaps a bubble of light, a shield of energy, or simply a clear boundary that allows love and compassion to flow while preventing you from absorbing others' emotional intensity.

This visualization isn't about shutting others out or becoming defensive. It's about creating a clear energetic distinction between your emotional experience and theirs, allowing you to remain open and caring while maintaining your own emotional equilibrium.

Language patterns can also help you maintain emotional detachment with love. Instead of saying "I'm so worried about you" (which fuses your emotional state with their situation), you might say "I can see you're going through a difficult time, and I care about you." Instead of "This is so stressful" (which absorbs their stress as your own), you might say "This sounds really stressful for you."

These linguistic shifts might seem subtle, but they reflect and reinforce important internal boundaries between your emotional experience and others' emotional experiences. They allow you to express care and concern without taking on others' emotions as your own responsibility.

The technique of conscious perspective-taking involves deliberately stepping back from the immediate emotional intensity of a situation and considering it from a broader viewpoint. This might involve asking yourself: "How will this situation look in a week, a month, or a year?" "What would I tell a friend who was dealing with this same situation?" "What's the difference between what's actually happening and what my anxiety is telling me might happen?"

This perspective-taking helps you respond to the actual situation rather than to your emotional reactions to the situation. It allows you to offer support that's grounded in reality rather than driven by emotional intensity.

Patricia, whose story opened the previous chapter, described using perspective-taking when her adult daughter was struggling with work stress: "Instead of immediately absorbing her anxiety and jumping into crisis mode, I stepped back and asked myself what was actually happening. She was dealing with a challenging project and feeling overwhelmed, but she wasn't in danger, she had handled difficult projects before, and she had resources available to help her. That perspective allowed me to offer calm support rather than adding my own anxiety to her stress."

The practice of emotional refocusing involves consciously redirecting your attention from others' emotional states to your own emotional center. When you notice yourself becoming absorbed in someone else's emotions, you can deliberately shift your focus to your own breathing, your own body sensations, your own emotional needs, or your own sense of groundedness.

This refocusing isn't selfish—it's actually essential for maintaining the emotional stability that allows you to offer genuine support. When you're emotionally centered, you can provide the calm presence and clear thinking that's most helpful during emotional crises.

Maintaining Compassion While Protecting Your Peace

One of the greatest challenges in developing emotional detachment with love is learning to maintain genuine compassion and care while protecting your own emotional peace and wellbeing. Many people fear that creating emotional boundaries will make them cold, uncaring, or unavailable to the people they love.

However, protecting your emotional peace actually enhances your ability to offer genuine compassion. When you're not overwhelmed by others' emotions, when you're not depleted by constantly absorbing emotional intensity, when you're not reactive to every emotional crisis, you have much more capacity for sustained, meaningful support.

Compassion that comes from emotional stability is far more valuable than compassion that comes from emotional fusion. Stable compassion can be sustained over time, it doesn't burn out or become resentful, and it actually helps others develop their own emotional regulation skills rather than creating dependency on your emotional management.

The key to maintaining compassion while protecting your peace lies in understanding that love doesn't require you to suffer along with others. You can care deeply about someone's pain without taking their pain into your own body and psyche. You can offer support and comfort without absorbing their distress as if it were your own emergency.

This distinction becomes clearer when you consider what kind of support is actually most helpful during emotional crises. People in distress rarely need someone else to become as upset as they are. They need someone who can remain calm and stable, who can offer perspective and hope, who can model emotional regulation rather than adding to the emotional chaos.

Dr. Kristin Neff, who studies self-compassion and emotional regulation, explains: "When we're emotionally overwhelmed ourselves, we can't offer the kind of presence and support that's actually most helpful. Maintaining our own emotional equilibrium isn't selfish—it's essential for being able to show up as our most helpful selves."

The practice of loving detachment involves holding space for others' emotions without taking responsibility for changing those emotions. This means you can witness someone's pain without immediately trying to fix it, you can acknowledge someone's fear without taking on the job of eliminating it, and you can offer comfort without becoming responsible for their emotional state.

This kind of presence is actually much more supportive than emotional fusion because it communicates trust in the other person's ability to handle their own emotional experiences. When you remain calm and stable in the face of someone's distress, you're sending the message that their emotions, however intense, are manageable and that you have confidence in their resilience.

The boundary between compassion and fusion becomes clearer when you examine your motivations for wanting to help. Are you responding from genuine care for the other person's wellbeing, or are you trying to relieve your own discomfort with their distress? Are you offering support because it serves their growth and healing, or because their emotional intensity triggers your own anxiety?

Compassion that serves others comes from a place of emotional stability and conscious choice. It's offered freely rather than compulsively, and it respects the other person's autonomy and capacity for growth. Fusion-based "compassion" is often driven by your own need to feel better, to be needed, or to control outcomes, and it frequently undermines rather than supports others' emotional development.

Jennifer discovered this distinction when her teenage daughter was going through a difficult breakup: "My initial response was to absorb all her heartbreak and try to fix her pain by offering solutions, distractions, and constant reassurance. But I realized this approach was actually preventing her from learning to process difficult emotions herself. When I stepped back and offered a calm presence without trying to eliminate her sadness, she was able to work through her feelings much more effectively."

The practice of compassionate detachment also involves accepting that you can't save others from all emotional pain, and that trying to do so often prevents them from developing emotional resilience and wisdom. Some emotional experiences are necessary for growth, and your attempts to prevent or minimize them may actually interfere with important developmental processes.

This doesn't mean being indifferent to others' suffering or refusing to offer support during genuine difficulties. It means recognizing that emotional pain is a normal part of human experience and that your job isn't to eliminate it but to offer love and support while others navigate their own emotional journeys.

The Power of "I Love You AND You Can Handle This"

One of the most powerful phrases for maintaining emotional detachment with love is "I love you AND you can handle this." This simple statement communicates both your care and your confidence in the other person's capability, both your emotional connection and your trust in their resilience.

The word "AND" is crucial in this formulation because it holds both realities simultaneously: your love and their capability, your care and their autonomy, your support and their responsibility. This is different from saying "I love you BUT you need to handle this yourself," which communicates withdrawal of love conditional on their handling things independently.

The "I love you AND you can handle this" approach allows you to maintain emotional connection while establishing appropriate boundaries around responsibility. It communicates that your love isn't dependent on your ability to fix their problems, and that their worth isn't dependent on their need for your management.

This phrase can be adapted to many different situations and relationships: "I care about you AND I believe in your ability to figure this out." "I'm here for you AND I trust you to make good decisions about your situation." "I love you AND I have confidence that you can handle whatever comes next."

The power of this approach lies in its ability to communicate two essential messages that are often seen as contradictory: unconditional love and expectation of competence. Many people believe they have to choose between being supportive and expecting independence, between being loving and maintaining boundaries, between caring and allowing others to handle their own challenges.

But these are false dichotomies. The most loving thing you can often do is express confidence in others' capabilities. The most supportive approach is often trusting others to handle their own lives. The best way to care for someone is frequently to refuse to take over their responsibilities while maintaining emotional connection and encouragement.

David, a father who had been learning to disengage from managing his adult son's career decisions, described using this approach: "When my son was stressed about whether to take a job offer, my old pattern would have been to research the company, analyze the pros and cons, and essentially make the decision for him. Instead, I told him, 'I love you and I have complete confidence in your ability to make the right decision for your life.' It was amazing how much more confident he became when he knew I trusted his judgment."

The "AND" approach also helps you maintain emotional equilibrium during challenging situations. When you're focused on both loving someone AND trusting their capability, you're less likely to become absorbed in their emotional intensity or feel compelled to take over their responsibilities.

This approach requires genuine belief in others' capabilities, which can be challenging if you've been in management mode for a long time. You may have become so focused on problems, deficits, and areas where others need help that you've lost sight of their strengths, resources, and capacity for growth.

Developing authentic confidence in others' capabilities often requires consciously looking for evidence of their competence, resourcefulness, and resilience. Most people have more capabilities than their managed relationships allow them to demonstrate, and shifting your focus to their strengths can help you develop genuine trust in their ability to handle their own challenges.

The Emotional Firewall Method

Creating sustainable emotional detachment with love requires developing what I call an "emotional firewall"—a systematic approach to maintaining emotional boundaries while remaining open to genuine connection and support. Like a computer firewall that filters information and prevents harmful intrusions while allowing beneficial communication, an emotional firewall helps you distinguish between emotions that serve your relationships and emotions that overwhelm your capacity to be helpful.

The first component of the emotional firewall is recognition—developing the ability to notice when you're beginning to absorb others' emotional states. This requires cultivating awareness of your own emotional patterns and triggers, understanding what situations tend to activate your fusion responses, and recognizing the early warning signs that you're losing your emotional boundaries.

These warning signs might include physical sensations like tightness in your chest or stomach when others are distressed, mental symptoms like obsessive thinking about others' problems, emotional symptoms like feeling anxious or depressed when others are struggling, or behavioral patterns like immediately jumping into problem-solving mode when others share difficulties.

The second component is assessment—evaluating whether the emotions you're experiencing are arising from your own authentic response to the situation or whether you're absorbing emotions that belong to others. This involves asking yourself questions like: "Is this feeling coming from my own experience of this situation, or am I taking on someone else's emotional state?" "Does the intensity of my emotional response match the actual circumstances, or am I amplifying it through fusion?"

The third component is choice—consciously deciding how to respond based on what would truly serve the situation rather than what would relieve your immediate emotional discomfort. This might involve choosing to listen without immediately trying to fix, offering support without taking over, or maintaining your own emotional stability while the other person works through their challenges.

The fourth component is action—implementing your chosen response while monitoring your emotional boundaries and adjusting as needed. This requires following through on your decision to maintain detachment even when others' emotional intensity increases, even when they pressure you to take on more responsibility, and even when your own anxiety about stepping back becomes uncomfortable.

Rachel, whose story opened this chapter, described developing her emotional firewall during her sister's relationship crises: "I learned to notice when Anna's anxiety about her marriage was starting to become my anxiety. I would literally feel it happening—my chest would tighten, my thoughts would start racing about her problems, and I would feel this urgent need to fix everything for her. Once I could recognize this pattern, I could choose to respond differently."

The emotional firewall method also includes what I call "emotional hygiene" practices—regular activities that help you clear absorbed emotions and return to your own emotional center. This might involve physical exercise, meditation, journaling, time in nature, creative activities, or simply quiet time to process and release emotions that don't belong to you.

These practices are particularly important for people who are naturally empathetic or highly sensitive to others' emotions. Just as physical hygiene helps you maintain health by removing harmful substances from your body, emotional hygiene helps you maintain psychological health by clearing emotions that you've absorbed from others.

The firewall method requires ongoing maintenance and adjustment as you learn more about your own patterns and as your relationships evolve. Some situations may require stronger boundaries, while others may allow for more emotional engagement. The key is developing the flexibility to adjust your emotional firewall based on what each situation requires.

The Compassionate Detachment Practice

Developing sustainable emotional detachment with love requires regular practice in situations that aren't emotionally intense, so you can maintain these skills when challenging situations arise. The Compassionate Detachment Practice provides a framework for developing these capabilities in a systematic way.

The practice begins with daily mindfulness of your emotional boundaries during routine interactions. Throughout the day, notice when you're taking on others' emotions unnecessarily, when you're feeling responsible for others' emotional states, or when you're becoming activated by others' stress or upset.

This might involve checking in with yourself during conversations: "Whose emotions am I feeling right now?" "Am I responding to what's actually happening, or to my own anxiety about what might happen?" "Is my emotional intensity proportional to my actual involvement in this situation?"

The second component involves practicing emotional differentiation in low-stakes situations. When someone shares a frustration about traffic, a concern about work, or disappointment about a canceled plan, practice feeling empathy without taking on their emotional state as your own. Notice the difference between caring about their experience and carrying their experience.

The third component involves experimenting with supportive responses that maintain emotional boundaries. Instead of automatically trying to fix others' problems or manage their emotions, practice offering presence, empathy, and confidence in their capability. Notice how these responses feel different from your usual patterns and how others respond to this different kind of support.

The fourth component involves processing and releasing emotions that you do absorb, either intentionally or unconsciously. At the end of each day, take time to notice what emotions you might be carrying that don't belong to you, and consciously choose to release them. This might involve visualization, journaling, physical movement, or simply taking deep breaths while imagining the emotions flowing out of your body.

Margaret, the physician whose transformation we've followed throughout this book, described her compassionate detachment practice: "I started with small situations—noticing when I would take on a colleague's stress about a difficult patient or absorb a friend's anxiety about her children. I practiced feeling concerned without feeling responsible, caring without carrying. It took months of daily practice before I could maintain these boundaries during really intense situations, but the practice made all the difference."

The practice also involves developing what Buddhist traditions call "loving-kindness" meditation—cultivating feelings of genuine care and goodwill for others while maintaining clear boundaries around responsibility and emotional management. This practice helps you develop the capacity to love deeply without losing yourself in others' experiences.

As you develop greater skill with compassionate detachment, you may notice that your relationships actually become deeper and more satisfying. When you're not constantly absorbing others' emotions or feeling responsible for managing their emotional states, you have more capacity for genuine connection, meaningful conversation, and authentic support.

The Energy Protection Toolkit

Maintaining emotional detachment with love requires protecting your energetic and emotional resources so you can offer sustained support without becoming depleted. The Energy Protection Toolkit provides practical strategies for managing your emotional energy in relationships that have historically been draining or overwhelming.

The first tool involves energy budgeting—consciously allocating your emotional energy based on your capacity and priorities rather than automatically spending it on whatever seems most urgent or dramatic. This means recognizing that your emotional energy is a finite resource that needs to be managed intentionally.

Energy budgeting might involve limiting the amount of time you spend in emotionally intense conversations, spacing out interactions with particularly draining people, or reserving emotional energy for situations where your support can genuinely make a difference rather than spending it on chronic complaining or crisis that could be handled independently.

The second tool involves creating energetic boundaries around specific types of interactions. You might decide that you're available for genuine requests for support but not for chronic venting, that you'll engage with problem-solving conversations but not with repeated rehearsals of the same issues, or that you'll offer empathy for current difficulties but not for ongoing drama about past grievances.

The third tool involves developing what I call "emotional aikido"—the ability to redirect emotional intensity rather than absorbing it. When someone is highly activated emotionally, instead of taking on their activation, you can acknowledge their feelings while redirecting the energy back to them in a supportive way.

This might sound like: "I can see you're really upset about this. What do you think would be most helpful for you right now?" or "This sounds incredibly frustrating. How are you thinking about handling it?" These responses validate the person's emotional experience while maintaining the boundary that their emotions and their solutions belong to them.

The fourth tool involves regular energy restoration practices that help you recover from emotionally demanding interactions. This might involve spending time alone after intense conversations, engaging in activities that bring you joy and vitality, connecting with people who energize rather than drain you, or simply taking time to rest and recharge.

Jennifer found that she needed to build energy restoration into her daily routine as she learned to maintain emotional boundaries: "I realized that certain conversations with my mother would leave me completely drained for hours afterward. I started scheduling these calls when I had time to recover afterward, and I developed a routine of taking a walk and calling a friend who always makes me laugh after particularly intense conversations."

The fifth tool involves what I call "compassionate limit-setting"—learning to say no to emotional demands that exceed your capacity while maintaining love and care for the relationship. This might involve setting time limits on crisis conversations, declining to participate in repetitive problem discussions, or simply saying, "I care about you and I'm not in a position to help with this particular issue right now."

These limits aren't punitive or meant to control others' behavior—they're protective boundaries that allow you to maintain your own emotional wellbeing so you can continue to be present and supportive in sustainable ways.

The energy protection toolkit requires ongoing attention and adjustment as you learn more about what drains your energy and what restores it. Some relationships may require more protective boundaries, while others may be naturally more balanced and energizing. The key is developing the awareness and skills to protect your energy intentionally rather than unconsciously depleting it through emotional fusion and over-functioning.

Living in Loving Detachment

The ultimate goal of developing emotional detachment with love is not to become distant or uncaring, but to love others in ways that truly serve their highest good while maintaining your own emotional wellbeing and autonomy. This loving detachment creates the foundation for relationships that are based on mutual respect, genuine support, and healthy interdependence rather than codependency and emotional fusion.

Loving detachment allows you to be present with others' pain without taking it on as your own emergency. It allows you to offer support and encouragement without feeling responsible for others' emotional states. It allows you to care deeply while maintaining the emotional stability that makes your caring genuinely helpful rather than just reactive.

When you master emotional detachment with love, you discover that you can actually love others more fully because your love isn't contaminated by your own anxiety, guilt, or need to control outcomes. You can offer the gift of your calm presence, your steady support, and your unshakable faith in others' capability to handle their own lives.

This transformation doesn't happen overnight, and it requires ongoing practice and refinement. There will be times when you slip back into fusion, when you absorb others' emotions despite your best intentions, when you feel guilty for maintaining boundaries, or when you wonder if you're being too detached.

These experiences are part of the learning process, and they provide valuable information about what adjustments you need to make in your approach. The goal isn't perfection—it's progress toward relationships that honor both your wellbeing and others' autonomy, that support growth rather than dependency, and that are based on choice rather than compulsion.

As you develop greater skill with loving detachment, you'll likely find that others begin to relate to you differently as well. When you stop absorbing their emotions and taking responsibility for their problems, they often develop greater emotional regulation skills themselves. When you express confidence in their capability rather than anxiety about their struggles, they often become more confident and resourceful.

The art of emotional detachment with love ultimately transforms not just how you relate to others, but how you relate to yourself. You learn to trust your own emotional experience, to value your own wellbeing, and to recognize that taking care of yourself isn't selfish—it's essential for being able to show up as your best self in all your relationships.

This is the foundation upon which you can build an authentic life—one where your energy is directed toward your own growth and dreams, where your relationships are based on mutual respect and healthy boundaries, and where your love for others empowers rather than enables, supports rather than suffocates, and honors the full capability and potential of everyone involved.

CHAPTER 8

Rediscovering Your Own Life Vision

On a quiet Saturday morning in October, Linda sat in her kitchen staring at a blank piece of paper. Her therapist had given her what seemed like a simple assignment: "Write down three things you want for your own life that have nothing to do with anyone else's needs or problems."

It should have been easy. Linda was fifty-one years old, successful in her career, financially stable, and respected in her community. She had spent decades making decisions, solving problems, and creating outcomes. But as she sat with her pen poised over the paper, she realized something that shook her to her core: she had no idea what she actually wanted for herself.

For the past twenty-five years, Linda's life had been organized entirely around other people's visions, dreams, and needs. She had supported her husband's career moves, managed her children's educational paths, helped her aging parents navigate their health challenges, and built her own professional life around what would best serve her family's financial needs. She had become incredibly skilled at identifying what others needed and figuring out how to provide it, but somewhere along the way, she had completely lost touch with her own desires, dreams, and sense of purpose.

The blank paper seemed to mock her. How could someone who had been so competent at managing everyone else's life have so little clarity about her own? How could she have spent decades making important decisions without ever stopping to ask herself what she actually wanted those decisions to create?

As Linda sat in that kitchen, confronting the vast emptiness where her personal vision should have been, she was experiencing what millions of over-managers discover when they finally step back from managing everyone else: they don't know who they are underneath all the roles they've been playing. They've become so skilled at anticipating and meeting others' needs that they've forgotten how to recognize their own.

This discovery can be terrifying, but it's also the doorway to freedom. Underneath all the management, fixing, and caretaking lies your authentic self—the person you were before you learned that your value came from what you could do for others, the person you still are beneath all the roles and responsibilities you've accumulated. Rediscovering this self and creating a vision for your own life is perhaps the most important work you can do, both for your own fulfillment and for your ability to truly serve others from a place of wholeness rather than depletion.

The Identity Archaeology Process: Who Are You Beneath the Manager Role?

Rediscovering your authentic self after years or decades of over-managing others requires what I call "identity archaeology"—a careful excavation of the layers of roles, expectations, and adaptations you've accumulated to uncover the core self that exists beneath them all.

This archaeological process begins with recognizing that you are not the roles you've been playing. You are not just a parent, partner, employee, friend, or family member, though you may fulfill all these roles beautifully. You are a complete person with your own interests, preferences, values, dreams, and ways of experiencing the world. The manager role may have become so dominant that it obscures these other aspects of yourself, but they haven't disappeared—they've simply been buried under years of focusing on everyone else's needs.

The first layer to excavate is the layer of automatic responses and people-pleasing patterns. Over-managers often develop sophisticated systems for reading others' needs and adapting their own behavior to meet those needs. While this adaptability can be a strength, it can also lead to a loss of contact with your own authentic preferences and responses.

To begin uncovering your authentic responses, start paying attention to your immediate, uncensored reactions to situations before you modify them to please others or meet their expectations. What do you actually think about the movie before you consider whether your opinion will disappoint your partner? What do you genuinely feel about the family vacation plans before you worry about whether your preferences will cause conflict? What are your instinctive reactions to social invitations before you calculate whether attending will meet others' needs or expectations?

Dr. Harriet Lerner, who studies authenticity in relationships, describes this process as "recovering your own voice." She explains: "Many people, especially women, become so skilled at harmonizing with others that they lose track of their own melody. The work of authenticity involves learning to hear and trust your own voice again, even when it doesn't blend perfectly with everyone else's preferences."

The second layer to excavate involves exploring the interests and activities you've abandoned or never pursued because they didn't fit with your management role. Over-managers often sacrifice their own hobbies, creative pursuits, and personal interests to make time for managing others' lives. This sacrifice can happen so gradually that you don't notice it until you realize you can't remember the last time you did something purely for your own enjoyment.

Margaret, the physician whose story has appeared throughout this book, discovered this when she tried to remember what she used to enjoy before her life became consumed with managing her family's needs. "I realized I hadn't painted in fifteen years," she said. "I used to love art, used to spend hours lost in creative projects. But somewhere along the way, those hours got filled with everyone else's activities, everyone else's needs. I had convinced myself that I didn't have time for 'frivolous' pursuits, but really I had forgotten that my own interests mattered."

The process of rediscovering abandoned interests often involves giving yourself permission to be "selfish" in ways that feel uncomfortable at first. You might need to schedule time for activities that serve no one but yourself, spend money on pursuits that don't benefit your family, or decline requests for help so you can focus on your own projects. This can trigger guilt and anxiety, especially if you've been conditioned to believe that good people always put others first.

The third layer involves exploring the dreams and aspirations you've deferred or dismissed as impractical. Over-managers often become so focused on immediate, practical needs that they lose touch with their own long-term visions and possibilities. They may have once had clear ideas about what they wanted to create, experience, or contribute, but these dreams got pushed aside to handle more urgent demands from others.

This exploration requires creating space to dream without immediately censoring your visions based on practical constraints or others' needs. What would you want to do with your life if you knew you couldn't fail? What would you pursue if money weren't a concern? What would you create if you had unlimited time and resources? What would you attempt if you weren't worried about others' reactions or expectations?

These questions aren't meant to create unrealistic fantasies, but to help you reconnect with the fundamental desires and values that motivate you. Even if your dreams seem impractical in their current form, they contain important information about what brings you alive, what gives your life meaning, and what direction you want to move toward.

Jennifer, whose journey we've followed throughout these chapters, discovered that underneath her role as family manager lay a long-buried dream of starting her own business. "I had always been interested in design and had even started developing some ideas in my twenties," she recalled. "But when we had children, I convinced myself that entrepreneurship was too risky, too time-consuming, too selfish. It took me years to realize that dismissing my own dreams didn't actually serve my family—it just made me resentful and depleted."

The fourth layer of identity archaeology involves examining the values and principles that truly matter to you, as distinct from the values you've adopted to fit in with others or meet their expectations. Over-managers often become so skilled at adapting to others' value systems that they lose touch with their own core beliefs and principles.

This exploration might involve asking yourself: What do you believe is most important in life? What principles do you want to guide your decisions? What kind of person do you want to be, regardless of what others expect from you? What matters to you so much that you would be willing to face conflict or disapproval to honor it?

Understanding your authentic values is crucial because it provides the foundation for making decisions that align with your true self rather than with others' expectations. When you're clear about what matters most to you, you can make choices that honor your integrity even when they disappoint others or require difficult conversations.

Reconnecting with Buried Dreams and Desires

Once you've begun the archaeological process of uncovering your authentic self, the next step involves actively reconnecting with the dreams and desires that have been buried under years of focusing on everyone else's needs. This reconnection requires both courage and patience, as buried dreams often emerge gradually and may feel foreign or unrealistic after years of neglect.

The process of reconnecting with buried dreams often begins with small experiments in self-expression and exploration. Rather than trying to immediately pursue major life changes, start with small ways of honoring your interests and curiosities. This might involve taking a class in something that's always intrigued you, reading books in areas you've never explored, or simply spending time in environments that inspire you.

These small experiments serve multiple purposes. They help you gather information about what truly energizes and excites you, they provide evidence that you can pursue your own interests without neglecting your responsibilities to others, and they gradually rebuild your capacity to focus on your own growth and development.

Patricia, whose story has appeared in previous chapters, described her process of reconnecting with buried dreams: "I started by giving myself permission to spend an hour each weekend doing something purely for my own enjoyment. At first, I could barely think of anything—I was so out of practice with focusing on my own preferences. But gradually, I remembered my love of hiking, my interest in photography, and my curiosity about different cultures. Each small step helped me remember more about who I was underneath all the managing and fixing."

The reconnection process often involves grieving for the time you've lost and the opportunities you've missed while focused on managing others. This grief is natural and important—it honors the cost of your over-management patterns and creates space for you to move forward with clarity about what you want to create going forward.

This grieving process might involve sadness about deferred dreams, anger about the ways you've neglected your own life, or regret about choices you made based on others' needs rather than your own values and desires. These emotions can be intense, but they're also healing, clearing away the accumulated resentment and regret that often accompany years of self-sacrifice.

It's important during this process not to blame others for your choices or to become bitter about the support you've provided. The goal isn't to regret your caring and generosity, but to learn from your experience and make different choices going forward. Most over-managers made their choices with good intentions, often based on genuine love and concern for others. The goal now is to find ways to maintain that love and concern while also honoring your own life and dreams.

The process of reconnecting with buried dreams also involves distinguishing between dreams that still resonate with who you are now and dreams that may have been appropriate for an earlier stage of your life but no longer fit your current circumstances and values. People change and evolve, and some dreams that seemed important in your twenties may not align with who you've become in your forties or fifties.

This doesn't mean that all your early dreams are obsolete, but it does mean that you need to evaluate them through the lens of who you are now rather than who you were then. Some dreams may need to be adapted or evolved rather than pursued in their original form. Others may need to be released entirely to make room for new dreams that better reflect your current values and circumstances.

Sarah discovered this when she reconnected with her teenage dream of becoming a professional musician. "I realized that what I had really loved wasn't the idea of being famous or performing on big stages," she reflected. "What I loved was the creative process, the collaboration with other musicians, and the way music could touch people's hearts. I didn't want to become a touring musician at this stage of my life, but I could find ways to incorporate music and creativity into my life that honored what I had really been seeking."

The reconnection process also involves developing tolerance for uncertainty and imperfection as you explore new directions. After years of focusing on managing and controlling outcomes for others, it can feel uncomfortable to pursue goals where the outcome is uncertain or where you might not excel immediately.

This tolerance for uncertainty is crucial because authentic dreams often involve growth, challenge, and learning. They require you to step outside your comfort zone and risk failure or disappointment. If you only pursue goals where success is guaranteed, you're likely still operating from a management mindset rather than embracing the vulnerability that comes with authentic growth and exploration.

Creating a Personal Vision Independent of Others' Needs

Once you've begun reconnecting with your authentic self and your buried dreams, the next step involves creating a compelling vision for your own life that's independent of others' needs, expectations, and problems. This personal vision serves as your North Star, guiding your decisions and helping you allocate your time and energy in ways that serve your own growth and fulfillment.

Creating a personal vision that's truly independent of others requires examining how much of your current life structure is organized around meeting others' needs versus pursuing your own goals and values. For many over-managers, this examination reveals that virtually every aspect of their life has been shaped by what others need from them rather than what they want to create for themselves.

This doesn't mean you need to become selfish or stop caring about others. It means developing a clear sense of your own direction so you can make conscious choices about how to balance your own goals with your relationships and responsibilities. When you have a strong personal vision, you can support others from a place of choice and abundance rather than from obligation and depletion.

The process of creating a personal vision begins with exploring what you want your life to stand for, what legacy you want to create, and what kind of person you want to become. These big-picture questions help you connect with your deeper sense of purpose and meaning, which provides the foundation for more specific goals and plans.

This exploration might involve asking yourself: What impact do you want to have on the world? What do you want to be remembered for? What values do you want to embody in how you live your life? What kind of person do you want to be in your relationships, your work, and your community? What would make you feel proud of how you've spent your time and energy?

David, a father and business executive whose transformation we've followed, described his process of creating a personal vision: "I realized that I had been living by default rather than by design. I had just been responding to whatever seemed most urgent or whatever others needed from me. When I stepped back and asked myself what I actually wanted to create with my life, I discovered that I had deep interests in mentoring young professionals and contributing to environmental sustainability. These weren't things anyone had asked me to focus on—they were directions that emerged from my own values and passions."

The vision creation process also involves imagining your ideal life in concrete, specific terms. This means going beyond vague desires like "being happy" or "having more balance" to envision specific experiences, achievements, relationships, and ways of spending your time that would feel deeply satisfying and meaningful to you.

This concrete visioning might involve imagining a typical day in your ideal life: What time would you wake up? What activities would fill your day? What kind of work would you be doing? What kinds of relationships would you have? How would you spend your free time? What kind of environment would you live in? What would you have accomplished that would make you feel proud and fulfilled?

The key to effective visioning is making it as specific and sensory as possible. The more vividly you can imagine your ideal life, the more motivating and compelling it becomes. This specificity also helps you identify concrete steps you can take to move toward your vision, rather than feeling overwhelmed by vague desires for change.

Linda, whose story opened this chapter, eventually created a vision that included starting a nonprofit organization focused on financial literacy for women, traveling to at least three new countries each year, and building deeper friendships based on shared interests rather than just convenience or family connections. "Having a specific vision gave me something to work toward instead of just feeling dissatisfied with my current life," she explained.

The personal vision should also include both internal and external goals. External goals might involve achievements, experiences, or contributions you want to make in the world. Internal goals might involve qualities you want to develop, ways you want to grow as a person, or emotional and spiritual states you want to cultivate.

This balance between internal and external goals is important because it ensures that your vision includes both doing and being, both achievement and personal development. Many over-managers are skilled at setting and achieving external goals but have neglected their own internal development and emotional wellbeing.

Creating a personal vision also requires honestly examining the constraints and responsibilities in your life and finding ways to honor your vision within realistic parameters. This doesn't mean abandoning your vision to accommodate others' needs, but it does mean being strategic about how you pursue your goals given your current circumstances.

This might involve breaking your vision down into phases, with some elements that you can begin pursuing immediately and others that might require more time or significant life changes. It might involve finding creative ways to incorporate elements of your vision into your current life structure while you work toward larger changes.

Overcoming the Guilt of Focusing on Yourself

One of the biggest obstacles to creating and pursuing a personal vision is the guilt that often accompanies focusing on your own needs, dreams, and goals. After years or decades of putting others first, redirecting energy toward your own life can feel selfish, irresponsible, or somehow wrong.

This guilt is particularly intense for people who have been praised and valued for their selflessness, their availability to help others, and their willingness to sacrifice their own needs for others' comfort. When your identity and self-worth have been built around being needed and useful to others, focusing on yourself can feel like a betrayal of everything you've been taught about how to be a good person.

Understanding the source of this guilt is crucial for working through it effectively. Much of the guilt stems from internalized messages about gender roles, family responsibilities, and social expectations that equate love with self-sacrifice and caring with constant availability. These messages are often so deeply ingrained that they feel like moral truths rather than cultural conditioning.

Challenging these messages requires developing a more nuanced understanding of what it means to care for others and contribute to their wellbeing. The most loving thing you can often do for the people in your life is to model what it looks like to live authentically, pursue your dreams, and take responsibility for your own happiness and fulfillment.

When you live from your own vision and purpose, you have more energy, enthusiasm, and genuine love to offer others. When you're fulfilled and engaged with your own life, you're less likely to become resentful or depleted in your relationships. When you demonstrate that it's possible to pursue your own goals while maintaining loving relationships, you give others permission to do the same.

Dr. Kristin Neff's research on self-compassion has shown that people who treat themselves with kindness and pursue their own wellbeing are actually more capable of genuine compassion toward others. She explains: "When we're constantly depleted and resentful from self-sacrifice, we don't have the emotional resources to offer authentic love and support. Taking care of ourselves isn't selfish—it's essential for being able to show up as our best selves in our relationships."

Working through the guilt of self-focus also involves examining the fears that often underlie the guilt. Many over-managers fear that if they stop focusing primarily on others' needs, they'll become selfish, narcissistic, or uncaring. They worry that pursuing their own goals will damage their relationships or that others will see them as bad people.

These fears are usually based on false dichotomies that assume you must choose between caring for yourself and caring for others, between pursuing your own dreams and maintaining loving relationships, between having boundaries and being loving. In reality, these are not either-or choices—they're both-and opportunities to create a more balanced, sustainable, and authentic way of living.

The guilt often intensifies when others react negatively to your shift toward self-focus. Family members who have benefited from your over-functioning may express hurt, confusion, or anger when you begin directing more energy toward your own life. They may accuse you of being selfish or suggest that you don't care about them anymore.

These reactions can be particularly difficult to handle because they often trigger your own fears about becoming selfish or uncaring. It's important to remember that others' discomfort with your changes doesn't mean your changes are wrong. People often resist changes in relationship dynamics, even when those changes are healthier for everyone involved.

Responding to others' negative reactions requires maintaining clarity about your motivations and values while acknowledging their feelings without taking responsibility for managing them. You might say something like: "I understand this feels different and maybe uncomfortable. I love you just as much as I always have, and I'm learning to balance caring for you with caring for myself. I believe this will actually make me a better partner/parent/friend in the long run."

Margaret faced this challenge when she began pursuing her research interests again after years of focusing entirely on her family's needs. Her husband initially reacted with concern and some resentment about the time and energy she was directing away from family management. "He was used to having me available for everything, and he worried that my research work meant I cared less about our family," she recalled. "It took time for him to see that I was actually happier and more engaged when I had my own meaningful work to focus on, and that made me more present and loving when I was with the family."

Overcoming the guilt of self-focus also involves reframing what it means to be responsible to others. True responsibility in relationships involves being authentic, maintaining appropriate boundaries, and encouraging others' growth and independence. It doesn't involve sacrificing your own life to manage others' comfort and convenience.

You can be deeply committed to others' wellbeing while still maintaining commitment to your own growth and fulfillment. You can love others fiercely while refusing to make their problems your primary focus. You can support others generously while insisting that they take responsibility for their own lives and choices.

Building a Life That Energizes Rather Than Depletes You

Creating and pursuing a personal vision ultimately means building a life structure that energizes and sustains you rather than constantly depleting your resources. This requires making conscious choices about how you spend your time, energy, and attention, prioritizing activities and relationships that align with your values and goals, and gradually eliminating or reducing commitments that drain you without providing corresponding fulfillment.

Building an energizing life begins with conducting an honest audit of how you currently spend your time and energy. For one week, track not just what you do, but how different activities and interactions affect your energy levels. Notice which activities leave you feeling energized, engaged, and alive, and which leave you feeling drained, resentful, or depleted.

This energy audit often reveals surprising patterns. You might discover that activities you thought were relaxing actually drain your energy, while activities you've been avoiding actually energize you. You might find that certain relationships consistently leave you feeling depleted, while others reliably restore your sense of vitality and connection.

The audit also helps you identify the difference between activities that are temporarily tiring but ultimately energizing (like challenging creative work or meaningful service) and activities that are simply draining without providing corresponding fulfillment (like managing others' responsibilities or engaging in obligations that don't align with your values).

Once you have clarity about what energizes and depletes you, you can begin making conscious choices about how to restructure your life. This doesn't mean immediately eliminating everything that's challenging or demanding—it means being strategic about which challenges you take on and ensuring that your life includes enough energizing activities to sustain you through the demanding ones.

This restructuring process often requires saying no to commitments that don't serve your vision or values, even when these commitments seem worthy or when others expect you to continue them. It might mean stepping down from volunteer positions that no longer inspire you, declining social invitations that feel obligatory rather than enjoyable, or reducing your involvement in family dynamics that consistently drain your energy.

These choices can be difficult because they often involve disappointing others or letting go of roles that have been important to your identity. However, learning to say no to what doesn't serve you is essential for creating space for what does serve you. Every yes to something that drains you is a no to something that could energize you.

The restructuring process also involves actively adding elements to your life that align with your vision and values. This might mean pursuing new interests, developing new skills, building new relationships, or creating new professional opportunities. The key is to be as intentional about what you add to your life as you are about what you remove.

Jennifer discovered this when she began restructuring her life around her entrepreneurial dreams. "I realized I was spending 80% of my time on activities that were either managing other people's lives or fulfilling obligations that didn't really matter to me. When I started saying no to these things and yes to activities that supported my business goals, my energy levels increased dramatically. I had more enthusiasm for everything, including my relationships with my family."

Building an energizing life also requires attention to your physical environment, daily routines, and lifestyle choices. Over-managers often neglect these foundational elements because they're so focused on others' needs, but your environment and routines have a significant impact on your energy levels and overall wellbeing.

This might involve creating a physical space in your home that's entirely yours, establishing morning or evening routines that center and energize you, making changes to your diet or exercise habits that better support your energy levels, or simply paying attention to the small daily choices that either add to or subtract from your sense of vitality.

The goal isn't to create a perfect life free from all challenges or demands, but to create a life structure that supports and sustains your authentic self while allowing you to contribute meaningfully to others' lives. When your life is aligned with your values and vision, when you're energized by your daily activities and relationships, you have much more to offer others from a place of genuine abundance rather than resentful obligation.

The Identity Excavation Exercise

To facilitate the process of rediscovering your authentic self, I've developed a comprehensive exercise that helps you systematically explore different aspects of your identity that may have been buried under years of over-managing others. This exercise is designed to be completed over several sessions, allowing time for reflection and discovery between different sections.

The first section involves exploring your authentic preferences and responses. For one week, pay attention to your immediate, uncensored reactions to everyday situations before you modify them to accommodate others. Notice what you genuinely think about movies, books, restaurants, vacation ideas, social plans, and daily decisions before you consider others' preferences or needs.

Keep a journal of these authentic responses, noting when they differ from what you eventually choose to express or act upon. This awareness helps you distinguish between your genuine preferences and the adaptations you make to please others or avoid conflict.

The second section involves rediscovering abandoned interests and activities. Make a list of everything you used to enjoy doing but have stopped pursuing. Include hobbies, creative activities, sports, social activities, learning interests, and any other pursuits that once brought you pleasure or satisfaction.

For each item on your list, explore what you loved about that activity and whether some version of it might still appeal to you. Consider whether you abandoned these activities because you genuinely lost interest or because they didn't fit with your management role and responsibilities.

The third section involves exploring deferred dreams and aspirations. Write about the dreams you had for your life at different stages—in childhood, adolescence, young adulthood, and at various points throughout your adult life. Include career aspirations, creative goals, travel dreams, relationship hopes, and any other visions you once held for your future.

Examine which of these dreams still resonate with who you are now and which might need to be adapted or evolved to fit your current circumstances and values. Consider what core desires or values these dreams represented that might be fulfilled in new ways.

The fourth section involves identifying your authentic values and principles. Write about what matters most to you, independent of others' expectations or approval. Consider what principles you want to guide your decisions, what kind of person you want to be, and what you want your life to stand for.

Compare these authentic values with the values you've been living by in your over-management role. Notice where they align and where they diverge, and consider how you might make choices that better honor your true values going forward.

The fifth section involves envisioning your ideal life. Write a detailed description of how you would like to spend your time, what kind of work you would do, what your relationships would look like, and what you would accomplish if you were free to design your life according to your own vision rather than others' needs.

Include both practical elements (daily routines, work activities, living situation) and intangible elements (emotional states, relationship qualities, sense of purpose). The more specific and vivid your vision, the more useful it will be for guiding your choices and actions.

The Personal Vision Canvas

Once you've completed the identity excavation process, the Personal Vision Canvas provides a framework for organizing your insights into a coherent, actionable vision for your life. This canvas helps you integrate what you've learned about your authentic self into a clear direction for moving forward.

The canvas is divided into several interconnected sections that together create a comprehensive picture of your vision. The first section focuses on your core values and principles—the fundamental beliefs and priorities that will guide your decisions and actions.

The second section identifies your unique strengths, talents, and capabilities—the qualities and abilities you bring to any situation and that can serve as the foundation for pursuing your goals. This includes both skills you've already developed and potential you'd like to cultivate.

The third section outlines your major life domains—areas like career, relationships, health, creativity, service, learning, and spirituality—and describes your vision for each domain. This helps ensure that your vision is comprehensive and addresses all aspects of your life that matter to you.

The fourth section identifies specific goals and milestones you want to achieve in each life domain, broken down by timeframe (one year, three years, five years, etc.). These goals should be concrete enough to guide action but flexible enough to allow for adjustment as you learn and grow.

The fifth section describes the kind of person you want to become—the character qualities, ways of being, and internal states you want to cultivate. This internal dimension of your vision is just as important as external achievements and ensures that your growth includes both doing and being.

The sixth section identifies potential obstacles and challenges you might face in pursuing your vision, along with strategies for addressing them. This realistic assessment helps you prepare for difficulties without becoming discouraged by them.

The final section describes how your personal vision connects with your relationships and responsibilities to others. This helps you integrate your individual goals with your ongoing commitments and shows how pursuing your own vision can actually enhance your ability to contribute to others' lives.

The Dream Recovery Protocol

For many over-managers, reconnecting with buried dreams requires a systematic approach that helps overcome the fear, guilt, and practical obstacles that have kept these dreams dormant. The Dream Recovery Protocol provides a step-by-step process for gradually bringing your dreams back to life.

The first step involves creating a safe space for dreaming without immediate pressure to act on your dreams. This might involve setting aside regular time for reflection and imagination, creating a private journal for exploring your aspirations, or finding a trusted friend or therapist who can support your exploration without immediately focusing on practical constraints.

The second step involves starting with small experiments that allow you to explore your interests without major life changes. If you've always dreamed of being an artist, start by taking a weekend art class or setting up a small creative space in your home. If you've imagined traveling to exotic places, begin by exploring new areas in your own region or learning about foreign cultures through books and documentaries.

These small experiments serve multiple purposes: they help you determine whether your dreams still resonate with who you are now, they provide evidence that you can pursue your interests without neglecting your responsibilities, and they gradually build your confidence in your ability to create positive changes in your life.

The third step involves gradually expanding your experiments as you gain confidence and clarity about what truly energizes and inspires you. This might involve taking more significant classes, joining groups related to your interests, or beginning to integrate elements of your dreams into your daily life and work.

The fourth step involves addressing the practical and emotional obstacles that have kept your dreams buried. This might require developing new skills, saving money for dream-related activities, creating time in your schedule for pursuing your interests, or working through guilt and fear about focusing on your own goals.

The fifth step involves creating an action plan for pursuing your dreams in realistic, sustainable ways. This doesn't necessarily mean making dramatic life changes immediately, but it does mean taking concrete steps toward bringing more of your authentic interests and aspirations into your daily life.

The final step involves building a support system that encourages your dream pursuit and holds you accountable for making progress toward your goals. This might include friends who share your interests, mentors who can guide your development, or professional coaches who can help you navigate the challenges of pursuing meaningful goals.

Living Your Authentic Vision

Rediscovering your own life vision is not a one-time event but an ongoing process of staying connected to your authentic self while navigating the demands and opportunities of daily life. As you grow and change, your vision may evolve, and new dreams may emerge while others fade in importance.

The key to living your authentic vision is making it a regular practice to check in with yourself about whether your choices and commitments align with your values and goals. This requires ongoing attention to how you're spending your time and energy, regular assessment of whether your life structure supports or undermines your vision, and the courage to make adjustments when you find yourself drifting away from what matters most to you.

Living authentically also means accepting that you can't pursue every dream simultaneously and that creating a meaningful life requires making choices about where to focus your limited time and energy. The goal isn't to do everything you've ever wanted to do, but to ensure that your life includes enough of what matters to you that you feel engaged, purposeful, and alive.

When you live from your own vision rather than from others' expectations and needs, you discover that you have much more energy and enthusiasm for all aspects of your life, including your relationships with others. You become someone who contributes to others' lives from choice rather than obligation, from abundance rather than depletion, and from authentic care rather than resentful duty.

This transformation ripples out to affect everyone around you. When you model what it looks like to live authentically and pursue your own dreams, you give others permission to do the same. When you take responsibility for your own happiness and fulfillment, you free others from the burden of trying to make you happy. When you live with purpose and passion, you inspire others to discover and pursue their own authentic visions.

Rediscovering your own life vision is ultimately about reclaiming your right to be the protagonist of your own story rather than just a supporting character in everyone else's drama. It's about remembering that your life matters, your dreams are valid, and your authentic self deserves to be expressed and celebrated. This isn't selfish—it's essential, both for your own wellbeing and for your ability to truly serve others from a place of wholeness and strength.

CHAPTER 9

The Time and Energy Reallocation Plan

At 6:15 on a Tuesday morning, Karen found herself sitting in her car in the parking lot of her daughter's college, having just driven two hours to deliver a textbook that Emma had forgotten for an important exam. As she watched other students walking across campus with their backpacks and coffee cups, Karen suddenly had a moment of startling clarity: she was a fifty-year-old woman who had just spent four hours of her life solving a problem that her twenty-year-old daughter could have solved herself with a phone call to a classmate or a quick trip to the campus bookstore.

This wasn't the first time Karen had made emergency rescue missions for her adult children. In the past month alone, she had driven across town to bring her son lunch when he texted that he was "too busy to eat," spent an entire Saturday helping her other daughter organize her apartment, and taken a day off work to handle car repairs that her children were perfectly capable of managing themselves.

Sitting in that parking lot, Karen began to calculate the time and energy she had spent over the past year managing crises and responsibilities that belonged to her adult children. The number was staggering: hundreds of hours that could have been spent on her own goals, her own interests, her own life. Hours that could have been invested in the photography business she'd been dreaming of starting, the novel she'd been wanting to write, the friendships she'd been neglecting, or simply the rest and relaxation she desperately needed.

For the first time, Karen understood viscerally that time and energy are finite resources that require intentional management. Every hour she spent solving other people's problems was an hour not spent on her own growth and fulfillment. Every burst of energy she directed toward managing others' lives was energy unavailable for creating the life she actually wanted to live.

This realization marked the beginning of Karen's journey toward what I call "time sovereignty"—the radical act of reclaiming control over how you spend your most precious resources and redirecting them toward what truly matters to you. For over-managers, learning to reallocate time and energy away from constant crisis management and toward personal growth represents one of the most challenging but essential aspects of breaking free from the management trap.

Conducting a Time Audit: Where Your Energy Really Goes

The first step in reclaiming your time sovereignty involves conducting a comprehensive audit of how you currently spend your time and energy. Most over-managers have only a vague sense of where their resources go because they've become so accustomed to responding automatically to whatever seems most urgent or whoever seems most needy.

This automatic responsiveness creates what I call "time leakage"—the gradual erosion of your time and energy through countless small interventions, rescues, and management activities that seem insignificant in the moment but add up to enormous resource drains over weeks and months.

A thorough time audit requires tracking not just your activities but your energy levels, emotional states, and sense of choice around how you spend your time. For two weeks, keep a detailed log of how you spend each hour of your day, noting not only what you're doing but whether you chose to do it or felt obligated to do it, whether it energized or depleted you, and whether it served your own goals or someone else's needs.

This tracking process often reveals shocking patterns. Patricia, whose transformation we've followed throughout these chapters, discovered that she was spending approximately thirty hours per week managing various aspects of her adult children's lives—from researching solutions to their problems to providing transportation they could arrange themselves to handling administrative tasks they could easily manage independently.

"I had no idea the extent of my involvement in their lives until I started tracking it," Patricia reflected. "I was essentially working a part-time job as their personal assistant, problem-solver, and crisis manager, but I was doing it for free and at the expense of my own goals and well-being."

The time audit also reveals what researchers call "attention residue"—the mental and emotional energy that continues to be consumed by other people's problems even when you're not actively working on them. Over-managers often carry others' concerns in their minds throughout the day, thinking about solutions, worrying about outcomes, and maintaining mental availability for the next crisis or request for help.

This mental energy drain can be just as significant as the time spent on actual helping activities. When your mind is constantly occupied with other people's problems, you have little mental space available for your own creative thinking, planning, and problem-solving. You exist in a state of perpetual mental fragmentation, never fully present to your own experience or fully focused on your own priorities.

The audit should also track what I call "invisible labor"—the emotional and mental work of managing family and social dynamics that rarely gets acknowledged or appreciated. This might include remembering everyone's schedules and preferences, mediating conflicts between family members, managing the emotional temperature of social situations, or simply holding space for others' feelings and needs.

This invisible labor is often overlooked because it doesn't produce tangible outcomes, but it can consume enormous amounts of energy and create chronic stress and depletion. Women, in particular, often carry disproportionate amounts of invisible labor, managing the emotional and social functioning of their families and social groups without recognition or compensation.

Marcus, a father and business executive, was surprised to discover through his time audit how much mental energy he was spending managing his wife's mood and his children's conflicts with each other. "I thought I was just being a good husband and father by staying tuned in to everyone's emotional needs," he said. "But I realized I was essentially working as an unpaid family therapist, constantly monitoring and intervening in emotional situations that the family members could have learned to handle themselves."

The time audit also helps you identify what I call "pseudo-emergencies"—situations that feel urgent but aren't actually time-sensitive or critical. Over-managers often operate in a state of chronic crisis response, treating every request for help or every expression of distress as an emergency requiring immediate attention.

Learning to distinguish between genuine emergencies and manufactured urgency is crucial for time sovereignty. Most situations that feel urgent can actually wait hours or even days without any negative consequences. Most problems that seem to require immediate intervention can be handled effectively by the person experiencing them if they're given the space and expectation to do so.

The 80/20 Rule Applied to Relationships and Responsibilities

Once you have clarity about how you're currently spending your time and energy, the next step involves applying the Pareto Principle—commonly known as the 80/20 rule—to your relationships and responsibilities. This principle suggests that 80% of results come from

20% of efforts, and it can be a powerful tool for identifying where your time and energy investments are most and least effective.

In the context of over-management patterns, the 80/20 rule often reveals that 80% of your helping and management activities produce only 20% of meaningful positive outcomes, while 20% of your efforts produce 80% of the genuine value you provide to others. Most of your interventions and rescue missions don't actually improve others' lives in significant ways—they just prevent them from developing their own problem-solving capabilities while exhausting your own resources.

Jennifer discovered this when she analyzed her pattern of helping her adult daughter with career decisions. "I was spending hours every week researching job opportunities, reviewing her résumé, and coaching her through interview preparation," Jennifer recalled. "But when I looked at the actual outcomes, most of this effort didn't make any real difference in her success. The 20% that actually helped was offering emotional support and occasionally providing perspective when she specifically asked for it."

Applying the 80/20 rule to relationships involves identifying which relationships give you energy versus which consistently drain you, which relationships involve mutual support versus one-sided caretaking, and which relationships encourage your growth versus those that keep you stuck in managing and fixing patterns.

This doesn't mean abandoning relationships that are going through difficult periods or that require more support than usual. It means recognizing which relationships have become structured around your over-functioning and making conscious choices about how much energy to invest in trying to change these dynamics versus accepting them and protecting your own resources.

The 80/20 analysis often reveals that certain relationships consistently require disproportionate amounts of energy while providing little fulfillment or genuine connection in return. These might be relationships with people who chronically create drama, who consistently expect you to solve their problems, or who take your support for granted while offering little reciprocal care.

Sarah applied this analysis to her extended family relationships and discovered that her relationship with her sister consistently consumed enormous amounts of emotional energy while providing very little satisfaction or mutual support. "I realized I was spending more time managing my sister's anxiety and problems than I was spending on all my other relationships combined," Sarah said. "It was a difficult realization because I love her, but I had to acknowledge that this level of investment wasn't sustainable or healthy for either of us."

The 80/20 rule also applies to your various responsibilities and commitments. Most over-managers have accumulated numerous obligations that seemed important when they accepted them but that now consume time and energy without providing corresponding value or satisfaction.

This might include volunteer positions that no longer inspire you, social commitments that feel obligatory rather than enjoyable, professional responsibilities that don't align with your goals or values, or family traditions that have become burdens rather than sources of connection and joy.

Applying the 80/20 analysis to your commitments requires honestly evaluating which activities provide the most satisfaction, growth, and positive impact relative to the time and energy they require. This evaluation should consider not just immediate outcomes but long-term alignment with your values and goals.

David used this analysis to examine his extensive volunteer commitments and discovered that he was serving on five different nonprofit boards, only one of which truly engaged his passion and utilized his skills effectively. "I had said yes to so many requests over the years that I had diluted my impact across multiple organizations instead of making a real difference in the areas I cared most about," he realized.

The goal of 80/20 analysis isn't to become calculating or transactional in your relationships and commitments, but to become more intentional about where you invest your limited resources. When you focus your time and energy on the relationships and activities that provide the greatest fulfillment and impact, you become more effective and satisfied while having more genuine enthusiasm for your commitments.

Creating Protected Time for Personal Pursuits

One of the most radical acts an over-manager can take is creating protected time—regularly scheduled periods that are dedicated exclusively to your own interests, goals, and wellbeing. This protected time is non-negotiable, meaning it doesn't get sacrificed when others have needs or when crises arise. It's time that belongs to you and serves your own development and fulfillment.

Creating protected time requires overcoming several significant obstacles. The first is the belief that your own interests and activities are less important than others' needs and problems. Over-managers often operate from the assumption that their personal pursuits are "selfish" luxuries that can be postponed indefinitely in favor of more pressing demands from others.

This belief is both false and destructive. Your personal growth, creative expression, and emotional wellbeing are not luxuries—they're necessities for maintaining your capacity to contribute meaningfully to others' lives. When you consistently sacrifice your own development for others' immediate comfort, you gradually become depleted, resentful, and less capable of offering genuine support.

The second obstacle is the fear that protecting time for yourself will damage your relationships or lead others to see you as selfish and uncaring. This fear is often based on the assumption that love requires constant availability and that caring means never prioritizing your own needs over others' requests.

However, relationships that can't survive you having protected time for your own growth are relationships that have become unhealthily dependent on your over-functioning. Healthy relationships not only tolerate but encourage each person's individual development and interests. When you model the importance of personal time and self-care, you give others permission to do the same.

Creating protected time begins with identifying specific periods in your schedule that will be dedicated exclusively to your own pursuits. This might be early morning hours before others wake up, evening time after family responsibilities are handled, or weekend blocks that are reserved for your personal interests and goals.

The key to successful protected time is making it specific and consistent rather than vague and sporadic. Instead of hoping you'll find time for your interests "when things calm down," you need to schedule specific hours that are dedicated to your personal pursuits regardless of what else is happening in your life.

Margaret, the physician whose transformation we've followed, created protected time by scheduling two hours every Saturday morning for her photography hobby. "I treated this time as seriously as I would treat a medical appointment," she explained. "I didn't cancel it for family events, I didn't use it to catch up on household tasks, and I didn't feel guilty about being unavailable for other people's needs during those hours."

Protected time also requires physical and mental boundaries that prevent encroachment from others' needs and demands. This might mean turning off your phone during protected time, establishing clear expectations with family members about your availability, or physically leaving your home to pursue your interests in a space where you won't be interrupted.

The third obstacle to creating protected time is your own tendency to sacrifice it when others seem to need you or when you feel guilty about focusing on yourself. Over-managers often struggle to maintain protected time consistently because they convince themselves that this particular situation is an exception that justifies abandoning their personal time.

Maintaining protected time requires developing what I call "emergency discernment"—the ability to distinguish between genuine emergencies that require immediate attention and pseudo-emergencies that can wait until your protected time is finished. True emergencies involving safety, health, or genuine crises are rare. Most situations that feel urgent can be addressed after you've honored your commitment to your own wellbeing.

Creating protected time also involves choosing activities that truly serve your growth, interests, and restoration rather than using the time for more obligation-based activities. This time should be dedicated to pursuits that energize you, challenge you in positive ways, or simply bring you joy and satisfaction.

This might include creative activities like writing, art, or music; physical activities like exercise, hiking, or dancing; learning activities like reading, classes, or skill development; social activities with people who share your interests; or simply solitary activities that restore your sense of peace and connection with yourself.

Energy Management Strategies for Highly Sensitive People

Many over-managers are what researchers call "highly sensitive people"—individuals with nervous systems that process sensory and emotional information more deeply and thoroughly than average. While this sensitivity can be a tremendous strength, allowing for empathy, intuition, and creative insight, it can also make energy management particularly challenging.

Highly sensitive people often become overwhelmed more easily by stimulation, absorb others' emotions more readily, and require more downtime to process their experiences and restore their energy. These characteristics can make them particularly vulnerable to over-management patterns because they feel others' distress so acutely that it becomes difficult to maintain appropriate boundaries.

Dr. Elaine Aron, who pioneered research on high sensitivity, explains that highly sensitive people have a lower threshold for stimulation and need more time to process experiences before moving on to new activities. She notes that "what looks like shyness or withdrawal is often just the need for processing time that allows sensitive people to function at their best."

For highly sensitive over-managers, energy management requires particular attention to overstimulation, emotional boundaries, and recovery time. Overstimulation can come from too much social interaction, too many demands for decision-making, too much sensory input, or too many emotional situations requiring response and attention.

Learning to recognize your early warning signs of overstimulation is crucial for managing your energy effectively. These signs might include feeling irritable or overwhelmed by normal sounds or activities, difficulty concentrating or making decisions, increased emotional reactivity, physical symptoms like headaches or fatigue, or simply a sense of being "peopled out" or needing solitude.

When you notice these signs, it's important to take steps to reduce stimulation and create space for processing and recovery. This might mean declining social invitations, postponing non-essential decisions, creating quiet time in your schedule, or simply taking breaks from problem-solving and helping activities.

Emotional boundaries are particularly important for highly sensitive people because they often absorb others' emotions unconsciously and automatically. The emotional firewall techniques discussed in the previous chapter are especially crucial for sensitive individuals who need extra protection from emotional overwhelm.

This protection might involve limiting exposure to highly emotional people or situations, creating physical distance during emotionally intense conversations, using visualization techniques to maintain energetic boundaries, or simply being more selective about which emotional situations you choose to engage with deeply.

Recovery time is essential for highly sensitive people to process their experiences and restore their energy. This recovery time needs to be built into your schedule regularly rather than waiting until you're completely depleted. It might involve daily periods of solitude, regular time in nature, meditative or contemplative practices, or simply quiet activities that allow your nervous system to settle and reset.

Karen, whose story opened this chapter, discovered that her sensitivity made her particularly vulnerable to her children's emotional crises. "I realized that when one of my kids was upset, I would feel their distress more intensely than they did," she said. "I had to learn to create boundaries that allowed me to be supportive without absorbing their emotions as my own crisis to solve."

Managing energy as a highly sensitive person also requires being strategic about your environment and daily routines. This might mean creating calming spaces in your home, managing noise levels and visual clutter, being mindful of lighting and temperature, or simply paying attention to how different environments affect your energy and wellbeing.

It also means being realistic about your capacity and not trying to maintain the same pace or level of stimulation that works for less sensitive people. This isn't a limitation—it's simply a characteristic that requires accommodation and strategic planning, just as any other individual difference would require.

Building Sustainable Self-Care That Doesn't Feel Selfish

For over-managers, developing sustainable self-care practices often feels impossibly selfish, especially when others seem to need so much help and support. The key to overcoming this resistance lies in reframing self-care not as a luxury or indulgence, but as a necessary foundation for your ability to show up as your best self in all areas of your life.

Sustainable self-care differs from emergency self-care in several important ways. Emergency self-care happens when you're already depleted, overwhelmed, or burned out, and it focuses on crisis intervention rather than prevention. Sustainable self-care is built into your regular routines and lifestyle, preventing depletion before it occurs and maintaining your resources rather than just restoring them after they've been exhausted.

This proactive approach to self-care requires viewing your wellbeing as a prerequisite for effective functioning rather than as a reward you earn after taking care of everyone else. Just as you wouldn't expect a car to run indefinitely without fuel and maintenance, you can't expect yourself to function effectively without regular attention to your physical, emotional, and mental needs.

Sustainable self-care also needs to be personally meaningful rather than based on generic recommendations about what you "should" do for wellness. What restores and energizes you may be very different from what works for others, and your self-care practices need to align with your personality, preferences, and lifestyle rather than conforming to external expectations.

For some people, self-care might involve vigorous physical exercise, social activities, and stimulating environments. For others, it might involve quiet contemplation, solitary activities, and calm environments. The key is paying attention to what actually makes you feel restored, energized, and connected to yourself rather than what you think you should find restorative.

This personalized approach to self-care requires experimenting with different activities and practices to discover what truly serves your wellbeing. You might find that certain activities that are supposed to be relaxing actually drain your energy, while activities that seem indulgent actually restore your capacity for caring about others.

Patricia discovered that her most effective self-care involved creative activities like painting and writing, which she had dismissed as "hobbies" that weren't important enough to prioritize. "I thought self-care had to involve things like bubble baths and spa treatments," she said. "But what actually restored my energy was having time to create something beautiful. When I made space for creative expression, I felt more alive and had more genuine enthusiasm for everything else in my life."

Sustainable self-care also needs to be integrated into your daily and weekly routines rather than relegated to special occasions or vacation time. This integration might involve small daily practices that support your wellbeing, weekly activities that provide restoration and enjoyment, and monthly or seasonal practices that support deeper renewal and reflection.

The daily practices might include morning routines that center and energize you, brief breaks throughout the day for breathing or movement, or evening routines that help you transition from work and caregiving responsibilities to rest and restoration. These don't need to be time-consuming—even five or ten minutes of intentional self-care can make a significant difference in your energy and wellbeing.

Weekly practices might involve longer periods dedicated to activities you enjoy, social time with people who energize you, or simply protected time for rest and doing nothing productive. These weekly practices provide more substantial restoration and help prevent the accumulation of stress and depletion over time.

Monthly or seasonal practices might involve longer retreats, significant creative projects, travel or adventure activities, or simply extended periods of rest and reflection. These practices support deeper renewal and help you maintain perspective on your life and priorities over longer time periods.

Building sustainable self-care also requires addressing the guilt and resistance that often arise when you prioritize your own wellbeing. This guilt is often based on the false belief that caring for yourself means caring less about others, or that time spent on your own needs is time taken away from more important responsibilities.

In reality, the opposite is true. When you're well-rested, energized, and connected to your own sense of purpose and joy, you have much more to offer others. When you model healthy self-care, you teach others that their wellbeing matters too. When you take responsibility for your own emotional and physical needs, you free others from the burden of trying to manage your wellbeing for you.

The Energy Investment Portfolio

Just as financial advisors recommend diversifying investment portfolios to maximize returns while minimizing risk, effective energy management requires diversifying how you invest your time and attention across different areas of your life. The Energy Investment Portfolio provides a framework for evaluating and optimizing these investments.

The portfolio consists of several different categories of energy investment, each serving different purposes and providing different types of returns. The first category is maintenance energy—the time and attention required to maintain your basic functioning, health, and responsibilities. This includes activities like sleep, nutrition, exercise, basic household management, and essential work responsibilities.

While maintenance energy might not feel exciting or fulfilling, it's the foundation that makes everything else possible. Neglecting maintenance activities often leads to crisis situations that consume much more energy than would have been required for prevention. Investing adequately in maintenance creates stability and prevents energy drains that can derail your other goals and priorities.

The second category is growth energy—time and attention dedicated to developing new skills, pursuing learning opportunities, and expanding your capabilities. This investment might include formal education, skill development, creative projects, or professional development activities that enhance your long-term capacity and effectiveness.

Growth investments often require significant energy in the short term but provide increasing returns over time as your enhanced capabilities make you more effective and open new opportunities for fulfillment and contribution. These investments are often the first to be sacrificed when life becomes overwhelming, but they're crucial for maintaining vitality and preventing stagnation.

The third category is relationship energy—time and attention invested in building and maintaining meaningful connections with others. This includes both intimate relationships with family and close friends and broader social connections that provide community, support, and shared experiences.

Effective relationship investments involve mutual support and genuine connection rather than one-sided caretaking or management. The goal is to invest in relationships that energize and fulfill you while also contributing meaningfully to others' wellbeing and growth.

The fourth category is service energy—time and attention dedicated to contributing to causes, communities, or individuals beyond your immediate circle. This might include volunteer work, professional service, community involvement, or informal helping activities that align with your values and sense of purpose.

Service investments provide meaning and connection to something larger than yourself, but they need to be chosen consciously rather than accepted automatically. The most fulfilling service opportunities align with your skills, interests, and values rather than simply filling gaps where help is needed.

The fifth category is restoration energy—time and attention dedicated to activities that restore your vitality, creativity, and sense of wellbeing. This includes not just relaxation and rest, but also activities that bring you joy, peace, inspiration, or a sense of connection to yourself and the world around you.

Restoration investments are often dismissed as selfish or unproductive, but they're essential for maintaining your capacity for all other activities. Without adequate restoration, your energy investments in other areas become less effective and sustainable over time.

The final category is legacy energy—time and attention invested in creating something that will outlast your immediate presence and contribute to the world in lasting ways. This might involve creative projects, mentoring others, building institutions or systems, or simply living in ways that model positive values and possibilities for others.

Legacy investments provide deep satisfaction and meaning, connecting your daily activities to your larger sense of purpose and contribution. These investments often require long-term thinking and patience, as their impacts may not be immediately visible or measurable.

Evaluating your current energy portfolio involves assessing how much time and attention you're currently investing in each category and whether this distribution aligns with your values and goals. Many over-managers discover that they're over-investing in maintenance and service energy while under-investing in growth, restoration, and legacy energy.

Rebalancing your portfolio doesn't necessarily require dramatic changes, but it does require conscious choices about how to reallocate your resources over time. This might involve gradually reducing energy spent on low-value maintenance activities, being more selective about service commitments, or creating more intentional space for growth and restoration activities.

The Time Sovereignty System

Achieving true time sovereignty—the ability to make conscious choices about how you spend your time based on your own priorities rather than others' demands—requires implementing systematic approaches to time management that protect your autonomy while allowing you to maintain important relationships and responsibilities.

The Time Sovereignty System begins with establishing what I call "time boundaries"—clear limits around when you're available for others' needs and when you're focused on your own priorities. These boundaries need to be communicated clearly and maintained consistently, even when others pressure you to abandon them.

Time boundaries might include specific hours when you're not available for non-emergency requests, days of the week that are protected for your own activities, or periods when you're not checking email or responding to phone calls. The key is creating predictable periods when others know you're not available while also ensuring that you are accessible when genuine needs arise.

These boundaries require distinguishing between actual emergencies and manufactured urgency. Most requests for help or attention can wait hours or even days without negative consequences, but over-managers often respond to all requests as if they were urgent crises requiring immediate attention.

Learning to evaluate urgency realistically involves asking questions like: Will waiting to address this issue create genuine harm or negative consequences? Is this truly time-sensitive, or does it just feel urgent because someone is anxious about it? Can this person handle this situation themselves if given the expectation and space to do so? Am I being asked to help because of a genuine need or because it's easier for them to have me handle it?

The Time Sovereignty System also includes what I call "priority protection"—actively safeguarding time for your most important goals and values against the constant pressure to respond to others' immediate needs. This protection requires treating your own priorities as seriously as you treat others' requests, scheduling time for your important activities, and refusing to consistently sacrifice your goals for others' convenience.

Priority protection often requires saying no to requests that would interfere with your important commitments, even when these requests seem worthy or when others express disappointment in your unavailability. Learning to say no without extensive justification or apology is crucial for maintaining your time sovereignty.

This might sound like: "I'm not available to help with that, but I hope you find a good solution." Or "That sounds important, but I have other commitments during that time." Or simply "I won't be able to do that." The key is being clear and direct without feeling obligated to convince others that your boundaries are reasonable.

The system also includes "time budgeting"—allocating specific amounts of time for different activities and relationships based on their importance to your goals and values rather than their urgency or others' expectations. This budgeting process involves making conscious choices about how much time you want to invest in various areas of your life.

Time budgeting might involve allocating specific hours per week for helping family members, limiting the amount of time you spend in problem-solving conversations, or dedicating certain percentages of your available time to different categories of activities. The goal is to make intentional choices about your time investments rather than allowing them to be determined by whoever makes the most urgent or persistent requests.

Jennifer implemented time budgeting by deciding that she would spend no more than two hours per week helping her adult children with their various challenges and decisions. "I realized I had been spending more time managing their lives than they were," she said. "Setting a specific limit helped me be more strategic about when and how I offered help, and it created clear boundaries that protected time for my own priorities."

The Time Sovereignty System also requires regular evaluation and adjustment of your time allocation based on changing circumstances and evolving priorities. This evaluation involves assessing whether your current time investments are producing the outcomes and satisfaction you desire, and making adjustments when you discover misalignments between your values and your actual time allocation.

This ongoing evaluation helps prevent the gradual erosion of time sovereignty that often occurs when small compromises and exceptions accumulate over time. Regular assessment ensures that you're making conscious choices about your time rather than simply defaulting to old patterns of automatic responsiveness to others' needs.

The Self-Care Sustainability Model

Creating sustainable self-care requires moving beyond the cultural narrative that self-care is a luxury or reward that you earn after taking care of everyone else. The Self-Care Sustainability Model reframes self-care as essential infrastructure for your ability to function effectively and contribute meaningfully to others' lives.

This model recognizes that self-care exists on multiple levels, each requiring different types of attention and investment. The foundation level involves basic physical and emotional maintenance—adequate sleep, nutrition, exercise, medical care, and emotional processing. Without this foundation, all other activities become more difficult and less effective.

The restoration level involves activities that actively restore your energy, creativity, and sense of wellbeing rather than just maintaining basic functioning. This might include creative pursuits, time in nature, social activities that energize you, or spiritual practices that connect you to your sense of purpose and meaning.

The growth level involves activities that challenge and develop you in positive ways, expanding your capabilities and understanding while providing a sense of progress and accomplishment. This might include learning new skills, pursuing meaningful projects, or engaging in activities that stretch your comfort zone in constructive ways.

The contribution level involves activities that allow you to use your gifts and talents in service of something meaningful beyond yourself, providing a sense of purpose and connection to larger values and goals. This contribution should align with your authentic interests and capabilities rather than being driven by obligation or guilt.

The sustainability model requires balancing investments across all these levels rather than focusing exclusively on any single level. Over-investing in foundation and restoration activities can lead to stagnation and lack of purpose, while over-investing in growth and contribution activities can lead to burnout and depletion.

This balance looks different for different people and may shift based on life circumstances, energy levels, and changing priorities. The key is maintaining awareness of your needs across all levels and making conscious choices about how to meet those needs rather than neglecting them until crisis intervention becomes necessary.

The model also recognizes that sustainable self-care requires both individual practices and supportive relationships and environments. This means not only taking personal responsibility for your wellbeing but also cultivating relationships and creating environments that support rather than undermine your self-care efforts.

This might involve setting boundaries with people who consistently drain your energy, seeking out relationships with people who encourage your wellbeing and growth, or making changes to your physical environment that support rather than stress your nervous system.

Sustainable self-care also requires addressing the systemic and cultural factors that make self-care challenging, particularly for people in caregiving roles. This might involve advocating for better support systems, challenging cultural messages that equate worth with self-sacrifice, or working to create communities that value everyone's wellbeing rather than expecting some people to consistently sacrifice their needs for others' comfort.

Reclaiming Your Life Energy

The ultimate goal of time and energy reallocation is not to become selfish or uncaring, but to reclaim conscious control over your most precious resources so you can invest them in ways that align with your values, support your growth, and contribute meaningfully to the world around you.

When you operate from a place of conscious choice rather than automatic reactivity, when you protect time for your own development and interests, when you maintain energy for your own goals and dreams, you discover that you have much more to offer others from a place of genuine abundance rather than resentful obligation.

This transformation ripples out to affect everyone in your life. When you model healthy boundaries around time and energy, you give others permission to do the same. When you demonstrate that it's possible to care deeply about others while also caring for yourself, you challenge the false dichotomy that suggests you must choose between selfishness and self-sacrifice.

When you invest in your own growth and fulfillment, you become someone who contributes to others' lives from strength rather than depletion, from choice rather than compulsion, and from authentic care rather than guilty obligation. This is the foundation for relationships and contributions that are sustainable, fulfilling, and genuinely beneficial for everyone involved.

The time and energy reallocation process requires patience, practice, and self-compassion as you learn new ways of managing your resources and relating to others' needs. There will be setbacks, guilt, and pressure to return to old patterns of automatic availability and endless giving.

But with consistent effort and commitment to your own wellbeing, you can reclaim sovereignty over your time and energy, creating a life that honors both your own authentic needs and your genuine desire to contribute to others' flourishing. This is not just a personal transformation—it's a model for a more sustainable and healthy way of living in relationship with others and with the world.

CHAPTER 10

Building Your Own Success Systems

Standing in her home office at 11 PM on a Sunday night, Maria stared at the vision board she had created six months earlier. Pinned to the cork board were images representing her dream of starting a consulting business: photos of confident women giving presentations, pictures of home offices with inspiring designs, articles about successful entrepreneurs, and a handwritten note with her financial goals for the first year.

But tonight, looking at those aspirational images felt more like mockery than motivation. Despite having a clear vision and genuine desire to build her own business, Maria had made virtually no progress toward her goals. She had attended a few networking events, read several business books, and even registered a domain name for her website. But six months later, she was still in the same job, still managing everyone else's priorities ahead of her own, still dreaming about a future that seemed as distant as ever.

The problem wasn't lack of vision or motivation. Maria could see exactly what she wanted to create, and she felt passionate about the work she hoped to do. The problem was that she had no systems in place to translate her vision into consistent action. She was approaching her personal goals the same way she approached helping others—through sporadic bursts of intense effort followed by long periods of distraction and delay.

While Maria had become incredibly skilled at creating systems that supported other people's success—helping her teenage children stay organized for school, managing her husband's schedule to optimize his work performance, coordinating her elderly mother's medical care with systematic precision—she had never applied that same systematic thinking to her own dreams and aspirations.

This disconnect is one of the most tragic ironies of over-management patterns. People who can create beautiful, effective systems for everyone else's success often live in complete chaos when it comes to pursuing their own goals. They become so skilled at organizing others' lives that they forget to organize their own. They become so competent at solving others' problems that they never develop systems for consistently working toward their own solutions.

Building your own success systems represents a fundamental shift from reactive helping to proactive creating, from managing others' goals to achieving your own, from being the supporting character in everyone else's story to becoming the protagonist of your own narrative. This shift requires not just new skills but a new mindset about what you deserve to invest in and what kinds of outcomes you can reasonably expect to create for yourself.

Goal Setting When You're Used to Focusing on Others' Goals

For over-managers, the process of setting personal goals often feels foreign and uncomfortable. After years or decades of orienting their energy around others' needs and aspirations, many discover that they've lost touch with their own authentic desires and have no experience with the systematic pursuit of personal objectives.

This discomfort with personal goal-setting often stems from several sources. First, over-managers frequently experience guilt about focusing on their own aspirations when others seem to need so much help and support. They may feel selfish for wanting to achieve personal success when family members or friends are struggling with their own challenges.

Second, many over-managers have developed what I call "vicarious achievement syndrome"—a pattern of experiencing satisfaction and accomplishment through others' successes rather than their own. They become so skilled at feeling proud of their children's achievements, their spouse's career progress, or their friends' personal victories that they lose touch with their own hunger for personal accomplishment and growth.

Third, over-managers often struggle with what psychologists call "imposter syndrome" when it comes to their own goals. While they have tremendous confidence in their ability to help others succeed, they often doubt their own capacity to create meaningful success in their own lives. They may believe they're not smart enough, talented enough, or deserving enough to pursue ambitious personal goals.

Overcoming these obstacles requires a fundamental reorientation toward personal goal-setting that honors both your individual aspirations and your caring nature. This reorientation begins with understanding that pursuing your own success doesn't diminish your care for others—it actually enhances your ability to support them from a place of fulfillment and strength rather than depletion and resentment.

The first step in effective personal goal-setting involves distinguishing between goals that are authentically yours and goals that you think you should have based on others' expectations or cultural messages. Over-managers often adopt goals that reflect what they believe will make others proud, what will earn approval and recognition, or what will maintain their image as successful, responsible people.

This external orientation can lead to pursuing goals that don't actually align with your values, interests, or vision for your life. You might find yourself working toward achievements that look impressive but don't bring genuine satisfaction, or pursuing objectives that serve others' needs more than your own authentic desires.

Jennifer discovered this when she examined her long-held goal of earning an advanced degree in her field. "I realized I wanted the degree not because I was passionate about the additional knowledge or because it would help me do work I loved, but because I thought it would make my family proud and prove that I was serious about my career," she reflected. "When I got honest about what I actually wanted, I discovered that I was more interested in starting my own business than in pursuing additional credentials."

Authentic goal-setting requires tuning into your own sense of excitement, curiosity, and motivation rather than trying to reverse-engineer goals from what you think the outcomes should be. This means paying attention to what energizes you when you think about it, what challenges excite rather than overwhelm you, and what achievements would feel personally meaningful regardless of others' reactions.

The process also involves setting goals at different time horizons and scales, from daily objectives that build momentum to long-term visions that provide direction and inspiration. Over-managers often struggle with both extremes—they may have difficulty setting small, manageable daily goals because they're used to crisis-driven reactivity, and they may resist setting ambitious long-term goals because they feel too vulnerable or unrealistic.

Effective goal-setting for recovering over-managers requires what I call "scaffolded ambition"—building your capacity for personal achievement gradually through progressively more challenging objectives. This might mean starting with small, easily achievable goals that build confidence and momentum before tackling larger, more complex aspirations.

This scaffolded approach serves several purposes. It helps you develop the skills and systems needed for consistent progress toward objectives. It provides regular experiences of success that build confidence in your ability to achieve what you set out to accomplish. It creates evidence that investing in your own goals produces positive outcomes, which helps overcome the guilt and resistance that often accompany personal ambition.

David applied this approach when he decided to transition from his corporate job to freelance consulting. Instead of immediately quitting his job and launching a full-scale business, he set a series of smaller goals: completing one freelance project while still employed, building a basic website for his services, connecting with ten potential clients through networking, and saving three months of expenses as a financial buffer.

"Each small goal I achieved made the bigger vision feel more realistic and less scary," David explained. "By the time I was ready to leave my corporate job, I had already proven to myself that I could successfully manage my own business objectives and create the outcomes I wanted."

Personal Productivity Systems That Work for Recovered Managers

Developing effective personal productivity systems requires understanding how your over-management patterns have shaped your current approach to organizing tasks and priorities. Many over-managers have developed sophisticated systems for tracking and managing others' responsibilities while operating in complete chaos when it comes to their own projects and goals.

This disparity often exists because managing others' tasks feels urgent and necessary, while managing your own tasks feels optional and selfish. When your teenage child has a school project due, you spring into action with detailed planning and systematic support. When you have a personal project with a self-imposed deadline, you may procrastinate, make excuses, or allow other priorities to take precedence.

Transforming this pattern requires developing productivity systems that treat your own goals and projects with the same seriousness and systematic attention that you've given to others' objectives. This doesn't mean becoming rigid or obsessive about personal productivity, but it does mean creating structure and accountability that support consistent progress toward your own aspirations.

The foundation of effective personal productivity for recovered managers is what I call "priority clarity"—having a clear, written understanding of what you're trying to accomplish and why it matters to you. Without this clarity, even the most sophisticated productivity systems become exercises in busy work rather than tools for meaningful progress.

Priority clarity begins with identifying your most important long-term objectives and breaking them down into smaller, actionable projects. Each project should have a clear definition of what completion looks like, a realistic timeline for achieving it, and an understanding of how it connects to your larger goals and vision.

This process requires overcoming the tendency to keep important goals vague and aspirational rather than specific and actionable. Over-managers often resist getting too specific about personal goals because specificity creates accountability, and accountability can trigger fears about failure or disappointment.

However, vague goals like "start a business," "get healthier," or "be more creative" provide little guidance for daily decision-making and action. Transforming these vague aspirations into specific, measurable objectives creates the clarity needed for systematic progress.

Margaret applied this principle when she decided to return to medical research after years focused on clinical practice and family management. Instead of the vague goal of "getting back into research," she created specific objectives: identify three research questions that excited her, connect with five potential collaborators in her field, write and submit one grant proposal within six months, and present her preliminary findings at a professional conference within one year.

"Having specific, measurable goals changed everything about how I approached my research aspirations," Margaret said. "Instead of feeling overwhelmed by the enormity of returning to academia, I had clear next steps that I could work on systematically."

The second element of effective personal productivity systems is what I call "project architecture"—organizing your goals and objectives into manageable projects with clear beginning, middle, and end phases. This architecture helps prevent the feeling of overwhelm that often accompanies ambitious personal goals and provides a framework for consistent progress.

Project architecture involves breaking larger objectives into smaller projects, each with its own timeline and deliverables. It also involves sequencing projects logically, so that completing earlier projects provides the foundation and momentum for later, more ambitious undertakings.

This systematic approach prevents the common pattern of jumping between different goals and projects without completing any of them. Over-managers often struggle with project completion because they're used to managing ongoing processes rather than discrete projects with clear endpoints.

The third element involves creating what productivity experts call "external scaffolding"—systems and structures outside your own memory and willpower that support consistent action toward your goals. This scaffolding might include calendar systems that protect time for important projects, task management systems that break projects into daily actions, accountability systems that provide external motivation and support, and environmental systems that make productive actions easier and distracting actions more difficult.

For over-managers, creating external scaffolding often requires overcoming the belief that they should be able to manage everything in their heads or through sheer willpower. The same people who would never expect others to manage complex projects without systems and support often resist creating similar support structures for their own goals.

Patricia discovered this when she began building her photography business. "I had helped my husband set up elaborate project management systems for his work and had created detailed organizational systems for my children's school activities, but I was trying to manage my business goals through random to-do lists and good intentions," she realized. "When I finally created proper systems for my own projects—calendar blocking, project folders, task tracking—my progress accelerated dramatically."

Building Skills and Pursuing Interests You've Neglected

One of the most common casualties of chronic over-management is the gradual abandonment of personal skill development and interest pursuit. Over-managers often become so focused on supporting others' growth and learning that they neglect their own intellectual curiosity, creative expression, and skill development.

This neglect often happens gradually and unconsciously. You might delay taking a class because a family member needs help with their studies. You might abandon a creative project because others need your time and attention. You might skip professional development opportunities because they seem less important than immediate demands from others.

Over time, this pattern creates what I call "skill stagnation"—a state where your abilities in areas unrelated to helping others begin to atrophy, while your helping and management skills become increasingly sophisticated. You become more and more competent at solving others' problems while becoming less and less confident in your own capacity for growth and learning.

Reversing skill stagnation requires intentional investment in your own development across multiple areas. This investment serves several purposes beyond just acquiring new capabilities. It restores your confidence in your ability to learn and grow. It provides evidence that you can successfully complete projects and achieve objectives for yourself. It creates new sources of satisfaction and accomplishment that aren't dependent on others' needs or approval.

The skill development process begins with conducting what I call a "capability audit"—an honest assessment of your current skills, interests, and growth areas. This audit involves identifying skills you once had but have allowed to deteriorate, interests you've always wanted to pursue but haven't made time for, and capabilities that would support your current goals and vision.

This assessment often reveals surprising patterns. Many over-managers discover that they've maintained and developed skills that serve others while neglecting skills that would serve their own goals and interests. They might be highly skilled at researching solutions to others' problems but out of practice with pursuing their own learning goals. They might be excellent at supporting others' creative projects but haven't developed their own creative abilities.

The capability audit also helps identify what I call "transfer skills"—abilities you've developed in your helping and management roles that could be applied to personal goals and projects. Over-managers often underestimate their own capabilities because they don't recognize how the skills they've developed in service of others could be redirected toward their own objectives.

For example, the project management skills you've used to coordinate family activities could be applied to personal business goals. The research abilities you've developed to solve others' problems could be used to support your own learning objectives. The interpersonal skills you've refined through helping others could be leveraged for your own networking and relationship-building goals.

Once you've identified priority areas for skill development, the next step involves creating systematic approaches to learning and growth. This systematic approach differs from the random, crisis-driven learning that often characterizes over-managers' attempts at personal development.

Instead of waiting for perfect conditions or trying to learn everything at once, systematic skill development involves choosing specific areas for focused improvement and creating consistent practices that support gradual mastery. This might involve enrolling in formal classes, finding mentors or coaches, joining groups with shared interests, or simply committing to regular practice in areas you want to develop.

Sarah applied this systematic approach when she decided to develop her business skills after years of focusing primarily on family management. "I realized I had sophisticated skills for managing household logistics and family finances, but I had no experience with marketing, sales, or business development," she said. "Instead of feeling overwhelmed by everything I didn't know, I chose one area to focus on each quarter—first marketing, then sales, then financial management—and committed to specific learning activities in each area."

The systematic approach also involves creating what I call "practice architecture"—regular structures and routines that support skill development even when motivation wanes or life becomes busy. This architecture might include daily practice sessions, weekly learning goals, monthly skill assessments, or quarterly project completions that demonstrate growing competence.

This practice architecture is particularly important for over-managers because they're accustomed to abandoning their own development when others need help or when life becomes demanding. Having systematic structures in place helps maintain momentum even during challenging periods.

The skill development process also involves overcoming what psychologists call "beginner's mind resistance"—the discomfort that competent adults often feel when starting to learn something new where they're not immediately proficient. Over-managers, who have often become experts at helping others, may find it particularly difficult to tolerate the vulnerability and uncertainty that comes with being a beginner.

Embracing a beginner's mind requires accepting that learning new skills involves temporary incompetence, mistakes, and frustration. It means being willing to be bad at something initially in order to eventually become good at it. This tolerance for temporary incompetence is essential for continued growth and development throughout life.

Creating Financial Independence and Security

For many over-managers, achieving financial independence represents both a practical necessity and a symbolic milestone in their journey toward personal freedom. Financial independence provides the resources and flexibility needed to make choices based on values and preferences rather than just survival needs. It also demonstrates the ability to create security and success through your own efforts rather than depending on others or sacrificing your own goals for financial stability.

However, over-managers often struggle with financial goal-setting and wealth-building because they've been conditioned to prioritize others' financial needs over their own. They might contribute generously to their children's education while neglecting their own retirement savings. They might help family members with financial emergencies while failing to build their own emergency funds. They might support their spouse's business ventures while avoiding investment in their own income-generating activities.

This pattern often stems from the belief that focusing on personal financial goals is selfish or that their own financial security is less important than others' immediate needs. Over-managers may also lack confidence in their ability to create wealth independently, especially if they've been financially dependent on others or have primarily earned income through employment rather than entrepreneurship.

Building financial independence requires shifting from reactive financial management—responding to others' needs and crises—to proactive wealth-building that prioritizes your own long-term security and freedom. This shift involves both practical strategies for increasing income and reducing expenses, and psychological changes in how you think about money, wealth, and your own financial priorities.

The foundation of financial independence is what financial advisors call "paying yourself first"—consistently allocating a portion of your income to your own savings, investments, and wealth-building activities before addressing others' financial needs or wants. This principle directly challenges the over-manager's tendency to give away financial resources that could be building their own security and independence.

Implementing "pay yourself first" often requires overcoming guilt about accumulating wealth while others have financial struggles. Over-managers may feel selfish for building savings while their adult children have student loans, or guilty about investing in their own business while family members face financial challenges.

However, building your own financial independence ultimately serves everyone in your life. When you're financially secure, you're less likely to become a financial burden on others, more able to provide genuine help during real emergencies, and better positioned to model financial responsibility and independence.

The pay-yourself-first principle also involves setting specific financial goals with clear timelines and measurable milestones. Instead of vague intentions to "save more money" or "be more financially secure," effective financial independence requires specific objectives like "save six months of expenses in an emergency fund within two years" or "invest 15% of income in retirement accounts consistently."

Jennifer implemented this approach when she realized that years of helping her adult children with various financial emergencies had prevented her from building adequate retirement savings. "I had to accept that my children's financial struggles were not my emergencies to solve," she said. "When I started automatically investing a percentage of my income before I could spend it on others' needs, my own financial security improved dramatically."

The second component of financial independence involves developing multiple income streams rather than depending solely on employment or a single source of revenue. Over-managers often have skills and knowledge that could be monetized through consulting, teaching, freelancing, or entrepreneurship, but they rarely pursue these opportunities because they're too busy managing others' lives and careers.

Creating additional income streams serves several purposes beyond just increasing total income. It reduces financial risk by diversifying revenue sources. It provides opportunities to develop new skills and explore different interests. It often allows for more flexible work arrangements that better support work-life integration. Most importantly, it demonstrates your capacity to create value and generate income independently.

The process of developing additional income streams often begins with what I call "skill monetization"—identifying knowledge and abilities you've developed that others would pay to access. Over-managers often underestimate the market value of their skills because they've primarily used these abilities to help others for free.

This skill monetization might involve offering consulting services in areas where you have expertise, teaching classes or workshops on subjects you know well, providing services that leverage your organizational and management abilities, or creating products that solve problems you've learned to address through helping others.

Patricia discovered this when she began offering organizational consulting to other busy parents. "I had spent years developing systems for managing complex family logistics, but I had never considered that other people would pay for this expertise," she said. "When I started offering my services professionally, I realized I had valuable skills that I had been giving away for free."

The third component involves strategic expense management that supports rather than undermines your financial goals. This doesn't mean extreme frugality or deprivation, but it does mean making conscious choices about spending based on your values and financial objectives rather than social pressure or others' expectations.

For over-managers, expense management often requires setting boundaries around financial gifts, loans, and support for others. This might mean establishing clear limits on how much you'll contribute to others' financial needs, requiring repayment plans for loans to family members, or simply saying no to requests for financial help that would compromise your own financial security.

Strategic expense management also involves investing in things that support your own goals and income generation rather than just others' comfort and convenience. This might mean spending money on education that enhances your earning potential, tools and resources that support your business goals, or services that free up time for income-generating activities.

Developing Your Own Support Network

One of the most crucial but often overlooked aspects of building personal success systems is developing a support network that encourages and supports your own goals and growth rather than just depending on you for help and assistance. Over-managers often have extensive networks of people who rely on their support, but they rarely cultivate relationships that provide mutual support and encouragement for their own aspirations.

This imbalance in support networks occurs because over-managers typically build relationships around their ability to help others rather than around shared interests, mutual support, or common goals. They become known as the person who can solve problems, provide assistance, and offer guidance, but they rarely position themselves as someone who also needs and deserves support, encouragement, and collaboration.

Developing a balanced support network requires intentionally seeking out and cultivating relationships with people who share your interests, support your goals, and can provide expertise, encouragement, and accountability for your own growth and development. This network should include several different types of relationships, each serving different functions in supporting your success.

The first type of relationship involves what I call "growth partners"—people who are also working on personal development and goal achievement and who can provide mutual support, accountability, and encouragement. These relationships are characterized by reciprocity, with both people offering and receiving support for their respective goals and challenges.

Growth partnerships often develop through shared activities like classes, workshops, professional associations, or interest-based groups. They're built around common interests and mutual support rather than one-sided helping relationships. These partnerships provide accountability, encouragement, and practical support while also offering opportunities to contribute meaningfully to others' success in balanced, sustainable ways.

The second type involves "expertise relationships"—connections with people who have knowledge, skills, or experience that can help you achieve your goals. These might include mentors who can provide guidance and wisdom, coaches who can offer specialized training and accountability, or colleagues who can share industry knowledge and professional opportunities.

Developing expertise relationships often requires overcoming the over-manager's tendency to be the expert and helper rather than the student and receiver of guidance. This shift can feel vulnerable because it requires admitting that you don't have all the answers and that you could benefit from others' knowledge and support.

However, positioning yourself as someone who's learning and growing often makes you more attractive as a connection rather than less. People generally enjoy sharing their expertise and supporting others' development, especially when the relationship involves mutual respect and appreciation rather than one-sided dependency.

Margaret developed several expertise relationships when she returned to medical research after years in clinical practice. "I had to overcome my pride about being behind in current research developments and position myself as someone who was eager to learn from colleagues who had stayed current in the field," she said. "Once I embraced being a student again, I found that people were incredibly generous with their knowledge and support."

The third type involves "inspiration relationships"—connections with people who model possibilities for growth, achievement, and authentic living that expand your sense of what's possible for your own life. These relationships might involve people who have achieved goals similar to yours, who have successfully made major life transitions, or who simply embody qualities and ways of being that you admire and want to develop.

Inspiration relationships don't necessarily require close personal connections. They might involve following thought leaders in your field, attending talks by people whose work inspires you, reading biographies of people who have overcome similar challenges, or simply observing how others navigate goals and challenges similar to yours.

The fourth type involves "celebration relationships"—people who genuinely celebrate your successes, progress, and achievements rather than feeling threatened or diminished by your growth. Over-managers often struggle to find people who can celebrate their success because their existing relationships may be built around being needed and helpful rather than being successful and accomplished.

These celebration relationships are crucial for maintaining motivation and momentum toward your goals. When you achieve milestones or make progress toward your objectives, having people who genuinely celebrate these accomplishments reinforces the value of pursuing your own goals and provides emotional support for continued effort.

Building a balanced support network also requires learning to ask for help and support rather than always being the person who provides it. This skill can be particularly challenging for over-managers who have built their identity around being helpful and self-sufficient rather than being vulnerable and receptive to others' assistance.

Learning to ask for help effectively involves being specific about what kind of support you need, being clear about how others can contribute to your goals, and being willing to receive assistance gracefully rather than immediately trying to reciprocate or minimize the help you've received.

David discovered this when he was launching his consulting business and needed to build a client base. "I had spent years helping others with their professional challenges, but I had never asked anyone to help me with my business goals," he said. "When I finally started reaching out to my network for introductions, referrals, and advice, I was amazed by how willing people were to support my success. Many people told me they had been waiting for years for me to ask for their help."

The Personal Success Architecture

Creating sustainable success in your own goals and aspirations requires building what I call "Personal Success Architecture"—systematic structures and processes that support consistent progress toward your objectives even when motivation wanes or life becomes demanding.

This architecture differs from the ad-hoc, crisis-driven approach that characterizes many over-managers' attempts at personal goal achievement. Instead of relying on bursts of inspiration or periods of intense effort, success architecture creates sustainable systems that support steady progress over time.

The foundation of personal success architecture is what project managers call "outcome definition"—clear, specific descriptions of what success looks like for each of your major goals and projects. These outcome definitions should be detailed enough to guide decision-making and action, but flexible enough to allow for adjustment and evolution as you learn and grow.

Effective outcome definition involves answering several key questions for each goal: What exactly will you have accomplished when this goal is complete? How will you know when you've achieved success? What will be different in your life as a result of achieving this objective? Who will benefit from your success, and how? What skills, resources, or support will you need to achieve this outcome?

This level of specificity helps prevent the vague goal-setting that often characterizes over-managers' personal aspirations. Instead of working toward nebulous objectives like "being more successful" or "having better work-life balance," you create clear targets that can guide daily decisions and actions.

The second component involves "milestone mapping"—breaking larger goals into smaller, measurable milestones that provide regular opportunities for progress assessment and celebration. These milestones serve as checkpoints that help you stay on track toward larger objectives while providing regular evidence of progress and achievement.

Milestone mapping also helps prevent the overwhelming feeling that often accompanies ambitious goals by creating a series of smaller, more manageable targets. Instead of focusing solely on a large, distant objective, you can concentrate on the next milestone while maintaining awareness of the larger direction.

The third component involves "system design"—creating consistent processes and routines that support progress toward your goals without requiring constant decision-making or motivation. These systems might include daily habits that support your objectives, weekly review processes that keep you on track, monthly planning sessions that adjust your approach based on progress and learning, and quarterly assessments that evaluate your overall direction and priorities.

System design also involves creating what behavioral psychologists call "environmental support"—structuring your physical and social environment to make productive actions easier and distracting actions more difficult. This might involve organizing your workspace to support focused work, scheduling time for important activities when your energy is highest, or surrounding yourself with visual reminders of your goals and priorities.

The fourth component involves "accountability integration"—building external accountability into your goal achievement process rather than relying solely on self-motivation and self-discipline. This accountability might come from coaches, mentors, peers, or formal programs that provide external support and encouragement for your goals.

Accountability integration is particularly important for over-managers because they're often excellent at maintaining accountability for others' goals while struggling to maintain consistency with their own objectives. Having external accountability helps bridge this gap by providing the same kind of support and expectation for your own goals that you naturally provide for others.

Sarah implemented comprehensive success architecture when she decided to transition from her corporate job to entrepreneurship. "I created detailed outcome definitions for my business goals, broke them down into quarterly and monthly milestones, designed daily and weekly systems for consistent progress, and joined a mastermind group for accountability and support," she said. "Having this architecture in place made the difference between another failed attempt at starting a business and actually building something sustainable and successful."

The Skill Development Accelerator

Developing new skills and capabilities efficiently requires systematic approaches that maximize learning while minimizing the time and energy required. The Skill Development Accelerator provides a framework for rapidly acquiring new abilities that support your goals and aspirations.

The accelerator begins with what learning experts call "skill stacking"—identifying sets of related skills that work together to create valuable capabilities rather than trying to develop isolated abilities. This approach leverages synergies between different skills and creates more versatile and marketable capability sets.

For example, instead of just learning graphic design, you might develop a skill stack that includes graphic design, basic marketing knowledge, and project management abilities. This combination creates more valuable and versatile capabilities than any single skill alone.

Skill stacking is particularly effective for over-managers because it builds on the systems thinking and integration abilities they've already developed through coordinating complex family and work situations. The same ability to see how different elements work together can be applied to building comprehensive skill sets that support your goals.

The second component involves "accelerated learning techniques"—methods for acquiring new skills more efficiently than traditional approaches. These techniques might include finding mentors who can provide direct guidance and feedback, using simulation and practice exercises that accelerate real-world learning, focusing on high-impact skills that provide the greatest return on learning investment, and creating intense learning experiences that compress typical learning timelines.

Accelerated learning also involves what psychologists call "deliberate practice"—focused, goal-oriented practice that specifically targets areas for improvement rather than just repeating existing capabilities. This type of practice requires stepping outside your comfort zone, seeking feedback on your performance, and continuously adjusting your approach based on results.

The third component involves "learning integration"—systematically connecting new skills to your existing knowledge and experience rather than treating them as completely separate additions to your capability set. This integration helps solidify new learning and makes it more accessible for practical application.

Learning integration might involve looking for connections between new skills and abilities you already have, finding ways to apply new learning to current projects and goals, or teaching new skills to others as a way of deepening your own understanding and retention.

The Independence Building Blocks

Achieving genuine independence—the ability to create the life you want without depending on others for essential resources, validation, or decision-making—requires building several foundational capabilities that work together to create personal autonomy and freedom.

The first building block involves "resource independence"—developing the ability to generate the financial, material, and practical resources you need to support your chosen lifestyle without depending on others for essential needs. This doesn't mean becoming completely self-sufficient in every area, but it does mean having the capability to meet your basic needs and pursue your goals through your own efforts.

Resource independence includes financial independence, but it also encompasses practical skills for managing daily life, emotional resources for handling challenges and stress, and intellectual resources for learning and problem-solving. The goal is developing sufficient capability across these areas to make choices based on your values and preferences rather than being constrained by dependency on others.

The second building block involves "decision independence"—developing confidence in your own judgment and the ability to make important choices without requiring external validation or approval. Over-managers often struggle with decision independence because they've become so skilled at helping others make decisions that they've lost confidence in their own decision-making abilities.

Decision independence requires trusting your own values, preferences, and judgment even when others disagree or express concern about your choices. It means taking responsibility for the outcomes of your decisions rather than trying to make choices that please everyone or avoid all possibility of criticism.

The third building block involves "emotional independence"—the ability to maintain your own emotional equilibrium and sense of well-being without depending on others for emotional regulation or validation. This doesn't mean becoming emotionally isolated, but it does mean taking responsibility for your own emotional state rather than making others responsible for managing your feelings.

Emotional independence allows you to offer genuine support to others without needing them to reciprocate in order to feel valuable and loved. It provides the foundation for authentic relationships based on choice rather than neediness or codependency.

The fourth building block involves "purpose independence"—having a clear sense of meaning and direction that comes from your own values and aspirations rather than from others' expectations or approval. This involves knowing what matters to you, what you want to contribute to the world, and what kind of life feels meaningful and fulfilling regardless of others' opinions.

Purpose independence provides the motivation and direction needed to sustain effort toward long-term goals even when others don't understand or support your choices. It allows you to persist through challenges and setbacks because your motivation comes from internal conviction rather than external validation.

Creating Your Personal Empire

The ultimate goal of building your own success systems is not just achieving individual goals, but creating what I call your "personal empire"—a comprehensive life structure that supports your values, enables your aspirations, and provides the foundation for ongoing growth and contribution.

Your personal empire includes all the systems, relationships, capabilities, and resources that work together to create the life you want to live. It's built intentionally over time through consistent effort and strategic choices rather than happening accidentally through responding to external demands and opportunities.

Creating a personal empire requires thinking strategically about how different elements of your life work together to support your overall vision and values. This might involve aligning your career choices with your personal interests, building relationships that support your growth and aspirations, developing skills that enhance your ability to create value and generate income, and creating lifestyle choices that support your health, relationships, and personal fulfillment.

The personal empire metaphor emphasizes that you are the architect and ruler of your own life rather than a subject in someone else's kingdom. You make the important decisions about how to spend your time and energy, what goals to pursue, and what kind of life to create. You take responsibility for building the structures and systems that support your chosen way of living.

This doesn't mean becoming selfish or isolated from others. The most successful personal empires are built on principles of mutual benefit and genuine contribution to others' wellbeing. But they're built from a foundation of personal strength, clarity, and independence rather than from a position of depletion, confusion, or dependency.

When you have strong personal success systems in place, when you're consistently making progress toward goals that matter to you, when you have the resources and support needed to handle challenges and pursue opportunities, you become someone who can contribute to others' lives from a place of abundance rather than obligation. You model what's possible when someone takes full responsibility for creating the life they want while maintaining loving, supportive relationships with others.

This transformation from over-manager to personal empire builder doesn't happen overnight, but it's one of the most rewarding journeys you can undertake. It leads not just to personal success, but to a way of living that honors both your individual potential and your genuine desire to contribute meaningfully to the world around you.

CHAPTER 11

The New Relationship Operating System

The conversation that changed everything for Robert happened on a quiet Thursday evening in his kitchen. His twenty-five-year-old son Michael had called to complain about his job, his girlfriend, and his financial situation—a weekly ritual that had been going on for nearly three years. As Robert listened to the familiar litany of problems and grievances, he felt the automatic response system kicking in: his mind began generating solutions, his body tensed with the urgency to fix and rescue, his emotional state synchronized with his son's distress.

But this time, instead of immediately jumping into problem-solving mode, Robert found himself asking a different question: "Michael, what do you think you want to do about this?"

The silence on the other end of the phone stretched for nearly thirty seconds—an eternity in their usual rapid-fire problem-solving sessions. Finally, Michael said, "I... I don't know, Dad. I guess I was hoping you'd tell me what to do, like you always do."

That moment of honest acknowledgment revealed the fundamental dysfunction in their relationship. For years, Robert had been operating as Michael's external brain, emotional regulator, and life manager. Michael had learned to outsource his problem-solving to his father, while Robert had become addicted to being needed and essential to his son's functioning.

"What if," Robert said carefully, "instead of me telling you what to do, I trusted you to figure this out yourself? What if I believed you were capable of handling your own life?"

Another long pause. Then Michael said something that surprised them both: "That would be terrifying... but also kind of exciting."

This conversation marked the beginning of Robert's transformation from a managing parent to what I call a "supportive partner" in his adult son's life. It was the start of implementing what I call the New Relationship Operating System—a fundamentally different approach to relationships that's based on mutual respect, shared responsibility, and loving empowerment rather than management, control, and codependent rescue.

The New Relationship Operating System represents a complete paradigm shift from the traditional over-manager approach to relationships. Instead of seeing yourself as responsible for others' emotional regulation, problem-solving, and life outcomes, you learn to see yourself as a supportive partner in their journey toward competence, resilience, and authentic success. Instead of trying to prevent others from experiencing difficulty, you learn to trust their capacity to handle challenges and grow from their experiences.

This shift requires fundamentally rewiring how you think about love, support, and responsibility in relationships. It means learning to love without controlling, to care without carrying, and to help without taking over. Most importantly, it means creating relationships that are based on mutual growth and empowerment rather than dependency and management.

Shifting from Manager to Supportive Partner/Friend/Parent

The transition from relationship manager to supportive partner requires understanding the crucial difference between these two approaches to caring for others. The manager approach is based on the assumption that others need your oversight, intervention, and control to function effectively. The supportive partner approach is based on the assumption that others are capable of managing their own lives with appropriate encouragement and resources.

This shift begins with recognizing that your management approach, however well-intentioned, often undermines rather than supports others' development. When you consistently solve problems for others, make decisions for them, or shield them from natural consequences, you inadvertently communicate that you don't believe they're capable of handling their own lives. Over time, this message becomes a self-fulfilling prophecy as others gradually lose confidence in their own abilities and become increasingly dependent on your management.

The supportive partner approach, by contrast, is based on expressing confidence in others' capabilities while offering appropriate resources and encouragement. Instead of taking over when others face challenges, you provide emotional support, perspective, and resources while maintaining clear boundaries about who is responsible for what.

This shift requires developing what I call "supportive detachment"—the ability to care deeply about others' wellbeing while maintaining appropriate boundaries around responsibility and autonomy. Supportive detachment allows you to be emotionally available and caring without becoming emotionally responsible for others' feelings, choices, and outcomes.

Sarah, whose transformation we've followed throughout this book, described her experience of shifting from managing parent to supportive partner with her teenage daughter: "I had to learn the difference between supporting her through a difficult situation and taking over the situation to prevent her from experiencing difficulty. When she was struggling with a friendship conflict, instead of calling the other girl's mother or coaching her through every conversation, I learned to listen, validate her feelings, and express confidence that she could figure out how to handle it herself."

This supportive approach often feels more difficult initially because it requires tolerating others' struggles without immediately intervening. It means sitting with your own anxiety about their challenges without taking action to relieve that anxiety through control and management. However, the long-term outcomes are far superior because others develop genuine confidence and competence rather than learned dependency.

The shift from manager to supportive partner also requires changing your communication patterns in fundamental ways. Instead of giving advice and direction, you learn to ask questions that help others think through their own solutions. Instead of expressing anxiety about their choices, you learn to express faith in their ability to handle whatever consequences arise from their decisions.

This communication shift involves moving from what I call "directive language" to "empowering language." Directive language tells others what to do, how to feel, or what to think about their situations. Empowering language helps others access their own wisdom, confidence, and problem-solving abilities.

For example, instead of saying "You should break up with him—he's obviously not right for you," supportive partner language might be "It sounds like you're feeling conflicted about this relationship. What feels most important to you as you think about what you want?" Instead of "You need to start looking for a new job immediately," you might say "This work situation sounds really stressful. What options are you considering?"

This language shift reflects a fundamental change in your role from director to consultant, from decision-maker to advisor, from problem-solver to thinking partner. You're still involved and caring, but you're involved in ways that strengthen rather than weaken others' capacity for independent functioning.

The transition to a supportive partner requires developing tolerance for others making choices you wouldn't make and handling situations differently than you would handle them. This tolerance is essential because micromanaging others' approaches based on your preferences prevents them from developing their own judgment and confidence.

Jennifer discovered this when her adult daughter chose to handle a workplace conflict by having a direct conversation with her difficult colleague rather than following Jennifer's advice to involve human resources immediately. "My instinct was to insist that she follow my approach because I was worried she would make the situation worse," Jennifer said. "But I learned to express confidence in her judgment while making it clear that I was available if she wanted to discuss how things went. When her direct approach actually resolved the conflict successfully, I realized that my way wasn't the only good way."

The Difference Between Helping and Enabling

One of the most crucial distinctions in the New Relationship Operating System is understanding the difference between helping that empowers others and "helping" that actually enables dysfunction and dependency. This distinction is often subtle but has profound implications for the long-term health and growth of both individuals and relationships.

Empowering help supports others in developing their own capabilities, confidence, and independence. It provides resources, encouragement, and temporary assistance that helps others become more capable of handling similar situations in the future. Empowering help is strategic, time-limited, and focused on building rather than replacing others' abilities.

Enabling, by contrast, involves doing things for others that they could reasonably do for themselves, preventing them from experiencing natural consequences of their choices, or providing assistance that reduces rather than increases their motivation to develop their own capabilities. Enabling often feels loving and supportive in the moment, but it creates long-term dependency and undermines others' confidence and competence.

The difference between helping and enabling often lies not in what you do, but in the impact of your actions on others' development over time. Helping someone organize their closet might be empowering if you're teaching organizational skills they can apply independently in the future. The same action becomes enabling if you do it repeatedly because they've learned to depend on your organizational abilities rather than developing their own.

Dr. Melody Beattie, whose work on codependency has influenced thousands of families, explains this distinction: "Helping is doing something for someone else that they cannot do for themselves. Enabling is doing something for someone else that they can and should be doing for themselves. The key difference is whether your actions increase or decrease the other person's responsibility and capability."

This distinction becomes particularly important when helping people you love who are struggling with challenges that could be growth opportunities. Natural struggles with finances, relationships, work situations, or life transitions often provide valuable learning experiences that build resilience and wisdom. When you consistently intervene to prevent or minimize these struggles, you may be robbing others of important developmental experiences.

The enabling pattern often begins innocently with genuine crises where help is truly needed and appropriate. The problem arises when temporary help becomes permanent management, when emergency assistance becomes routine rescue, and when others learn to create or maintain crisis situations because they know you'll intervene.

Marcus recognized this pattern when he examined his relationship with his adult son who had been struggling with employment stability. "I had been helping with his rent payments for two years, telling myself it was temporary assistance while he got back on his feet," Marcus said. "But I realized that my financial help was actually reducing his motivation to find stable employment or develop better budgeting skills. My 'help' was enabling him to avoid taking full responsibility for his financial situation."

Distinguishing between helping and enabling requires asking several key questions about your assistance: Does this help increase or decrease the other person's capability over time? Am I doing something for them that they could reasonably do for themselves? Am I preventing them from experiencing consequences that could provide valuable learning? Am I more invested in solving their problem than they are? Is my help creating dependency or building independence?

These questions help you evaluate not just individual instances of help, but patterns of assistance over time. One-time help during a genuine crisis is very different from ongoing patterns of management and rescue that prevent others from developing their own problem-solving abilities.

The process of shifting from enabling to empowering often requires what I call "graduated withdrawal"—gradually reducing your level of involvement and assistance while increasing your expectations for others' independence and responsibility. This withdrawal needs to be communicated clearly and implemented consistently, often despite initial resistance from those who have become accustomed to your management.

This graduated approach might involve helping someone create a budget rather than managing their finances for them, teaching someone how to research solutions rather than researching for them, or providing emotional support while they handle a difficult conversation rather than having the conversation for them.

The goal isn't to become unhelpful or unsupportive, but to help in ways that build rather than replace others' capabilities. This type of help often requires more skill and creativity than simple rescue and management, but it creates much better long-term outcomes for everyone involved.

Creating Space for Others to Fail and Learn

One of the most challenging aspects of implementing the New Relationship Operating System is learning to create space for others to fail, struggle, and learn from their experiences without immediately intervening to rescue them. This space is essential for growth and development, but it requires enormous emotional discipline for people who have been conditioned to prevent others' discomfort at all costs.

Creating space for failure and learning doesn't mean becoming indifferent to others' struggles or refusing to provide appropriate support during genuine difficulties. It means recognizing that some level of failure and struggle is necessary for developing resilience, competence, and wisdom. It means understanding that your attempts to prevent all failure often prevent the very experiences that would help others become stronger and more capable.

This concept challenges deeply held beliefs about what it means to love and care for others. Many over-managers have been taught that love means protecting others from pain, that caring means preventing failure, and that good relationships involve shielding each other from life's difficulties. However, this protective approach often stunts rather than supports others' growth and development.

The space for failure and learning requires what I call "loving restraint"—the discipline to step back and allow others to experience the natural consequences of their choices even when you could intervene to prevent those consequences. This restraint is motivated by long-term love and care rather than short-term comfort and rescue.

Patricia learned this lesson when her adult daughter was struggling with chronic lateness at work. "My automatic response was to start calling her every morning to make sure she was awake and offer to drive her to work when she was running late," Patricia said. "But I realized that my interventions were preventing her from experiencing the natural consequences of her choices and learning to manage her own schedule."

Instead of rescuing her daughter from the consequences of lateness, Patricia chose to express confidence in her daughter's ability to solve the problem while making it clear that the responsibility belonged to her daughter. When her daughter was eventually written up at work for tardiness, it was a difficult experience, but it motivated her to develop better morning routines and time management skills.

"It was hard to watch her struggle and face consequences I could have prevented," Patricia reflected. "But the skills she developed by handling that situation herself were much more valuable than the temporary comfort my rescue would have provided."

Creating space for failure also requires distinguishing between consequences that provide valuable learning opportunities and consequences that are genuinely harmful or disproportionate. Not all failures are equally instructive, and some situations do require intervention to prevent serious harm.

The key is evaluating consequences based on their potential for learning versus their potential for genuine damage. Learning-rich consequences are typically manageable, reversible, and directly related to the choices that created them. Dangerous consequences involve genuine threats to safety, health, or long-term wellbeing that could cause irreparable harm.

This evaluation requires developing what I call "consequence discernment"—the ability to assess situations objectively and determine when natural consequences will be instructive versus when intervention is necessary to prevent genuine harm. This discernment improves with practice and often involves consulting with others who can provide objective perspective.

The space for failure and learning also requires developing emotional tolerance for others' discomfort and your own anxiety about their struggles. Over-managers often intervene not because others truly need help, but because witnessing struggle creates intolerable anxiety for the over-manager. Learning to tolerate this anxiety without taking action is essential for creating healthy relationship dynamics.

This emotional tolerance develops through practice and often requires support from others who understand the importance of allowing natural learning processes to occur. It also requires developing self-care practices that help you manage your own anxiety without taking action to control others' experiences.

Creating space for failure becomes particularly important in relationships with young adults who are transitioning to independence. This developmental stage naturally involves increased responsibility and autonomy, along with the mistakes and struggles that accompany learning to manage adult responsibilities. Parents who intervene too heavily during this stage often delay rather than support their children's development into capable adults.

The same principle applies to other relationships where one person is developing new capabilities or handling new challenges. Spouses learning to manage new responsibilities, friends developing new skills, or colleagues taking on expanded roles all need space to struggle and learn without constant oversight and intervention.

Building Relationships Based on Mutual Respect, Not Dependency

The foundation of the New Relationship Operating System is mutual respect—a genuine appreciation for each person's autonomy, capability, and right to make their own choices and handle their own life challenges. This mutual respect creates the conditions for healthy interdependence rather than unhealthy codependency.

Mutual respect involves recognizing and honoring each person's inherent worth and capability independent of their need for your help or their ability to meet your expectations. It means treating others as whole, competent people who are capable of growth and learning rather than as fragile beings who need your protection and management.

This respect is expressed through both what you do and what you don't do in relationships. It's expressed by asking for others' input before making decisions that affect them, by honoring their choices even when you disagree with them, and by expressing confidence in their ability to handle their own challenges. It's also expressed by not taking over their responsibilities, not making decisions for them without their request, and not treating them as extensions of yourself rather than separate individuals.

Building relationships based on mutual respect requires examining the power dynamics in your current relationships and identifying areas where respect may be compromised by patterns of over-functioning and under-functioning. These dynamics often develop gradually and may not be immediately obvious to either party.

Over-functioning involves taking on responsibilities that belong to others, making decisions for others without their request, or generally doing more than your fair share of the work required to maintain the relationship or handle shared responsibilities. Under-functioning involves consistently relying on others to handle responsibilities that you could manage yourself, avoiding decision-making, or generally doing less than your fair share.

These imbalanced dynamics create relationships where one person is consistently in a one-up position (the over-functioner) while the other is in a one-down position (the under-functioner). While this arrangement might feel stable, it undermines mutual respect because it's based on inequality rather than partnership.

David recognized this dynamic in his marriage when he realized that he had gradually taken over most decision-making responsibilities because it seemed easier than dealing with conflict or delays. "I was making decisions about our social calendar, our vacation plans, even our home decoration choices because my wife seemed overwhelmed by these decisions," he said. "But I realized that by taking over, I was treating her as incompetent and denying her the opportunity to contribute equally to our shared life."

Rebalancing these dynamics requires honest conversation about how responsibilities and decision-making authority are distributed in your relationships. This conversation often reveals assumptions and expectations that have never been explicitly discussed but that significantly impact the relationship's functioning.

The process of creating mutual respect also involves what I call "capability assumption"—choosing to assume that others are capable of handling their responsibilities and challenges unless evidence clearly suggests otherwise. This assumption is the opposite of the deficit mindset that characterizes many over-management relationships, where the assumption is that others need help unless proven otherwise.

Capability assumption doesn't mean ignoring genuine limitations or avoiding appropriate support when others are struggling. It means starting from the premise that others are competent and resourceful, and offering help as a choice rather than imposing it as a necessity.

This assumption shift often requires overcoming deeply ingrained habits of scanning for problems, anticipating needs, and intervening before others have a chance to handle situations themselves. It means learning to wait for requests for help rather than offering unsolicited assistance, and to express confidence in others' abilities rather than anxiety about their potential struggles.

Mutual respect also requires what I call "outcome detachment"—caring about others' wellbeing while not being attached to specific outcomes or methods they choose for handling their lives. This detachment allows you to love and support others while honoring their autonomy to make choices you wouldn't make and to handle situations differently than you would.

This outcome detachment is particularly challenging for over-managers who have become invested in specific outcomes as evidence of their successful helping. Learning to care about others' growth and happiness while not being attached to how they achieve these states requires a fundamental shift in how you define successful relationships.

Jennifer experienced this shift when her adult son chose to handle his career transition very differently than she would have recommended. "I had clear ideas about what steps he should take, what timeline would be most effective, and what approach would minimize risk," she said. "Learning to support his process while detaching from my preferred outcomes was difficult, but it allowed him to develop confidence in his own judgment and approach."

The Art of Loving Detachment

Loving detachment represents the pinnacle of the New Relationship Operating System—the ability to love others deeply while maintaining appropriate emotional and psychological boundaries that allow both people to remain whole, autonomous individuals. This type of love is more mature and sustainable than the enmeshed, codependent love that characterizes many over-management relationships.

Loving detachment involves what spiritual traditions call "unconditional love"—love that isn't dependent on others behaving in specific ways, making choices you approve of, or needing your help and management. This love is based on appreciation for others' inherent worth and potential rather than on their ability to meet your expectations or needs.

This detached love allows you to care deeply about others' wellbeing while not taking responsibility for their emotional states, life choices, or personal growth. You can offer support and encouragement while maintaining clear boundaries about what belongs to you and what belongs to them.

The development of loving detachment often requires healing from what psychologists call "enmeshment"—the blurring of boundaries between yourself and others that leads to taking on their emotions, problems, and responsibilities as if they were your own. Enmeshment often feels like love because it involves intense emotional connection and investment, but it actually undermines both people's ability to develop as whole, independent individuals.

Healing from enmeshment involves learning to distinguish between your own emotional experience and others' emotional experiences, between your own problems and others' problems, and between your own life path and others' life paths. This process often feels threatening initially because enmeshment can create a sense of closeness and importance that feels like evidence of deep love and connection.

However, relationships based on loving detachment are actually closer and more intimate than enmeshed relationships because they allow both people to show up authentically rather than playing roles designed to meet each other's emotional needs. When you're not responsible for managing others' emotions, you can be genuinely present with their experiences. When you're not taking over their problems, you can offer real support and companionship.

Sarah described her experience of developing loving detachment with her teenage daughter: "I had to learn the difference between empathy and emotional fusion. I could feel compassion for her struggles without taking on her anxiety as my own emergency. I could care about her happiness without making her emotional state my responsibility. This shift actually brought us closer because she could share her experiences with me without worrying that I would become upset or take over."

Loving detachment also involves what I call "growth trust"—faith in others' capacity to learn, develop, and become who they're meant to become through their own experiences and choices. This trust allows you to step back from management and control while maintaining love and support for their journey.

This growth trust often requires overcoming fears about what might happen if you stop managing and controlling. Many over-managers fear that without their intervention, others will make terrible mistakes, fail to reach their potential, or experience unnecessary pain. However, these fears often overestimate the dangers of independence while underestimating others' capacity for growth and resilience.

The practice of loving detachment involves several specific skills and attitudes. It requires learning to witness others' experiences without immediately trying to fix or change them. It involves offering presence and support without taking over or taking on others' problems. It means expressing faith in others' capabilities while remaining available for appropriate assistance when requested.

Loving detachment also requires developing what Buddhist traditions call "non-attachment to outcomes"—caring about others' wellbeing while not being invested in specific ways they achieve that wellbeing. This non-attachment allows you to support others' choices even when those choices differ from what you would prefer or recommend.

This non-attachment doesn't mean becoming indifferent or uncaring. It means caring in a way that honors others' autonomy and supports their growth rather than caring in a way that seeks to control their choices and outcomes to reduce your own anxiety.

Margaret practiced loving detachment when her adult daughter chose to move across the country for a job opportunity that Margaret thought was risky and poorly planned. "Every instinct I had wanted to research the job market in that city, help her negotiate a better offer, and basically manage her decision-making process," Margaret said. "Instead, I learned to express my love and confidence in her judgment while staying available for support if she requested it. When the move turned out to be a wonderful opportunity for growth, I realized that my management would have robbed her of the confidence that came from making and implementing her own major life decision."

The Healthy Relationship Redesign Process

Implementing the New Relationship Operating System often requires intentionally redesigning existing relationships that have become structured around over-management and codependency. This redesign process involves honest assessment of current dynamics, clear communication about desired changes, and consistent implementation of new patterns over time.

The redesign process begins with what I call "relationship mapping"—examining the current structure of your important relationships to identify patterns of over-functioning and under-functioning, areas where boundaries are unclear or violated, and dynamics that support dependency rather than mutual growth.

This mapping involves asking several key questions about each important relationship: Who typically initiates problem-solving conversations? Who takes responsibility for managing logistics and details? Who makes decisions about shared activities or concerns? Who provides emotional support, and who receives it? Who takes action when problems arise? Who carries the mental and emotional load for maintaining the relationship?

This analysis often reveals patterns that have developed gradually and may not be immediately obvious. You might discover that you consistently take more responsibility for maintaining the relationship, managing shared logistics, or solving problems that arise. Or you might find that others consistently look to you for emotional regulation, decision-making, or crisis management.

The mapping process also involves examining how these patterns serve both parties. Over-functioning and under-functioning dynamics persist because they meet certain needs for both people, even when they create long-term problems. Understanding what needs these patterns serve helps in designing healthier alternatives that meet the same underlying needs in more balanced ways.

Once you have clarity about current patterns, the next step involves envisioning what you want the relationship to look like based on mutual respect, shared responsibility, and healthy interdependence. This vision should address how responsibilities will be shared, how decisions will be made, how support will be offered and received, and how conflicts will be handled.

This envisioning process requires thinking about the relationship as a partnership between equals rather than a caretaking arrangement between a helper and a helped person. Even relationships that involve natural power differences—like parent-child relationships—can be structured to honor each person's autonomy and capability within appropriate developmental and situational limits.

The communication phase involves having honest conversations about the current dynamics and your desires for change. These conversations require skill and sensitivity because they often challenge established patterns that others may be comfortable with or invested in maintaining.

Effective communication about relationship redesign involves taking responsibility for your own role in creating current dynamics rather than blaming others for their participation. It means expressing your needs and desires for change while acknowledging others' perspectives and concerns. It also means being clear about what changes you're committed to making regardless of others' choices.

This might sound like: "I've realized that I've been taking over a lot of decisions and responsibilities that we could be sharing more equally. I'd like to work together to create a more balanced approach where we both contribute more equally. How does that sound to you?" Or "I've noticed that I tend to jump in with advice and solutions when you're dealing with challenges. I'd like to be more supportive by listening and asking questions rather than taking over. Would that be helpful for you?"

The implementation phase involves consistently practicing new patterns while expecting and working through the discomfort that naturally accompanies change. Both parties often experience anxiety, confusion, or resistance as they adjust to new roles and expectations. This discomfort is normal and temporary, but it requires patience and commitment to work through.

Implementation also requires what I call "pattern interruption"—consciously choosing different responses when old dynamics begin to emerge. This might mean pausing before offering unsolicited advice, asking for others' input before making decisions that affect them, or stepping back when you notice yourself taking over responsibilities that belong to others.

Robert used this pattern interruption approach when redesigning his relationship with his adult son. "I had to learn to pause when Michael called with problems and ask myself whether he was looking for a conversation partner or a problem-solver," Robert said. "Instead of automatically jumping into fix-it mode, I started asking him what kind of support he was looking for. Sometimes he wanted advice, but often he just wanted someone to listen and validate his experience."

The relationship redesign process also involves regular check-ins and adjustments as both parties learn new ways of relating. These check-ins provide opportunities to assess how the changes are working, address any problems or concerns that arise, and fine-tune the new dynamics based on what you learn through experience.

This ongoing adjustment process recognizes that relationship change is gradual and requires patience with both yourself and others as you develop new skills and comfort with different ways of relating. It also acknowledges that relationships continue to evolve, and the redesign process may need to be revisited as circumstances and needs change over time.

The Help Versus Enable Decision Matrix

Making real-time decisions about when to help and when to step back requires a systematic framework that helps you evaluate specific situations quickly and consistently. The Help Versus Enable Decision Matrix provides a tool for making these evaluations based on clear criteria that support empowerment rather than dependency.

The matrix evaluates potential helping situations along several key dimensions. The first dimension examines capability: Can this person reasonably handle this situation themselves, or do they genuinely lack the resources, skills, or capacity to manage it independently? Help is more appropriate when genuine incapacity exists, while stepping back is more appropriate when the person has the basic capability to handle the situation.

The second dimension examines urgency and consequences: Is this a genuine emergency that requires immediate intervention, or is it a manageable problem that can be handled at a reasonable pace? Are the potential consequences of not helping truly serious, or are they primarily uncomfortable but not harmful? Emergency situations may warrant more direct help, while non-urgent situations provide better opportunities for independent problem-solving.

The third dimension examines learning opportunities: Will your help increase or decrease this person's capacity to handle similar situations in the future? Does this situation provide valuable learning opportunities that your intervention would prevent? Help that builds capacity and teaches skills is more empowering than help that replaces the person's own efforts.

The fourth dimension examines motivation and investment: Is this person actively working to address the situation themselves, or are they looking for someone else to take over? Are they more invested in solving the problem, or are you? Help is more appropriate when the person is actively engaged in their own problem-solving and genuinely wants assistance rather than rescue.

The fifth dimension examines patterns and history: Is this a one-time situation requiring temporary help, or is it part of a chronic pattern where the person consistently relies on others for situations they could handle themselves? Occasional help during genuine difficulties is different from ongoing patterns of rescue and management.

The sixth dimension examines your motivation: Are you offering help because it would genuinely serve this person's growth and wellbeing, or because their distress makes you uncomfortable and you want to relieve your own anxiety? Help motivated by your own discomfort often becomes enabling, while help motivated by genuine care for the other person's development is more likely to be empowering.

Using this matrix involves quickly evaluating situations along these dimensions to determine whether offering help would empower or enable. Situations that score high on genuine incapacity, real urgency, learning opportunities, recipient motivation, unusual circumstances, and appropriate helper motivation suggest that help would be empowering. Situations that score low on these dimensions suggest that stepping back would be more beneficial.

Patricia used this matrix when her adult daughter called asking for help with apartment hunting. "I ran through the dimensions quickly: she was capable of searching for apartments herself, it wasn't urgent since she had several weeks to find a place, my taking over would prevent her from learning the process, she seemed to want me to do the work rather than help her do it, this was becoming a pattern of her outsourcing adult responsibilities to me, and I was motivated more by my own anxiety about her housing situation than by what would actually help her develop," Patricia said. "The matrix helped me realize that stepping back and offering emotional support while she handled the search herself would be more empowering than taking over the process."

The matrix also helps identify situations where help is genuinely appropriate and empowering. When someone is facing a situation beyond their current capability, dealing with a real emergency, actively working on their own solutions, and asking for specific assistance that would build their capacity, offering help supports rather than undermines their development.

The key to using the matrix effectively is making these evaluations quickly and consistently rather than getting caught up in extensive analysis or guilt about your decisions. The goal is developing better instincts about when to help and when to step back, not creating perfect decisions in every situation.

The Mutual Growth Partnership Model

The ultimate vision of the New Relationship Operating System is what I call the Mutual Growth Partnership Model—relationships where both people support each other's development, celebrate each other's successes, and maintain their own individual identity and autonomy while enjoying genuine connection and mutual support.

This model recognizes that healthy relationships involve two whole people choosing to share their lives and support each other's journey rather than two partial people trying to complete each other through enmeshment and codependency. In mutual growth partnerships, each person takes responsibility for their own happiness, growth, and life outcomes while offering appropriate support and encouragement for their partner's development.

The mutual growth partnership model applies to all types of relationships—romantic partnerships, friendships, parent-child relationships, and professional relationships. While the specific dynamics vary based on the type of relationship and the developmental stage of the people involved, the underlying principles remain consistent.

These principles include mutual respect for each person's autonomy and capability, shared responsibility for the relationship's health and growth, support that empowers rather than enables, communication that encourages honesty and authenticity, and commitment to each person's individual development as well as the relationship's growth.

In mutual growth partnerships, both people are encouraged to pursue their own interests, develop their own capabilities, and maintain their own social connections while also investing in their shared relationship. Neither person is expected to sacrifice their individual identity or goals for the relationship, and both people are expected to contribute actively to the relationship's wellbeing.

This model often requires unlearning patterns of self-sacrifice and other-sacrifice that have been taught as expressions of love. Many people have been conditioned to believe that love requires giving up your own needs for others, or that good relationships involve one person taking care of the other rather than both people taking care of themselves and supporting each other.

The mutual growth partnership model offers a different vision: relationships where love is expressed through supporting each other's authentic development, where care is demonstrated by encouraging rather than managing each other's growth, and where commitment involves choosing each other repeatedly from a place of wholeness rather than neediness.

Jennifer and her husband worked to implement this model in their marriage after recognizing that their relationship had become structured around her managing most aspects of their shared life while he under-functioned in areas like social planning, household management, and family communication.

"We had to have honest conversations about how we had both contributed to this imbalance," Jennifer said. "I had to stop taking over responsibilities that he could handle, and he had to step up and take more active ownership of our shared life. It was uncomfortable at first because we were both so used to our old roles, but gradually we developed a partnership where we both contributed more equally and both felt more respected and valued."

The mutual growth partnership model also involves celebrating each other's individual successes and growth rather than feeling threatened by them. In codependent relationships, one person's growth can feel threatening to the other because it changes the established dynamic and may reduce dependency. In mutual growth partnerships, individual development is celebrated because it enhances both people's capacity to contribute to the relationship.

This celebration of individual growth requires developing what I call "abundance thinking"—the belief that others' success and happiness enhances rather than diminishes your own wellbeing. This thinking challenges the scarcity mindset that often underlies codependent relationships, where one person's gain is seen as another person's loss.

The mutual growth partnership model recognizes that healthy relationships require ongoing attention, communication, and adjustment as both people continue to grow and change throughout their lives. Rather than assuming that relationships should remain static once established, this model embraces the reality that relationships must evolve to remain healthy and fulfilling for both parties.

This evolution requires regular communication about how the relationship is working, what adjustments might be needed, and how both people can better support each other's continued growth and development. It also requires flexibility and willingness to adapt relationship patterns as circumstances and needs change over time.

The ultimate goal of implementing the New Relationship Operating System is creating relationships that honor both individual autonomy and genuine connection, that support both personal growth and relational intimacy, and that are based on choice and mutual respect rather than obligation and dependency. These relationships provide the foundation for a life where you can pursue your own authentic development while maintaining loving, supportive connections with others who are also committed to their own growth and wellbeing.

When relationships are based on the New Relationship Operating System, they become sources of energy and inspiration rather than drain and obligation. They support your freedom to live authentically while providing genuine love and connection. They model for others what healthy relationships can look like and create ripple effects that extend far beyond your immediate circle.

This transformation doesn't happen overnight, and it requires patience, practice, and commitment from everyone involved. There will be setbacks, misunderstandings, and moments when old patterns resurface. But with consistent effort and clear commitment to mutual respect and empowerment, you can create relationships that truly serve everyone's highest good while honoring the fundamental truth that each person is responsible for their own life journey.

The New Relationship Operating System ultimately recognizes that the best way to love others is to trust them, support them, and believe in their capacity to create their own meaningful, successful lives. When you operate from this foundation of respect and empowerment, your relationships become demonstrations of what's possible when people choose to love each other without trying to control each other, to support each other without taking over for each other, and to care deeply while maintaining the healthy boundaries that make genuine intimacy possible.

This is love without management, care without control, and support without sacrifice. It's the foundation for relationships that last not because people are dependent on each other, but because they choose each other from a place of freedom, wholeness, and mutual respect. These relationships become the context within which everyone involved can flourish as their most authentic, capable, and fulfilled selves.

CHAPTER 12

Communication That Empowers Others

The moment of realization came for Lisa during what should have been a simple phone conversation with her twenty-eight-year-old daughter. Emma had called to share the exciting news that she'd been offered a promotion at work, but within minutes, Lisa found herself taking over the conversation with a barrage of questions and advice.

"That's wonderful, honey! Now, did you negotiate the salary? You need to make sure you're getting paid what you're worth. And what about the benefits package? Don't just accept the first offer—you should always counter-negotiate. Have you researched what people in similar positions are making? I can help you look that up. And make sure you understand the expectations for the new role. Sometimes promotions come with unrealistic workloads..."

Lisa continued for several more minutes, her excitement for her daughter quickly transforming into management mode, offering solutions to problems Emma hadn't mentioned and advice she hadn't requested. When she finally paused to take a breath, the silence on the other end of the line stretched uncomfortably long.

"Mom," Emma said quietly, "I just wanted to share some good news with you. I wasn't asking for help with anything."

The hurt in Emma's voice hit Lisa like a physical blow. In her eagerness to be helpful and supportive, she had completely hijacked her daughter's moment of celebration and turned it into a problem-solving session. She realized that her automatic response to any information was to immediately start managing, advising, and fixing, even when none of that was requested or needed.

This conversation became a turning point for Lisa in understanding how her communication patterns had been undermining rather than supporting her relationships. Despite her good intentions, her habitual way of talking with others—especially family members—was based on the assumption that they needed her guidance, oversight, and problem-solving expertise rather than her presence, listening, and faith in their capabilities.

Lisa's experience illustrates one of the most common challenges facing over-managers: learning to communicate in ways that empower rather than diminish others. For years or decades, over-managers develop communication patterns that reflect their role as helper, advisor, and problem-solver. They become skilled at giving advice, offering solutions, and providing direction, but they often lose the ability to simply be present with others' experiences without immediately trying to manage or fix them.

Transforming your communication style from managing to empowering requires fundamental changes in how you listen, how you respond, and what you believe your role should be in others' lives. It means learning to trust others' wisdom and capability rather than assuming they need your guidance. It means becoming curious about others' perspectives rather than immediately offering your own. Most importantly, it means understanding that the goal of communication is connection and empowerment rather than control and management.

Shifting from Advice-Giving to Question-Asking

One of the most powerful shifts in empowering communication involves moving from automatically offering advice and solutions to asking thoughtful questions that help others access their own wisdom and problem-solving abilities. This shift challenges the over-manager's deeply ingrained habit of immediately jumping into fix-it mode whenever someone shares a challenge or concern.

The tendency to give unsolicited advice often stems from genuine desire to help combined with unconscious assumptions about others' capabilities. When someone shares a problem with you, your immediate impulse might be to offer solutions based on your experience, knowledge, or perspective. This impulse feels helpful and caring, but it often communicates that you don't believe the other person is capable of finding their own solutions.

Advice-giving also serves the advice-giver's psychological needs in ways that aren't always conscious. Offering solutions can make you feel useful, important, and competent. It can relieve your own anxiety about others' problems by creating the illusion that you've solved them. It can maintain your identity as someone who has answers and can fix things for others.

However, unsolicited advice often has the opposite effect of what's intended. Instead of feeling supported and helped, the recipient may feel diminished, controlled, or misunderstood. They may feel that their own thoughts and feelings aren't valued, that their capability is questioned, or that their autonomy is being undermined.

Question-asking, by contrast, demonstrates respect for others' intelligence and capability while helping them access their own problem-solving resources. Thoughtful questions can help others clarify their thinking, explore different perspectives, identify their own values and priorities, and develop confidence in their own judgment.

The shift from advice-giving to question-asking requires developing what I call "curiosity over certainty"—approaching others' situations with genuine interest in their perspective rather than immediate confidence that you know what they should do. This curiosity involves recognizing that others may have insights, information, or values that you don't have, and that their solutions may be different from but equally valid as the ones you would choose.

Jennifer discovered the power of this shift when her adult son was struggling with a career decision. Instead of immediately offering her perspective on which job he should choose, she began asking questions: "What aspects of each opportunity excite you most? What concerns do you have about each option? How do these choices align with your longer-term goals? What would help you feel most confident about your decision?"

"I was amazed by how much more thoughtful and confident he became when I asked questions instead of giving advice," Jennifer said. "The questions helped him think through aspects of the decision that I wouldn't have considered, and he came up with solutions that were much better suited to his personality and goals than anything I would have suggested."

Effective question-asking involves several key principles. The questions should be genuinely open-ended rather than leading questions designed to guide others toward answers you prefer. They should focus on helping others explore their own thoughts and feelings rather than gathering information for you to use in formulating advice. They should demonstrate curiosity about others' perspectives rather than testing whether they've considered options you think are important.

The most empowering questions often help others clarify their own values, priorities, and desires rather than focusing immediately on practical solutions. Questions like "What matters most to you in this situation?" or "What would you want to be true if you could design the ideal outcome?" help people connect with their own internal guidance system rather than looking externally for answers.

Process-focused questions can also be powerful for helping others develop their own problem-solving skills. Questions like "What options are you considering?" or "What information would help you feel more confident about this decision?" or "Who else might have useful perspectives on this situation?" help others think systematically about their challenges without taking over their thinking process.

The question-asking approach also requires learning to tolerate the discomfort that comes from not immediately offering solutions. When someone you care about is struggling, your automatic impulse might be to relieve their discomfort as quickly as possible by providing answers. Learning to sit with their uncertainty while supporting their own problem-solving process requires emotional discipline and faith in their capabilities.

This tolerance for others' temporary discomfort is essential because the process of working through challenges and developing solutions is often more valuable than the specific solutions themselves. When you immediately provide answers, you rob others of the opportunity to develop their own thinking skills, confidence, and sense of capability.

The Power of Reflective Listening

Reflective listening represents one of the most profound shifts available to over-managers in their communication style. Instead of listening for problems to solve or advice to give, reflective listening involves fully receiving and reflecting back others' experiences, emotions, and perspectives without immediately trying to change or fix anything.

This type of listening is fundamentally different from the problem-focused listening that characterizes most over-management communication. Problem-focused listening involves scanning what others say for issues that need addressing, challenges that require solutions, or emotions that need managing. The listener is primarily focused on what they can do to help rather than on simply receiving and understanding the speaker's experience.

Reflective listening, by contrast, involves what psychologists call "empathic presence"—being fully available to others' experiences without immediately moving into action or advice. This presence communicates that their thoughts and feelings are valuable in themselves, not just as problems to be solved or situations to be managed.

The practice of reflective listening involves several key skills. The first is what listening experts call "bracketing"—temporarily setting aside your own thoughts, reactions, and impulses to offer advice in order to fully focus on understanding others' perspectives. This bracketing allows you to receive what others are sharing without immediately filtering it through your own lens of how to help or what to do.

This bracketing can be challenging for over-managers because their automatic response to others' sharing is often to start generating solutions, advice, or actions they could take to help. Learning to temporarily suspend these responses in order to simply receive and understand requires conscious effort and practice.

The second skill involves "emotional mirroring"—reflecting back the emotional content of what others are sharing to demonstrate that you've heard and understood their feelings. This might involve statements like "It sounds like you're feeling really frustrated about this situation" or "I can hear how excited you are about this opportunity" or "This seems to be bringing up a lot of anxiety for you."

Emotional mirroring serves several important functions. It demonstrates that you're paying attention to others' emotional experience, not just the factual content of what they're sharing. It helps others feel seen and understood rather than just heard. It also helps others become more aware of and comfortable with their own emotional responses.

The third skill involves "content reflection"—summarizing or paraphrasing what others have shared to demonstrate understanding and help them clarify their own thinking. This might sound like "So if I understand correctly, you're trying to decide between staying in your current job where you feel secure but unfulfilled, or taking a risk on this new opportunity that excites you but feels uncertain."

Content reflection helps others organize their thoughts, feel understood, and sometimes gain new insights into their own situations through hearing their experiences reflected back. It also provides an opportunity to correct any misunderstandings and ensure that you're truly grasping their perspective.

The fourth skill involves "inquiry expansion"—asking follow-up questions that help others explore their experiences more deeply rather than moving quickly to solutions. These questions might focus on emotional responses ("What's it like for you when that happens?"), values and priorities ("What's most important to you in this situation?"), or desired outcomes ("What would you want to be different?").

Patricia learned the power of reflective listening when her teenage daughter was struggling with social dynamics at school. Instead of immediately offering advice about how to handle difficult friendships, Patricia focused on listening and reflecting what she heard.

"I realized that my daughter didn't need me to solve her social problems," Patricia said. "She needed someone to witness her experience and help her process her feelings. When I stopped trying to fix everything and just listened reflectively, she became much more open about what she was going through, and she started developing her own insights about how to handle the situations."

Reflective listening also requires learning to be comfortable with silence and emotional intensity without immediately trying to relieve discomfort through action or advice. This comfort develops through practice and often involves managing your own anxiety about others' struggles without taking action to make yourself feel better.

The goal of reflective listening isn't to become passive or unhelpful, but to provide a different type of support that's often more valuable than immediate problem-solving. When others feel truly heard and understood, they often discover their own clarity and solutions. When they feel that their experiences are valued and respected, they develop more confidence in their own ability to handle challenges.

How to Express Concern Without Taking Responsibility

One of the most delicate communication challenges for recovering over-managers involves learning to express genuine care and concern for others' wellbeing without automatically taking responsibility for their problems or emotions. This balance requires developing language and approaches that communicate love and support while maintaining appropriate boundaries around responsibility and autonomy.

The traditional over-manager approach to expressing concern often involves immediate problem-solving, advice-giving, or emotional caretaking. When someone you care about is struggling, your automatic response might be to ask what you can do to help, offer suggestions for how to handle the situation, or take on their emotional distress as your own responsibility.

While these responses come from genuine care, they often communicate that you don't believe the other person is capable of handling their own situation. They can also create pressure for others to accept your help or follow your advice even when they prefer to handle things themselves.

Learning to express concern without taking responsibility requires developing what I call "supportive presence"—a way of being with others that communicates care and availability without automatically moving into management mode. This presence involves acknowledging others' struggles, expressing confidence in their ability to handle challenges, and offering specific, limited support while maintaining clear boundaries about responsibility.

This supportive presence often begins with validation and empathy rather than immediate problem-solving. Instead of asking "What can I do to help?" you might begin with "This sounds really difficult" or "I can see how much this means to you" or "It makes sense that you're feeling overwhelmed by this situation."

This validation communicates that you understand and care about their experience without immediately moving to fix or change it. It allows others to feel seen and supported in their struggle rather than rushed toward solutions they may not be ready for or want.

The expression of concern can also include what I call "capability affirmation"—statements that express confidence in others' ability to handle their challenges. This might sound like "I trust your judgment about how to handle this" or "You've handled difficult situations well before, and I believe you can navigate this one too" or "I know this is challenging, and I have confidence in your ability to figure out what's right for you."

These affirmations serve multiple purposes. They communicate respect for others' competence and autonomy. They provide emotional support without creating dependency. They help others connect with their own inner resources and confidence rather than looking externally for solutions.

When offering specific support, it's important to make offers that are truly optional rather than implicit expectations. This means framing support in terms of what you're available for rather than what you think others need. It also means being genuinely comfortable with others declining your offers of help.

This might sound like "I'm happy to listen if you want to talk through what you're thinking" or "If you'd like a different perspective on this situation, I'm available" or "I'm here if you need someone to bounce ideas off of, but I also completely understand if you prefer to handle this on your own."

The key to these offers is making them without attachment to whether others accept them. The goal is to communicate availability and care rather than to actually provide help or solve problems. When others know that support is available without pressure to accept it, they often feel more supported than when help is offered with implicit expectations for acceptance.

David learned this approach when his adult daughter was going through a difficult divorce. Instead of immediately offering to help with legal research, childcare arrangements, or emotional processing, he focused on expressing care while respecting her autonomy.

"I told her that I could see how much pain she was in and that I loved her and believed in her strength to get through this difficult time," David said. "I let her know that I was available if she wanted to talk or if there were specific ways I could support her, but I made it clear that I trusted her to handle the situation in whatever way felt right to her. This approach actually brought us closer because she felt supported without feeling managed."

Expressing concern without taking responsibility also requires managing your own anxiety about others' struggles without taking action to relieve that anxiety. This often means tolerating your own discomfort with their discomfort without immediately trying to fix their situation to make yourself feel better.

This emotional discipline is crucial because actions taken primarily to relieve your own anxiety rather than to genuinely serve others' well-being often create more problems than they solve. Learning to sit with your concern while respecting others' autonomy and capability is one of the most loving things you can do.

Setting Expectations Versus Imposing Control

Effective communication in empowering relationships involves learning to set clear expectations and boundaries while avoiding the imposition of control over others' choices and behaviors. This distinction is often subtle but crucial for maintaining respect and autonomy in relationships while still addressing practical needs and concerns.

Setting expectations involves communicating your own needs, boundaries, and standards while leaving others free to choose how they respond. Imposing control involves trying to dictate others' choices or behaviors through pressure, manipulation, or consequences designed to force compliance rather than encourage cooperation.

The difference often lies not in what you communicate, but in how you communicate it and what your attachment is to others' responses. Healthy expectation-setting focuses on clarifying your own position while respecting others' autonomy to make their own choices. Control-based communication focuses on getting others to do what you want them to do regardless of their own preferences or judgment.

Sarah learned this distinction when addressing chronic lateness issues with her teenage daughter. Instead of trying to control her daughter's time management through constant reminders and consequences, Sarah focused on setting clear expectations about how lateness affected her and what she was willing to accommodate.

"I told her that I was happy to provide transportation to her activities as long as she was ready at the agreed-upon time," Sarah said. "I explained that when she wasn't ready, it created stress for me and sometimes made me late for my own commitments. I let her know that if she wasn't ready when I needed to leave, I would go ahead with my schedule and she would need to find alternative transportation."

This approach communicated clear expectations and consequences while leaving Sarah's daughter free to choose how to manage her time. It focused on Sarah's own boundaries and needs rather than trying to control her daughter's behavior. When her daughter chose to be late and had to find her own rides to activities, she learned to manage her time better through natural consequences rather than through external control.

Expectation-setting also involves what I call "standards clarity"—being clear about what you will and won't accept in your relationships while avoiding attempts to control others' choices in areas that don't directly affect you. This might involve setting expectations about how you want to be treated, what behaviors you're willing to tolerate, or what you need in order to feel comfortable and respected in the relationship.

This standards clarity is different from trying to control others' general behavior or life choices. You can set expectations about how others treat you without trying to control how they live their lives. You can communicate what you need in the relationship without taking responsibility for their personal growth or development.

The communication of expectations works best when it focuses on specific, observable behaviors rather than vague character judgments or emotional demands. Instead of saying "You need to be more responsible," you might say "I need you to follow through on commitments you make to me." Instead of "You're too negative," you might say "I'm not available for conversations that focus primarily on complaints without exploring solutions."

This specificity helps others understand exactly what you're requesting while avoiding character attacks or emotional manipulation. It also makes it easier for others to choose whether and how they want to meet your expectations rather than feeling generally criticized or controlled.

Marcus applied this approach when addressing his adult son's pattern of asking for financial help during every visit. Instead of trying to control his son's financial behavior or lecturing him about money management, Marcus set clear expectations about his own boundaries around financial assistance.

"I told him that I loved spending time with him but that I wasn't comfortable with our visits consistently including requests for money," Marcus said. "I explained that I was happy to talk about his financial situation if he wanted perspective or advice, but that I wouldn't be providing financial assistance except in genuine emergencies. I also let him know that I hoped we could develop a relationship that wasn't focused on financial help."

This communication focused on Marcus's own comfort and boundaries rather than trying to control his son's financial choices. It set clear expectations while leaving his son free to decide how he wanted to handle their relationship going forward.

Setting expectations also requires being prepared to follow through on boundaries and consequences without becoming punitive or controlling. This follow-through demonstrates that your expectations are genuine rather than just threats or manipulations designed to force compliance.

The goal of expectation-setting is to create clarity and respect in relationships rather than to control others' behavior. When expectations are communicated clearly and respectfully, they often improve relationships by reducing confusion and conflict while increasing mutual respect and understanding.

Language Patterns That Promote Independence

The specific words and phrases you use in communication have powerful effects on others' sense of capability, autonomy, and confidence. Learning to use language patterns that promote independence rather than dependence can transform your relationships and help others develop greater confidence in their own abilities.

Language that promotes independence is characterized by several key patterns. It expresses confidence in others' capabilities rather than anxiety about their potential struggles. It focuses on their strengths and resources rather than their deficits and needs. It encourages their own thinking and decision-making rather than providing ready-made solutions.

One of the most powerful shifts involves moving from "you should" language to "you might consider" or "one option could be" language. "You should" statements position you as the authority who knows what's best, while "you might consider" language positions you as a thinking partner who's offering possibilities for consideration.

This shift might sound subtle, but it has significant psychological effects. "You should call your boss about this situation" positions the listener as someone who needs direction about obvious next steps. "You might consider talking directly with your boss about this" positions the listener as someone who's capable of evaluating options and making their own decisions about how to proceed.

Similarly, moving from "you need to" language to "it might be helpful to" language communicates respect for others' autonomy while still offering perspective. "You need to set better boundaries with your coworkers" suggests that the person is failing to do something obvious. "It might be helpful to think about what boundaries would feel comfortable for you in this situation" invites consideration without imposing judgment.

Another powerful pattern involves what I call "ownership language"—phrasing that keeps responsibility and ownership with the person who has the problem rather than transferring it to you. This might involve saying "What are you thinking about that?" instead of "Here's what I think you should do," or "How are you feeling about your options?" instead of "I'm worried about the choice you're making."

This ownership language helps others stay connected to their own experience and judgment rather than immediately looking to you for answers. It reinforces that they are the experts on their own life and that their thoughts and feelings are the most important factors in their decision-making.

Jennifer discovered the power of ownership language when her adult son was struggling with a relationship decision. Instead of offering her opinion about whether he should break up with his girlfriend, she asked questions that helped him stay connected to his own experience: "What feels most important to you in a relationship? How do you feel when you're with her? What would help you feel more confident about whatever decision you make?"

"I realized that my opinions about his relationship weren't nearly as important as helping him clarify his own feelings and values," Jennifer said. "When I used language that kept the ownership with him, he became much more confident in his ability to make good decisions about his own relationships."

Independence-promoting language also involves what I call "capability assumption"—speaking to others as if you assume they're competent and resourceful rather than fragile and needy. This might involve asking "What's your plan for handling this?" instead of "Do you need help figuring out what to do?" or saying "I'm curious how this turns out for you" instead of "I'm worried about whether you can handle this."

These seemingly small shifts in language communicate powerful messages about your assessment of others' capabilities. When you speak to others as if you assume they're competent, they often rise to meet that expectation. When you speak to them as if you assume they need help or management, they often begin to doubt their own abilities.

The language of empowerment also involves what psychologists call "growth mindset" communication—language that emphasizes learning, development, and possibility rather than fixed limitations or deficits. This might involve focusing on what others are learning from challenging situations rather than just the difficulties they're experiencing, or highlighting their growth and development rather than their current struggles.

This growth-focused language helps others see challenges as opportunities for development rather than just problems to be solved or avoided. It reinforces that they're capable of learning, adapting, and becoming more competent over time rather than being fixed in their current level of capability.

Patricia used growth mindset language when her teenage daughter was struggling with a difficult class. Instead of focusing on how hard the subject was or offering to help with homework, Patricia highlighted her daughter's learning process: "I can see how much effort you're putting into understanding this material. What strategies are you finding most helpful? What's been most challenging about learning this new information?"

"This approach helped my daughter see herself as someone who was capable of learning difficult material rather than someone who needed rescue from academic challenges," Patricia said. "She developed much more confidence in her own learning abilities when I spoke to her as a capable student rather than someone who needed constant help."

The Empowering Communication Toolkit

Developing consistently empowering communication requires building a toolkit of specific phrases, questions, and approaches that you can use in various situations to support others' autonomy while maintaining connection and care. This toolkit serves as a practical resource for transforming automatic advice-giving and managing responses into empowering alternatives.

The toolkit begins with what I call "curiosity openers"—phrases that demonstrate genuine interest in others' perspectives rather than immediate certainty about what they should do. These might include "I'm curious about your thoughts on this," "What's your sense of the situation?" "How are you thinking about approaching this?" or "What feels most important to you about this decision?"

These openers set a tone of collaboration and respect rather than expertise and direction. They invite others to share their own thinking rather than positioning you as the person with answers. They also create space for you to learn about others' perspectives rather than immediately offering your own.

The toolkit also includes "validation statements" that acknowledge others' experiences and feelings without immediately trying to change or fix them. These might sound like "That sounds really challenging," "I can understand why you'd feel that way," "It makes sense that this would be difficult for you," or "I can see how much this matters to you."

These validation statements provide emotional support without creating dependency or taking over others' experiences. They help others feel heard and understood while maintaining appropriate boundaries around whose feelings and experiences belong to whom.

"Confidence expressions" form another crucial part of the toolkit—statements that communicate your faith in others' abilities and judgment. These might include "I trust your judgment about this," "You've handled difficult situations well before," "I have confidence in your ability to figure this out," or "I believe you'll know what's right for you when you've had time to think about it."

These expressions serve as powerful antidotes to the doubt and anxiety that often drive over-management. When others know that you believe in their capabilities, they often develop greater confidence in themselves. When they feel trusted to handle their own lives, they often rise to meet that trust.

The toolkit includes "boundary statements" that communicate your own limits and needs while respecting others' autonomy. These might sound like "I'm not in a position to help with that, but I hope you find a good solution," "I care about you and I'm not available to manage this situation for you," or "I love you and I trust you to handle this yourself."

These boundary statements allow you to maintain appropriate limits while communicating care and respect. They avoid both the extremes of taking over others' problems and completely withdrawing support and connection.

"Resource offering" represents another important category—ways of offering support that empower rather than enable. These might include "I'm happy to listen if you want to talk through your thinking," "Would it be helpful to brainstorm some options together?" "I could share some resources if you're interested," or "I'm available if you want someone to bounce ideas off of."

These offers provide genuine support while maintaining clear boundaries about responsibility and ownership. They position you as a resource that others can choose to utilize rather than as a manager who will take over their situations.

The toolkit also includes "process questions" that help others develop their own problem-solving skills rather than depending on your solutions. These might include "What options are you considering?" "What information would help you feel more confident about this decision?" "Who else might have useful perspectives?" "What would help you feel more prepared to handle this?" or "What's your next step?"

These questions guide others through systematic thinking about their challenges without taking over their thinking process. They help others develop confidence in their own ability to analyze situations and develop solutions.

Margaret found the empowering communication toolkit particularly helpful in her relationships with her adult children. "Having specific phrases and questions to use helped me break my automatic pattern of jumping into advice-giving mode," she said. "When I had alternative responses readily available, I could choose empowering communication even when my instinct was to take over and manage."

The toolkit requires practice and conscious application, especially in situations where your automatic response would be to offer advice or take over. Over time, these empowering communication patterns become more natural and automatic, transforming not just what you say but how you think about your role in others' lives.

The Question-Based Helping Method

The Question-Based Helping Method represents a systematic approach to providing support that empowers rather than enables, that builds rather than replaces others' capabilities, and that honors autonomy while maintaining connection and care. This method transforms the traditional advice-giving approach into a collaborative exploration that helps others access their own wisdom and develop confidence in their own judgment.

The method is based on several key principles. It assumes that others are capable of finding good solutions to their problems when given appropriate support and encouragement. It recognizes that others often know more about their own situations, values, and constraints than you do, even when they're feeling confused or overwhelmed. It understands that the process of working through challenges is often more valuable than the specific solutions that emerge.

The Question-Based Helping Method begins with what I call "exploration questions"—inquiries that help others clarify their own understanding of their situation without immediately moving toward solutions. These might include "What's most concerning to you about this situation?" "What would you want to be different?" "What's working well that you want to preserve?" or "What feels most important to you as you think about this?"

These exploration questions help others organize their thoughts and identify their own priorities rather than jumping immediately to problem-solving. They often reveal information and perspectives that wouldn't emerge if you immediately started offering advice based on your initial understanding of the situation.

The second phase involves "option-generating questions" that help others identify possibilities and alternatives without you providing ready-made solutions. These might include "What approaches have you considered?" "What options seem most appealing to you?" "What would you do if you knew you couldn't fail?" "What advice would you give a friend in this situation?" or "What possibilities haven't you explored yet?"

These questions help others access their own creativity and problem-solving abilities rather than depending on your ideas. They often lead to solutions that are more innovative and better suited to others' specific circumstances than anything you might have suggested.

The third phase involves "evaluation questions" that help others assess their options and make decisions based on their own values and priorities. These might include "What feels most aligned with your values?" "What option would you be most excited to try?" "What concerns do you have about each possibility?" "What would help you feel most confident about your decision?" or "What's your gut telling you?"

These evaluation questions help others develop confidence in their own judgment rather than looking to you for approval or direction. They reinforce that they are the best judge of what will work in their own life and circumstances.

The fourth phase involves "implementation questions" that help others develop their own plans for moving forward rather than depending on your guidance for execution. These might include "What would be your first step?" "What support would be helpful as you move forward?" "What obstacles might you encounter, and how could you handle them?" "How will you know if your approach is working?" or "What adjustments might you need to make along the way?"

These implementation questions help others develop confidence in their ability to execute their own plans and handle challenges that arise.

They also demonstrate your faith in their capability to manage their own follow-through rather than needing your ongoing oversight.

David used the Question-Based Helping Method when his adult daughter was struggling with a career transition. Instead of immediately offering advice about job search strategies or networking approaches, he guided her through a systematic exploration of her own thinking.

"I started by asking what aspects of her current job she most wanted to change and what elements she most wanted to preserve in a new role," David said. "Then we explored what types of organizations and positions might offer what she was looking for. I asked about her concerns and what information would help her feel more confident about making a transition. By the end of our conversation, she had developed her own clear plan for exploring new opportunities, and she felt confident about her ability to manage the process."

The Question-Based Helping Method often takes more time initially than simply offering advice, but it produces much better long-term outcomes. Others develop greater confidence in their own abilities, better problem-solving skills, and more ownership of their decisions and outcomes. They also become less dependent on your guidance and more capable of handling future challenges independently.

The method also creates more satisfying relationships because it's based on genuine collaboration and mutual respect rather than one-sided helping. When you approach others' challenges with curiosity rather than solutions, you often learn things that surprise you and develop deeper appreciation for their perspectives and capabilities.

The Concern Versus Control Language Guide

Learning to distinguish between language that expresses genuine concern and language that attempts to control others' choices is crucial for developing empowering communication patterns. This distinction is often subtle but has profound effects on how others experience your involvement in their lives and how they develop confidence in their own capabilities.

Concern-based language focuses on expressing care while respecting others' autonomy and capability. It acknowledges challenges and difficulties without immediately moving to fix or manage them. It communicates availability for support while maintaining clear boundaries about responsibility and ownership.

Control-based language, by contrast, focuses on getting others to make choices you prefer or handle situations in ways you think are best. It often involves subtle pressure, implicit expectations, or emotional manipulation designed to influence others' decisions. It may communicate care, but it's care that's conditional on others doing what you think they should do.

The difference often lies not just in the specific words used, but in the underlying intention and energy behind the communication. Concern comes from a place of respect and trust, while control comes from a place of anxiety and doubt about others' capabilities.

Examples of concern-based language include "I can see this is really difficult for you," "I trust your judgment about how to handle this," "I'm here if you want to talk through your thinking," "This sounds challenging, and I believe in your ability to work through it," or "I care about you and I'm confident you'll figure out what's right for you."

These statements communicate care and availability while maintaining respect for others' autonomy. They express faith in others' capabilities rather than anxiety about their choices. They offer support without creating pressure to accept it or handle situations in specific ways.

Examples of control-based language include "You really should consider..." "I'm worried that you're making a mistake," "Don't you think it would be better if..." "I can't support you if you choose to..." or "You're going to regret this decision."

These statements, while potentially coming from genuine care, communicate doubt about others' judgment and pressure to make choices you prefer. They often create defensiveness or compliance rather than genuine collaboration and respect.

The concern versus control distinction becomes particularly important when others are making choices you disagree with or handling situations differently than you would. In these moments, the temptation to use controlling language can be strong because their choices trigger your own anxiety or disagreement.

Learning to express concern without control requires developing what I call "outcome detachment"—caring about others' wellbeing while not being attached to specific ways they achieve that wellbeing. This detachment allows you to support others' decision-making process while respecting their autonomy to make choices you wouldn't make.

Jennifer faced this challenge when her adult son decided to quit his stable job to start a business that she thought was risky and poorly planned. "My automatic response was to use language that was designed to talk him out of his decision," she said. "I wanted to say things like 'Don't you think you should wait until you have more experience?' or 'I'm worried you're making a huge mistake.'"

Instead, Jennifer chose concern-based language that expressed care while respecting his autonomy: "I can see how excited you are about this opportunity, and I also imagine it feels a bit scary to make such a big change. I trust your judgment about what's right for your life, and I'm here if you want to talk through any aspects of your planning."

This language communicated care and availability while avoiding pressure or control. It allowed her son to feel supported in his decision-making process while knowing that his mother trusted his judgment and capability.

The concern versus control language guide also helps identify the emotional undertones that often drive controlling communication. When you notice yourself using language that's designed to influence others' choices rather than simply express care, it's often worth examining what fears or anxieties might be driving that impulse.

Sometimes controlling language emerges from genuine love and worry about others' wellbeing. Other times it comes from your own discomfort with uncertainty, your need to feel useful and important, or your attachment to being right about what others should do. Understanding these underlying motivations can help you choose more empowering communication even when you're feeling anxious or disagreeable about others' choices.

The guide also recognizes that there are times when expressing concerns about others' choices is appropriate and caring, particularly when those choices could result in genuine harm. The key is expressing these concerns in ways that respect others' autonomy while still communicating your perspective clearly.

This might sound like "I care about you and I have some concerns about this plan. Would you be interested in hearing my perspective?" This approach communicates that you have thoughts to share while making it clear that the other person can choose whether to hear them and what to do with them.

When others do want to hear your concerns, expressing them in terms of your own feelings and observations rather than judgments about their choices helps maintain respect and autonomy. "I feel worried about the financial risk involved" is different from "You're being financially irresponsible." "I'm concerned about the timeline you've outlined" is different from "You're rushing into this too quickly."

This language allows you to share your perspective while maintaining respect for others' right to make their own decisions based on their own values, priorities, and assessment of risks and benefits.

Building a New Communication Foundation

Transforming your communication from managing to empowering requires building an entirely new foundation for how you interact with others. This foundation is based on respect rather than control, curiosity rather than certainty, and empowerment rather than rescue. Building this foundation requires both unlearning old patterns and consciously developing new skills and approaches.

The new communication foundation begins with what I call "mindset shifts"—fundamental changes in how you think about your role in others' lives and what constitutes helpful communication. The first mindset shift involves moving from seeing yourself as the expert who has answers to seeing yourself as a supporter who helps others access their own wisdom.

This shift requires recognizing that others often know more about their own situations, values, and constraints than you do, even when they're feeling confused or overwhelmed. It means approaching others' challenges with humility and curiosity rather than immediate confidence in what they should do.

The second mindset shift involves moving from problem-focused communication to growth-focused communication. Instead of immediately scanning for problems to solve or emotions to manage, you learn to focus on others' strengths, capabilities, and potential for learning and development.

This growth focus helps others see themselves as capable of handling challenges and developing new skills rather than as people who need constant help and management. It communicates faith in their ability to learn and adapt rather than doubt about their capacity to handle their own lives.

The third mindset shift involves moving from outcome attachment to process support. Instead of being invested in specific solutions or decisions that others make, you learn to support their decision-making process while respecting their autonomy to choose directions you might not prefer.

This process support allows you to be genuinely helpful without becoming controlling or manipulative. It honors others' right to make their own choices while still providing care and encouragement for their journey.

Building the new communication foundation also requires developing what I call "emotional discipline"—the ability to manage your own anxiety, frustration, or disagreement without taking action to control others' experiences. This discipline allows you to remain supportive and available while respecting others' autonomy and learning process.

This emotional discipline often involves tolerating uncertainty about others' choices and outcomes without immediately trying to reduce that uncertainty through advice, management, or control. It means sitting with your own discomfort when others are struggling without taking action to relieve your anxiety by fixing their problems.

The new foundation also requires practicing empowering communication consistently, even when your automatic impulse is to revert to old patterns of advice-giving and managing. This consistency helps others learn to trust that your support comes without hidden agendas or pressure to handle things in specific ways.

Sarah discovered that building this new foundation required conscious attention and practice over many months. "I had to catch myself constantly reverting to old patterns of jumping in with advice or taking over when my family members were struggling," she said. "But gradually, as I practiced empowering communication consistently, my relationships became deeper and more respectful. My family members started sharing more with me because they knew I wouldn't immediately try to fix or manage their experiences."

The new communication foundation also creates space for genuine intimacy and connection that isn't based on neediness or management. When others know that your support doesn't come with expectations for them to handle things in specific ways, they often feel safer being vulnerable and authentic in their sharing.

This authentic sharing creates deeper relationships that are based on mutual respect and genuine interest in each other's experiences rather than on roles and functions. It allows everyone involved to show up as whole people rather than just in their helping or being-helped roles.

The transformation to empowering communication is one of the most challenging but rewarding aspects of breaking free from over-management patterns. It requires developing new skills, changing fundamental assumptions about what constitutes helpful communication, and learning to trust others' capabilities even when they're struggling.

But the outcomes of this transformation are profound. When you learn to communicate in ways that empower rather than diminish others, you create relationships that support everyone's growth and autonomy. You model a way of caring that honors both individual capability and genuine connection. You discover that you can love others deeply while trusting them completely to handle their own lives.

This empowering communication becomes one of the greatest gifts you can offer to the people in your life. It communicates that you see them as capable, valuable, and worthy of respect. It supports their development of confidence and competence. Most importantly, it creates the foundation for relationships that are based on choice rather than need, respect rather than control, and mutual empowerment rather than one-sided management.

When your communication empowers rather than manages, when your words build confidence rather than create dependency, when your presence supports growth rather than preventing it, you become someone who truly serves others' highest good while honoring your own need for authentic, respectful relationships. This is communication that creates freedom for everyone involved—freedom to be authentic, to make choices, to learn and grow, and to love without conditions or control.

CHAPTER 13

Navigating Resistance and Pushback

The text message arrived at 7:42 PM on a Wednesday: "Mom, I can't believe you're being so selfish. I really needed help with my presentation tomorrow, and you just blew me off. I guess your yoga class is more important than your own daughter's education. Thanks for nothing."

Reading these words, Karen felt the familiar stab of guilt and doubt that had derailed so many of her previous attempts to establish healthier boundaries. For the past three months, she had been working to reduce her involvement in her twenty-three-year-old daughter's academic and professional responsibilities. She had stopped doing research for Emma's projects, ceased editing her papers, and begun declining requests to help with assignments that Emma could reasonably handle herself.

Tonight's "emergency" had been a request for Karen to cancel her yoga class—one of the few activities she did purely for herself—to help Emma prepare a presentation for work. When Karen had gently suggested that Emma was capable of handling the preparation herself and offered to listen if Emma wanted to talk through her ideas afterward, Emma had responded with hurt and anger.

The text message was designed to trigger every fear Karen had about setting boundaries: that she was being selfish, that she was failing as a mother, that her daughter would suffer because of her unwillingness to help. For a moment, Karen felt the powerful urge to abandon her boundaries, cancel her plans, and rush to rescue her daughter from the consequences of poor planning.

But this time, instead of immediately capitulating to the emotional pressure, Karen recognized what was happening. Emma was experiencing what psychologists call "extinction burst"—an intensification of problematic behavior that often occurs when established patterns are disrupted. Rather than evidence that Karen's boundaries were wrong or harmful, Emma's reaction was actually a predictable response to changing dynamics in their relationship.

Karen's experience illustrates one of the most challenging aspects of transforming over-management patterns: navigating the resistance and pushback that almost inevitably occur when you begin establishing healthier boundaries and expectations. This resistance comes from multiple sources—the people who have benefited from your over-functioning, your own internal doubts and guilt, and sometimes even well-meaning friends and family who don't understand why you're changing patterns that seemed to be working.

Understanding this resistance as a normal and temporary part of the transformation process, rather than evidence that your changes are wrong or harmful, is crucial for maintaining your commitment to healthier relationship patterns. Learning to navigate pushback with compassion but firmness, to respond to manipulation without being controlled by it, and to stay true to your values even when others express disappointment or anger, represents one of the most important skills you can develop in your journey toward freedom.

Understanding Why People Resist Your Newfound Boundaries

When you begin establishing boundaries and reducing your over-management of others' lives, the resistance you encounter often feels personal and hurtful. You might interpret others' negative reactions as evidence that you're being selfish, uncaring, or irresponsible. However, understanding the psychological dynamics behind this resistance can help you respond more effectively while maintaining your commitment to healthier patterns.

The first source of resistance stems from what behaviorists call "intermittent reinforcement." When you've been consistently available to solve problems, provide assistance, and manage crises for extended periods, others develop expectations that this pattern will continue indefinitely. Your availability and help have become part of their normal operating system, and they've organized their lives around the assumption that you'll continue to function in this role.

When you suddenly become less available or stop providing the same level of management, it disrupts their established systems and creates genuine inconvenience and stress. Their resistance isn't necessarily manipulative or intentional—it often reflects real discomfort with having to develop new strategies for handling responsibilities they've become accustomed to outsourcing to you.

Dr. John Gottman, whose research on relationship dynamics has influenced thousands of therapists and coaches, explains this phenomenon: "When one person in a relationship system changes their behavior patterns, it creates disequilibrium that affects everyone in the system. The initial response is often resistance designed to restore the familiar dynamic, even when that dynamic wasn't healthy for everyone involved."

This systemic resistance means that others' negative reactions to your boundaries often say more about their attachment to familiar patterns than about the appropriateness of your changes. People naturally resist disruption to established systems, even when those systems aren't serving everyone's long-term interests.

The second source of resistance comes from what I call "competence anxiety." When you stop managing aspects of others' lives, they're forced to confront their own capability or lack thereof in areas they haven't had to handle independently. This confrontation can trigger anxiety, self-doubt, and insecurity that gets directed toward you as the person who's "causing" the discomfort.

For example, if you've been managing someone's schedule, they may have never developed strong time management skills. When you stop providing this service, they're faced with their own disorganization and may feel overwhelmed or incompetent. Rather than acknowledging their need to develop these skills, they may blame you for being "unhelpful" or "unsupportive."

This competence anxiety is often accompanied by what psychologists call "learned helplessness"—a state where people have become convinced they can't handle certain responsibilities because someone else has been handling them consistently. Even when they're perfectly capable of developing the necessary skills, they may genuinely believe they need your management to function effectively.

Sarah experienced this when she stopped managing her teenage daughter's homework schedule and study habits. "My daughter had genuine panic about keeping track of her assignments and deadlines because I had been doing it for her for so long," Sarah said. "She wasn't trying to manipulate me—she really felt overwhelmed and incapable. But her anxiety was actually evidence that she needed to develop these skills, not that I should continue doing everything for her."

The third source of resistance involves identity and role disruption. Many relationships develop identities and roles that become central to how people see themselves and each other. When you're the family problem-solver, the workplace crisis manager, or the friend everyone turns to for help, changing these patterns disrupts not just practical arrangements but fundamental identity structures.

Others may resist your boundaries because they challenge their sense of who they are in relationship to you. If someone's identity has become organized around being helped, supported, or managed by you, your withdrawal from that role can feel like a threat to their sense of self and their place in the relationship.

Similarly, if your identity has been built around being needed, helpful, and indispensable, others may resist your boundaries partly because they sense your own ambivalence about changing roles. They may unconsciously recognize that part of you misses being needed and may try to pull you back into familiar patterns.

The fourth source of resistance often involves emotional regulation challenges. Many over-management relationships develop because one person has become responsible for managing or absorbing another person's emotional states. When you stop providing this emotional management, others are forced to develop their own emotional regulation skills, which can be uncomfortable and challenging.

This emotional resistance often manifests as intensified emotional reactions designed to trigger your caregiving responses. Others may become more dramatic in their distress, more frequent in their crisis calls, or more intense in their expressions of hurt and disappointment. These reactions often represent attempts to restore the emotional management they've become accustomed to receiving.

Understanding these sources of resistance helps you respond with compassion while maintaining your boundaries. The resistance isn't evidence that your changes are wrong—it's evidence that the changes are significant enough to disrupt established patterns and require genuine adjustment from everyone involved.

Handling Guilt Trips and Manipulation Attempts

One of the most challenging aspects of establishing boundaries involves learning to recognize and respond effectively to guilt trips and manipulation attempts without either becoming defensive or abandoning your newly established limits. These emotional pressures can be particularly intense because they often come from people you love and are designed to trigger your deepest fears about being selfish, uncaring, or irresponsible.

Guilt trips typically involve statements or behaviors designed to make you feel responsible for others' negative emotions or circumstances. They often take the form of comparisons to how "other people" would handle the situation, reminders of past help you've received, or predictions of negative outcomes that will result from your boundaries.

Common guilt trip patterns include statements like "I guess I'll just have to figure this out on my own, even though I've never had to deal with anything like this before," or "Your sister would never refuse to help me with something this important," or "I can't believe you're abandoning me when I need you most."

These statements are designed to trigger your rescue impulses by suggesting that your boundaries are causing harm, that you're failing to meet reasonable expectations, or that you're being unusually selfish compared to others. The emotional charge behind these statements often makes them feel compelling even when you intellectually recognize them as manipulative.

Manipulation attempts often involve more sophisticated emotional pressure designed to override your judgment and decision-making. These might include creating artificial urgency around situations that aren't actually time-sensitive, presenting false choices that exclude reasonable alternatives, or using emotional blackmail to pressure you into compliance.

Dr. Susan Forward, whose research on emotional manipulation has helped thousands of people recognize and respond to these patterns, explains: "Manipulation works by bypassing rational thought and triggering emotional responses that lead to compliance. The key to resisting manipulation is learning to pause, breathe, and reconnect with your own values and judgment before responding."

The most effective response to guilt trips and manipulation involves what I call "emotional jujitsu"—acknowledging the emotional content without accepting responsibility for others' feelings or changing your boundaries to accommodate their pressure. This approach allows you to remain compassionate while maintaining your limits.

This might sound like: "I can see that you're really upset about this situation, and I care about you. I'm not available to handle this particular issue, but I hope you find a good solution." This response acknowledges their distress without taking responsibility for solving it or changing your boundaries to relieve their discomfort.

Another effective approach involves what I call "broken record technique"—calmly repeating your boundary without engaging in arguments, justifications, or defensive explanations. This technique prevents you from getting drawn into debates about whether your boundaries are reasonable while clearly communicating that your limits aren't negotiable.

Jennifer used this approach when her adult son pressured her to cosign a loan for a car purchase she thought was financially irresponsible. Despite his arguments about why he needed the car and his suggestions that she didn't trust or support him, Jennifer repeatedly stated: "I care about you and I'm not comfortable cosigning loans. I'm confident you can find another solution that works for your situation."

"The hardest part was not explaining or justifying my decision," Jennifer said. "My impulse was to give him all the reasons why cosigning seemed risky, but I realized that would just invite argument and negotiation. When I simply restated my boundary without explanation, he eventually stopped pressuring me and found another way to handle his transportation needs."

Responding to manipulation also requires developing what I call "pressure immunity"—the ability to maintain your boundaries even when others escalate their emotional intensity or expand their pressure tactics. This immunity develops through understanding that others' emotional reactions, however intense, don't create obligations for you to change your limits or take actions you're not comfortable with.

Pressure immunity often requires tolerating others' disappointment, anger, or distress without immediately taking action to relieve their discomfort. This tolerance can be particularly challenging when the pressure comes from people you love, but it's essential for maintaining healthy boundaries over time.

The development of pressure immunity also involves recognizing that giving in to manipulation often makes the pattern worse rather than better. When you change your boundaries in response to emotional pressure, you inadvertently teach others that sufficient emotional intensity can override your limits. This creates an escalating cycle where others learn to increase pressure until they achieve compliance.

Marcus learned this lesson when his adult daughter used increasingly dramatic emotional appeals to pressure him for financial assistance. "Each time I gave in to her tears and crisis presentations, the next request became more intense and emotional," he said. "I realized that my compliance was actually training her to use emotional manipulation rather than developing her own financial problem-solving skills."

Breaking this cycle required Marcus to maintain his boundaries consistently regardless of his daughter's emotional intensity. While this consistency initially led to increased pressure and drama, it eventually helped his daughter develop more mature approaches to financial challenges and communication.

Handling manipulation also involves learning to distinguish between genuine distress and manufactured crisis. People who have learned to use emotional pressure often become skilled at presenting normal life challenges as emergencies requiring immediate intervention. Developing discernment about what constitutes real crisis versus manipulative drama is crucial for responding appropriately.

This discernment often involves asking yourself: Is this situation genuinely time-sensitive and urgent, or is the urgency artificially created to pressure compliance? Is this person actively working on solutions themselves, or are they focused primarily on getting me to solve the problem? Have I seen this pattern of crisis presentation before, and what were the actual outcomes when I didn't intervene?

Managing Family Dynamics During Your Transformation

Family systems are particularly resistant to change because they often involve decades of established patterns, multiple people with invested interests in maintaining familiar dynamics, and complex emotional histories that make boundary-setting feel threatening to family stability and connection.

When you begin transforming your over-management patterns within your family, you're not just changing your individual behavior—you're disrupting a system that has organized itself around your over-functioning. This disruption often triggers reactions from multiple family members who may feel threatened, confused, or disadvantaged by the changes you're implementing.

Family resistance often manifests through what systems therapists call "homeostatic pressure"—collective efforts to restore familiar patterns and resist changes that disrupt the family's equilibrium. This pressure might come in the form of increased requests for help, family discussions about your "selfishness," or attempts to involve other family members in pressuring you to return to previous patterns.

Understanding family systems dynamics helps you anticipate and respond to this pressure more effectively. Family systems naturally resist change because disruption feels threatening to stability and connection. However, this resistance doesn't mean that your changes are harmful—it often means that the changes are significant enough to require genuine adjustment from the entire family system.

Dr. Murray Bowen, whose family systems theory has influenced thousands of therapists, explains that when one person in a family changes their functioning, it creates pressure throughout the system. He notes that "the person who changes their functioning level will experience pressure from the family to return to their previous level, but maintaining the changes consistently usually leads to improved functioning throughout the entire system."

One of the most common family dynamics during transformation involves what I call "replacement seeking"—family members' attempts to find someone else to fill the over-functioning role you're vacating. This might involve pressuring another family member to take over your previous responsibilities or bringing in outside helpers to maintain the family's previous level of external support.

While replacement seeking is natural, it often creates conflict and resentment within the family as others resist being assigned the roles you previously fulfilled. This conflict can create pressure for you to resume your over-functioning to restore family harmony, but giving in to this pressure usually prevents the family from developing healthier, more balanced dynamics.

Sarah experienced this dynamic when she stopped managing conflicts between her teenage children. "When I stopped mediating every disagreement and solving every problem between my kids, my husband initially tried to step into that role," she said. "But he quickly became overwhelmed and frustrated, and both kids started complaining that he wasn't as good at fixing their problems as I was. The whole family pressure was for me to go back to managing their conflicts."

Instead of resuming her previous role, Sarah maintained her boundaries while supporting the family's adjustment to new patterns. She expressed confidence in her children's ability to resolve their own conflicts and in her husband's capability to provide guidance when genuinely needed. Over time, the family developed healthier communication patterns and conflict resolution skills.

Managing family dynamics also involves dealing with what I call "loyalty pressure"—family members' suggestions that your boundaries demonstrate lack of love, commitment, or loyalty to family relationships. This pressure often takes the form of statements like "Family should always come first," "If you really loved us, you would help," or "We've always been there for each other."

These loyalty appeals can be particularly effective because they touch on fundamental values about family commitment and mutual support. However, it's important to distinguish between genuine family loyalty and codependent enmeshment. True family loyalty involves supporting each other's growth and independence, while codependent loyalty requires self-sacrifice and over-functioning that ultimately weakens rather than strengthens family bonds.

Responding to loyalty pressure often involves reframing your boundaries as expressions of love rather than withdrawals of support. You might say something like: "I love our family, which is why I want us to develop patterns that support everyone's growth and independence. I believe we're all capable of handling more responsibility, and I want to encourage that capability rather than preventing it."

Family transformation also requires patience with the adjustment period that naturally follows significant changes in family dynamics. Most family members need time to develop new skills, adjust to new expectations, and learn to function in roles they haven't previously filled. During this adjustment period, there may be increased conflict, temporary decreases in family functioning, and pressure to return to familiar patterns.

This adjustment period can be particularly challenging because it often involves watching family members struggle with responsibilities they haven't handled independently. Your instinct may be to jump back in and resume your previous role to reduce their discomfort and restore family stability.

However, moving through this adjustment period is essential for developing healthier family dynamics. Most family members adapt more quickly than expected when they're given clear expectations and confidence in their abilities. The temporary discomfort of adjustment is usually outweighed by the long-term benefits of more balanced, respectful family relationships.

Patricia navigated this adjustment period when she stopped managing her elderly mother's medical appointments and health care coordination. "Initially, my mother struggled with keeping track of appointments and communicating with her doctors," Patricia said. "The whole family was worried about her ability to manage her health care independently, and there was significant pressure for me to resume my previous level of involvement."

Instead of taking over again, Patricia worked with her mother to develop systems and resources that supported her independence while ensuring appropriate care. She helped her mother organize a medical binder, identified transportation resources, and connected her with a care coordinator through her insurance. While the transition required patience and adjustment, it ultimately resulted in her mother feeling more competent and engaged in her own health care.

Dealing with Workplace Resistance to Your New Approach

Professional environments often present unique challenges for implementing healthier boundaries because workplace dynamics frequently reward over-functioning and penalize appropriate limit-setting. Organizations often benefit from employees who consistently work beyond their job descriptions, take on others' responsibilities, and sacrifice personal boundaries for organizational needs.

When you begin establishing healthier boundaries at work—declining to consistently work excessive hours, refusing to take on responsibilities that belong to others, or stopping the practice of solving everyone else's problems—you may encounter resistance from colleagues, supervisors, and organizational cultures that have become dependent on your over-functioning.

This workplace resistance often manifests in several predictable patterns. Colleagues who have benefited from your over-functioning may express concern about your "reduced commitment" or "change in attitude." Supervisors may pressure you to maintain previous patterns by suggesting that boundary-setting demonstrates lack of dedication or team spirit. Organizational cultures may reinforce over-functioning through recognition systems that reward those who consistently exceed reasonable expectations.

Understanding workplace resistance as systemic rather than personal helps you respond more strategically while maintaining your professional reputation and effectiveness. Most workplace resistance to appropriate boundaries stems from organizational dysfunction rather than legitimate job requirements, but addressing it requires skill and diplomacy.

The first step in managing workplace resistance involves distinguishing between your essential job responsibilities and additional tasks you've assumed that aren't actually required for your role. This distinction helps you identify areas where you can establish boundaries without compromising your professional obligations.

Many over-managers have gradually expanded their job responsibilities beyond what's officially required, taking on tasks that belong to other departments, solving problems that others should handle, or working hours that far exceed reasonable expectations. Establishing boundaries often involves returning to your actual job description rather than refusing to do required work.

David faced this challenge when he realized he had been functioning as an unofficial human resources coordinator for his team, mediating conflicts, providing career counseling, and handling personnel issues that should have been managed by his supervisor or HR department.

"I had gradually taken on so many responsibilities that weren't actually part of my job that I was working sixty hours a week and constantly dealing with other people's workplace problems," David said. "When I started redirecting these issues to appropriate channels and focusing on my actual responsibilities, some colleagues complained that I wasn't being helpful anymore."

Rather than resuming his unofficial HR role, David consistently redirected personnel issues to proper channels while expressing confidence in his colleagues' ability to handle their own workplace challenges. He also communicated clearly with his supervisor about his decision to focus on his core responsibilities, framing it as improving his effectiveness in his primary role.

The second step involves communicating boundary changes proactively and professionally rather than allowing others to discover them through your unavailability or refusal to help. This proactive communication demonstrates respect for others while clearly establishing new expectations.

This communication might involve meetings with key colleagues or supervisors to discuss how you're restructuring your approach to work, email messages clarifying your availability and response times, or team discussions about redistributing responsibilities that you've been handling beyond your job description.

The key to effective boundary communication at work is framing changes in terms of professional effectiveness and organizational benefit rather than personal needs or preferences. Instead of saying "I need better work-life balance," you might say "I'm focusing my efforts on my core responsibilities to maximize my effectiveness in my primary role."

Jennifer used this approach when she stopped routinely staying late to help colleagues with projects that weren't related to her responsibilities. "Instead of just becoming unavailable, I proactively communicated that I was restructuring my schedule to focus more intensively on my key projects during regular work hours," she said. "I framed it as improving my performance in my primary responsibilities rather than just refusing to help others."

The third step involves developing strategic responses to pressure that acknowledge workplace relationships while maintaining appropriate boundaries. This often involves offering alternative solutions rather than simply declining requests, demonstrating your continued commitment to team success while establishing limits on your personal involvement.

For example, instead of agreeing to take on a project that belongs to another department, you might suggest connecting the requester with the appropriate person or department. Instead of working excessive hours to solve a crisis, you might suggest process improvements that would prevent similar situations. Instead of mediating workplace conflicts, you might recommend involving supervisors or HR professionals.

These alternative responses demonstrate continued engagement and problem-solving while establishing appropriate boundaries around your own responsibilities and time. They show that you're still committed to organizational success but are approaching it in more sustainable and appropriate ways.

The fourth step involves building alliances with colleagues and supervisors who support healthy workplace boundaries and professional sustainability. These alliances provide support for your boundary-setting efforts while demonstrating that your approach aligns with broader organizational health and effectiveness.

Many organizations are beginning to recognize the costs of employee burnout and over-functioning, and you may find more support for reasonable boundaries than expected. Identifying leaders, colleagues, or organizational policies that support work-life balance and sustainable work practices can provide backing for your boundary-setting efforts.

Margaret found this support when she stopped routinely sacrificing her continuing education time to cover for colleagues who were unprepared for their responsibilities. "I discovered that our department head actually supported my decision to protect time for professional development because it improved my effectiveness and prevented burnout," she said. "Having leadership support made it much easier to maintain boundaries with colleagues who wanted me to continue covering for their poor planning."

Managing workplace resistance also requires patience with the adjustment period that often follows boundary changes in professional environments. Colleagues and systems that have become dependent on your over-functioning need time to develop alternative solutions and adjust to new expectations.

During this adjustment period, there may be temporary decreases in team efficiency, increased pressure to resume previous patterns, or criticism of your "reduced helpfulness." However, most workplace systems adapt more quickly than expected when boundaries are maintained consistently and alternative solutions are supported.

The long-term benefits of maintaining appropriate workplace boundaries often include improved job satisfaction, better work-life integration, increased respect from colleagues, and enhanced effectiveness in your primary responsibilities. Organizations typically benefit from employees who work sustainably rather than those who burn out from over-functioning.

Staying Strong When Others Try to Pull You Back

One of the most challenging aspects of maintaining your transformation involves staying committed to healthy boundaries and patterns when people you care about actively try to pull you back into previous roles and dynamics. This pull-back pressure often intensifies just when you think you've successfully established new patterns, and it can be particularly difficult to resist because it often comes wrapped in expressions of need, love, or concern.

Pull-back attempts typically occur when others realize that your changes are permanent rather than temporary, when they encounter situations that would have previously triggered your rescue response, or when they feel stressed or overwhelmed and want to return to familiar patterns of support and management.

These attempts often take sophisticated forms that are designed to trigger your deepest fears and guilt. Others might create or exaggerate crises that seem to require your immediate intervention. They might appeal to your love and commitment to the relationship by suggesting that your boundaries demonstrate lack of caring. They might use comparison pressure by pointing to how other people in similar relationships handle support and assistance.

Understanding pull-back pressure as a normal part of the change process rather than evidence that your boundaries are harmful helps you respond with compassion while maintaining your limits. Most pull-back attempts reflect others' anxiety about change and their natural desire to return to familiar patterns rather than genuine emergencies requiring your intervention.

Staying strong during pull-back pressure requires developing what I call "boundary resilience"—the ability to maintain your limits even when others escalate their pressure tactics or present compelling reasons why you should abandon your boundaries in specific situations.

This resilience often involves recognizing that others' discomfort with your boundaries doesn't create obligations for you to change them. People naturally resist disruption to familiar patterns, and their negative reactions often reflect their adjustment challenges rather than problems with your approach.

Boundary resilience also requires distinguishing between genuine emergencies that warrant temporary flexibility and manufactured crises designed to override your limits. True emergencies involving safety, health, or genuine crises are relatively rare, and most situations presented as requiring immediate boundary abandonment are actually manageable challenges that others can handle with appropriate support.

Karen developed this discernment when her adult daughter began presenting increasingly dramatic "emergencies" that required Karen's immediate assistance. "I learned to ask myself whether the situation involved genuine danger or just inconvenience and stress," Karen said. "Most of the 'emergencies' were actually poor planning or normal life challenges that felt overwhelming because my daughter hadn't developed good problem-solving skills."

Instead of immediately responding to the urgency and drama, Karen learned to offer emotional support while maintaining expectations for her daughter's independent problem-solving. She would say things like: "This sounds really stressful, and I have confidence in your ability to handle it. Let me know how it goes, and we can talk about what you learned from the experience."

Staying strong also requires what I call "values anchoring"—regularly reconnecting with the reasons you established boundaries in the first place and the long-term outcomes you're working toward. When faced with intense pressure to abandon your limits, it's easy to lose sight of why the changes are important and focus only on the immediate discomfort they're creating.

Values anchoring might involve regularly reviewing your reasons for establishing boundaries, reminding yourself of the positive changes you've already seen, seeking support from others who understand and encourage your transformation, or simply taking time to reconnect with your own sense of purpose and direction.

This anchoring process helps you maintain perspective during difficult moments and remember that temporary discomfort often precedes significant positive change. It also helps you distinguish between pressure that's designed to serve others' comfort and guidance that genuinely serves everyone's long-term wellbeing.

Jennifer used values anchoring when her family pressured her to resume managing her elderly father's finances after he made some poor investment decisions. "Everyone was convinced that I needed to take over his financial management to protect him from further mistakes," she said. "But I remembered that my goal was to support his independence and dignity as long as safely possible, not to prevent him from ever making poor decisions."

Instead of taking over his finances, Jennifer helped her father connect with a financial advisor and supported him in developing better decision-making processes while maintaining his autonomy. While this approach involved some risk and temporary family tension, it ultimately supported her father's sense of competence and independence.

Staying strong during pull-back pressure also requires building and maintaining support systems that encourage your transformation rather than undermining it. This might involve working with therapists or coaches who understand boundary-setting processes, connecting with others who are navigating similar transformations, or simply ensuring that you have relationships that aren't based on your over-functioning.

These support systems provide perspective during challenging moments and help you remember that your changes are healthy and necessary rather than selfish or harmful. They also offer practical guidance for navigating specific situations and maintaining your boundaries in the face of intense pressure.

The most important aspect of staying strong involves recognizing that others' adjustment to your boundaries often takes longer than you expect but usually results in healthier, more respectful relationships. Most people who initially resist boundary changes eventually adapt and often come to appreciate the increased respect and autonomy that healthier patterns provide.

This adaptation process requires patience and consistency from you, but it typically leads to relationships that are more satisfying and sustainable for everyone involved. When you maintain your boundaries with love and firmness, you often discover that others are more capable and resilient than your over-management allowed them to demonstrate.

The Resistance Navigation System

Successfully navigating resistance and pushback requires a systematic approach that helps you respond consistently and effectively to various forms of pressure while maintaining your emotional equilibrium and commitment to healthy boundaries. The Resistance Navigation System provides a framework for anticipating, understanding, and responding to resistance in ways that support your transformation while maintaining compassion for others' adjustment challenges.

The system begins with what I call "resistance prediction"—anticipating the forms of pushback you're likely to encounter based on your specific relationships and the patterns you're changing. This prediction helps you prepare emotionally and practically for resistance rather than being surprised or overwhelmed by negative reactions.

Resistance prediction involves examining your current over-management patterns and considering how others might react when those patterns change. If you typically manage someone's schedule, you can predict they might express anxiety or resentment when you stop providing that service. If you consistently solve family conflicts, you can anticipate pushback when you refuse to mediate disputes.

This prediction process also involves identifying your own vulnerabilities to different types of pressure. Understanding which guilt trips, manipulation tactics, or emotional appeals are most likely to trigger your rescue impulses helps you prepare responses and maintain your boundaries when pressure intensifies.

The second component involves "pressure categorization"—distinguishing between different types of resistance and responding appropriately to each category. Not all pushback requires the same response, and understanding the motivations behind different forms of pressure helps you choose effective responses.

Some resistance reflects genuine adjustment challenges as others learn to handle responsibilities they haven't managed independently. This type of resistance often responds well to encouragement, support, and patience while maintaining clear expectations for increased independence.

Other resistance reflects attempts to manipulate you into resuming previous patterns through guilt, obligation, or emotional pressure. This type of resistance requires firmer boundaries and less accommodation, as giving in often reinforces manipulative patterns.

Still other resistance may reflect legitimate concerns about your changes or genuine requests for modified boundaries that address real needs. This type of resistance deserves careful consideration and potentially some flexibility while maintaining your core limits.

The third component involves "response scripting"—developing specific language and approaches for common resistance scenarios. Having prepared responses helps you maintain consistency and avoid getting drawn into arguments or defensive explanations that often undermine boundary-setting efforts.

These scripts might include phrases for acknowledging others' feelings while maintaining boundaries, language for redirecting responsibility back to appropriate people, responses for declining requests without extensive justification, and approaches for expressing confidence in others' capabilities.

Patricia developed response scripts for her mother's resistance to decreased involvement in medical management. "When my mother would express anxiety about handling doctor's appointments independently, I would say something like: 'I understand this feels overwhelming, and I have confidence in your ability to manage your health care. I'm happy to help you organize systems that support your independence, but I won't be scheduling appointments or attending visits unless there's a genuine emergency,'" Patricia said.

The fourth component involves "consistency maintenance"—implementing your boundaries uniformly regardless of the specific circumstances or emotional pressure surrounding each situation. Consistency is crucial because inconsistent boundary enforcement often leads to increased testing and pressure from others.

This consistency requires treating similar situations similarly rather than making exceptions based on others' emotional states or the apparent urgency of specific requests. It also means maintaining your boundaries even when doing so creates temporary inconvenience or discomfort for others.

The fifth component involves "adjustment support"—providing appropriate encouragement and resources to help others adapt to new patterns without resuming your previous over-functioning role. This support acknowledges that change is challenging while maintaining expectations for others' growth and adaptation.

Adjustment support might involve helping others develop systems and skills for handling increased responsibilities, connecting them with appropriate resources and assistance, or simply expressing confidence in their ability to adapt to new expectations.

The sixth component involves "progress tracking"—regularly assessing how resistance patterns are changing over time and adjusting your approach based on what you learn. Most resistance decreases significantly over time as others adapt to new patterns, but tracking this progress helps you maintain perspective during challenging periods.

This tracking also helps you identify which approaches are most effective for specific relationships and situations, allowing you to refine your responses and maintain your boundaries more easily over time.

The Resistance Navigation System recognizes that navigating pushback is one of the most challenging aspects of transformation but also one of the most important for creating lasting change. When you can maintain your boundaries consistently in the face of resistance, you demonstrate that your changes are permanent rather than temporary, which encourages others to adapt rather than continuing to test your limits.

The Manipulation Defense Protocol

Protecting yourself from manipulation while maintaining compassionate relationships requires developing systematic approaches for recognizing and responding to manipulative tactics without becoming defensive, aggressive, or emotionally reactive. The Manipulation Defense Protocol provides a framework for maintaining your boundaries and autonomy while preserving respect and care in your relationships.

The protocol begins with "manipulation recognition"—developing the ability to identify manipulative tactics quickly and accurately so you can respond consciously rather than react automatically. Manipulation often works by bypassing rational thought and triggering emotional responses that lead to compliance, so early recognition is crucial for effective defense.

Common manipulation tactics include emotional blackmail (threatening negative emotional consequences if you don't comply), guilt induction (making you feel responsible for others' problems or feelings), false urgency (creating artificial time pressure to prevent careful consideration), false choices (presenting limited options that exclude reasonable alternatives), and comparison pressure (suggesting that reasonable people would act differently than you're choosing to act).

Learning to recognize these tactics requires developing awareness of your own emotional triggers and the specific approaches that are most likely to override your judgment. Different people are vulnerable to different types of manipulation, and understanding your particular vulnerabilities helps you maintain stronger defenses.

The second component involves "emotional regulation"—maintaining your emotional equilibrium when faced with manipulative pressure so you can respond from a place of clarity rather than reactivity. This regulation often involves breathing techniques, grounding practices, or simply pausing before responding to intense emotional pressure.

Emotional regulation also involves recognizing that others' emotional states, however intense, don't create emergencies that require you to abandon your boundaries or judgment. Learning to witness others' distress without immediately taking action to relieve it is crucial for resisting manipulation that relies on triggering your rescue impulses.

Sarah used emotional regulation techniques when her teenage daughter would have dramatic emotional outbursts designed to pressure Sarah into changing decisions about privileges or consequences. "I learned to breathe deeply and remind myself that my daughter's emotional intensity didn't mean I needed to change my boundaries," Sarah said. "When I stayed calm and maintained my limits, her emotional storms usually passed much more quickly."

The third component involves "boundary reassertion"—calmly and consistently restating your limits without engaging in arguments or extensive justifications that often provide opportunities for further manipulation. This reassertion demonstrates that your boundaries are non-negotiable regardless of the emotional pressure applied.

Boundary reassertion often involves using what therapists call "broken record technique"—repeating your position calmly without getting drawn into debates about whether your boundaries are reasonable or fair. This technique prevents manipulation tactics that rely on engaging you in arguments where pressure and emotion can override rational judgment.

The fourth component involves "responsibility redirection"—consistently returning responsibility for problems and emotions to their appropriate owners rather than accepting responsibility that belongs to others. This redirection involves statements that acknowledge others' experiences while maintaining clear boundaries about whose responsibility it is to address them.

This might sound like: "I can see that you're upset about this situation, and it's your responsibility to decide how you want to handle it," or "I understand this is frustrating for you, and I'm confident you can find a solution that works for your needs."

These statements acknowledge others' feelings without accepting responsibility for managing those feelings or solving the problems that created them. They maintain compassion while preserving appropriate boundaries around responsibility and autonomy.

The fifth component involves "consequence tolerance"—accepting that maintaining your boundaries may result in others being disappointed, angry, or temporarily inconvenienced without changing your limits to relieve their discomfort. This tolerance is crucial because manipulation often relies on your discomfort with others' negative reactions.

Developing consequence tolerance involves recognizing that others' emotional reactions to your boundaries are their responsibility to manage, not yours to prevent or fix. It also involves understanding that temporary discomfort often precedes positive change, and that maintaining boundaries consistently usually leads to better relationships over time.

David learned consequence tolerance when his adult son used emotional manipulation to pressure him for financial assistance. "I had to accept that my son would be angry and disappointed when I refused to bail him out of financial difficulties he had created," David said. "Learning to tolerate his negative reactions without changing my boundaries was difficult, but it ultimately helped him develop better financial management skills."

The sixth component involves "support system activation"—reaching out to trusted friends, family members, or professionals who can provide perspective and encouragement when you're facing intense manipulative pressure. This support helps you maintain clarity about your boundaries and resist manipulation tactics that might otherwise be effective.

Support system activation is particularly important because manipulation often involves isolation tactics designed to make you feel alone in your perspective or cut off from others who might validate your boundaries. Having reliable sources of support and perspective helps counter these isolation attempts.

The Manipulation Defense Protocol recognizes that protecting yourself from manipulation doesn't require becoming defensive, aggressive, or uncaring. Instead, it involves developing skills for maintaining your autonomy and boundaries while preserving respect and compassion in your relationships.

When you can resist manipulation effectively while maintaining care for others, you often discover that relationships improve rather than deteriorate. People who use manipulative tactics often respect clear boundaries more than they appreciate compliance, and your refusal to be manipulated can lead to more honest and respectful communication.

The Consistency Maintenance Method

Maintaining your boundaries and new relationship patterns consistently over time requires systematic approaches that help you stay committed to healthy changes even when pressure mounts, when convenient exceptions arise, or when you experience doubt about your transformation. The Consistency Maintenance Method provides a framework for sustaining your progress and preventing gradual erosion of the boundaries you've worked hard to establish.

Consistency is crucial for boundary maintenance because inconsistent enforcement often leads to increased testing and pressure from others. When people learn that sufficient pressure, emotional intensity, or special circumstances can override your limits, they often increase their efforts to find exceptions to your boundaries rather than adapting to new patterns.

The method begins with "boundary documentation"—creating clear, written descriptions of your boundaries and the reasons behind them so you can refer to them during moments of doubt or pressure. This documentation serves as an anchor during challenging times when others' emotional pressure or your own guilt might make you question whether your boundaries are appropriate.

This documentation might include descriptions of specific boundaries you've established, examples of situations where these boundaries apply, reminders of why these changes are important for your wellbeing and relationships, and affirmations of others' capabilities that support your confidence in stepping back from over-management.

Jennifer created boundary documentation when she was establishing limits around her involvement in her adult children's financial decisions. "I wrote down my specific boundaries about financial assistance, my reasons for establishing these limits, and reminders of my children's capabilities and resources," she said. "When they pressured me to make exceptions, I could refer to my documentation to remember why these boundaries were important."

The second component involves "exception evaluation"—developing criteria for assessing requests for boundary flexibility to distinguish between genuine emergencies that warrant temporary accommodation and manipulation attempts disguised as special circumstances.

This evaluation involves asking specific questions about requests for exceptions: Is this situation genuinely different from others where I've maintained my boundary? Does this involve actual emergency circumstances beyond the person's control? Will making an exception support their growth and independence, or will it reinforce dependency patterns? Am I being asked to make an exception because of manipulation pressure or because of legitimate changed circumstances?

These questions help you respond thoughtfully to requests for flexibility rather than automatically saying yes or no to exception requests. They also help you distinguish between situations that genuinely warrant different responses and those that represent attempts to test or erode your boundaries.

The third component involves "accountability partnerships"—establishing relationships with trusted friends, family members, or professionals who understand your boundary-setting goals and can provide support and perspective when you're facing pressure to abandon your limits.

These accountability partnerships involve regular check-ins about how your boundaries are working, discussions about challenges you're facing, and support for maintaining consistency even when doing so is difficult. Having external accountability helps you maintain perspective during challenging periods and resist pressure that might otherwise overwhelm your resolve.

Patricia developed an accountability partnership with her sister who was also working on establishing healthier boundaries in her own family. "We would check in weekly about how our boundary-setting was going and support each other when we were facing pressure to revert to old patterns," Patricia said. "Having someone who understood what I was trying to accomplish made it much easier to stay consistent during difficult periods."

The fourth component involves "progress celebration"—regularly acknowledging the positive changes that result from maintaining your boundaries, even when those changes are subtle or gradual. This celebration helps you maintain motivation during challenging periods and remember why your transformation efforts are worthwhile.

Progress celebration might involve noting improvements in your relationships, increased respect from others, better work-life balance, reduced stress and resentment, or simply greater peace of mind about your choices and priorities. Recognizing these benefits helps you maintain commitment to healthy patterns even when maintaining them requires effort and discipline.

The fifth component involves "adjustment protocols"—systematic approaches for modifying your boundaries when you learn that adjustments are needed, while avoiding the complete abandonment of limits that often occurs when people become frustrated with boundary maintenance.

These protocols involve distinguishing between boundaries that need fine-tuning and boundaries that should be maintained regardless of pressure. They also involve making conscious adjustments based on learning and growth rather than reactive changes based on pressure or guilt.

The sixth component involves "relapse recovery"—having plans for getting back on track when you inevitably have moments of reverting to old patterns or abandoning boundaries under pressure. This recovery approach treats setbacks as normal parts of the change process rather than evidence of failure.

Relapse recovery involves acknowledging when you've reverted to old patterns without self-judgment, recommitting to your boundaries and goals, learning from what triggered the relapse, and implementing strategies for handling similar situations more effectively in the future.

The Consistency Maintenance Method recognizes that sustaining transformation requires ongoing attention and effort, but it becomes easier over time as new patterns become established and others adapt to your boundaries. When you maintain consistency despite pressure and challenges, you demonstrate that your changes are permanent, which encourages others to develop healthier ways of relating rather than continuing to test your limits.

Building Long-Term Resilience

The ultimate goal of navigating resistance and pushback is not just to survive the challenging period of transformation, but to build long-term resilience that allows you to maintain healthy boundaries and relationships throughout your life. This resilience involves developing internal resources and external support systems that sustain your commitment to healthy patterns regardless of the pressures and challenges you encounter.

Building resilience begins with developing what I call "identity integration"—incorporating your new understanding of healthy relationships and appropriate boundaries into your core sense of self rather than treating them as temporary behavior changes. This integration helps you maintain your transformation even when external pressures are intense.

Identity integration involves seeing yourself as someone who deserves respect, who has valuable boundaries, and who contributes to others' lives through empowerment rather than management. It means understanding that your worth isn't dependent on being needed or managing others' problems, and that you can love others deeply while maintaining appropriate limits.

This identity integration often requires ongoing work to challenge internalized messages about your value being tied to your usefulness to others. It involves developing new sources of meaning and self-worth that aren't dependent on others' dependency or appreciation for your over-functioning.

Margaret experienced this identity integration when she realized that her sense of self-worth had been entirely tied to being needed and helpful to others. "I had to develop a new understanding of my value that was based on who I was as a person rather than what I could do for others," she said. "This shift was fundamental to maintaining my boundaries because it meant I no longer needed others to need me in order to feel valuable."

Building resilience also involves developing what psychologists call "emotional regulation skills"—the ability to manage your own anxiety, guilt, and discomfort without taking action to control others' experiences or relieve their distress. These skills are crucial for maintaining boundaries when others are struggling or expressing negative emotions about your limits.

Emotional regulation skills include mindfulness practices that help you stay present with your own experience rather than getting caught up in others' emotional states, breathing techniques that help you maintain calm during intense situations, and self-soothing strategies that help you manage anxiety without reverting to controlling behaviors.

These skills also include developing tolerance for uncertainty about others' choices and outcomes. Much of over-management stems from anxiety about what might happen if you don't intervene, and building resilience requires learning to live with uncertainty while trusting others' capabilities.

Long-term resilience also requires building and maintaining support systems that encourage healthy boundaries and authentic relationships. This involves cultivating friendships that aren't based on your helpfulness, professional relationships that respect your limits, and family connections that support rather than undermine your growth.

These support systems provide perspective during challenging periods, encouragement when you're facing pressure to abandon your boundaries, and modeling of what healthy relationships can look like. They also offer practical advice and emotional support for navigating specific challenges while maintaining your commitment to transformation.

The final aspect of building resilience involves developing what I call "purpose clarity"—understanding how your boundary-setting and transformation serve not just your own wellbeing but also contribute to the wellbeing of others and the creation of healthier relationship patterns in your community and family.

This purpose clarity helps you maintain commitment to your transformation even when it's difficult because you understand that your changes benefit not just you but everyone involved. When you model healthy boundaries and empowering relationships, you teach others what's possible and create ripple effects that extend far beyond your immediate circle.

Purpose clarity also involves understanding that resistance and pushback are temporary challenges that often precede significant positive change. When you maintain your boundaries consistently despite pressure, you often discover that relationships become stronger and more respectful, that others develop greater capability and confidence, and that everyone involved benefits from healthier patterns.

Building long-term resilience ultimately means developing the internal resources and external supports that allow you to love others without losing yourself, to care without controlling, and to support without sacrificing your own wellbeing. This resilience provides the foundation for a life where your relationships enhance rather than drain your energy, where your care for others empowers rather than enables them, and where your love is expressed through trust and respect rather than management and control.

When you've built this resilience, you discover that navigating resistance becomes easier because you're grounded in your own sense of worth and purpose. You can weather others' temporary discomfort with your boundaries because you're confident that maintaining them serves everyone's long-term interests. You can love others deeply while trusting them completely to handle their own lives, and you can offer support without taking over because you understand that true love empowers rather than diminishes those we care about most.

CHAPTER 14

The Daily Practice of Freedom

The alarm clock rang at 5:30 AM, but for the first time in months, Patricia didn't immediately reach for her phone to check for overnight crisis messages from family members. Instead, she lay in bed for a few moments, taking three deep breaths and setting an intention for the day: "Today I will respond from choice rather than obligation, from my own center rather than others' urgency."

This simple morning ritual had become the foundation of what Patricia called her "freedom practice"—a collection of daily habits and check-ins that helped her maintain the healthy boundaries and empowering relationships she'd worked so hard to create. Over the past year, Patricia had transformed from someone who managed every crisis and solved every problem for her extended family into someone who offered support while trusting others to handle their own lives.

But Patricia had learned that transformation isn't a one-time event—it's a daily practice that requires ongoing attention, intention, and recommitment. Without consistent daily practices that reinforced her new way of being, she found herself gradually slipping back into old patterns of over-functioning and people-pleasing, especially during stressful periods or family crises.

The morning intention ritual was just the beginning of Patricia's daily freedom practice. Throughout the day, she had developed small but powerful habits that helped her stay connected to her own values and boundaries while maintaining loving relationships with others. These practices had become as essential to her wellbeing as brushing her teeth or eating healthy meals—simple daily actions that prevented problems and maintained the positive changes she'd created.

Patricia's experience illustrates a crucial truth about personal transformation: lasting change requires translating insights and breakthroughs into consistent daily practices that support and reinforce new ways of being. The most profound realizations about boundaries, empowerment, and healthy relationships mean little if they're not integrated into the routine patterns of daily life through intentional practices and habits.

The Daily Practice of Freedom represents the practical translation of everything you've learned about breaking free from over-management patterns into sustainable daily rhythms that support your ongoing growth and transformation. These practices serve as both protection against sliding back into old patterns and cultivation of the inner resources that allow you to love others without losing yourself.

Morning Routines That Reinforce Your New Boundaries

How you begin each day sets the tone for everything that follows. For recovering over-managers, morning routines that reinforce healthy boundaries and personal autonomy can be the difference between staying centered in your own values and getting swept away by others' urgency and needs before you've even had breakfast.

Traditional morning routines for over-managers often involve immediately checking messages to see what crises have emerged overnight, reviewing others' schedules and needs, and beginning the day in reactive mode—responding to whatever seems most urgent rather than starting from a place of intention and choice. This reactive approach often means that your entire day becomes organized around others' priorities rather than your own values and goals.

Creating morning routines that reinforce your freedom requires consciously choosing to begin each day from your own center rather than from others' needs. This doesn't mean becoming selfish or ignoring genuine emergencies, but it does mean starting each day with practices that connect you to your own sense of purpose, values, and autonomy before engaging with others' requests and expectations.

The most effective freedom-reinforcing morning routines typically include several key elements that work together to create a foundation of inner strength and clarity. These elements can be adapted to fit your schedule, preferences, and lifestyle, but they share the common goal of helping you start each day as the author of your own experience rather than a character in others' dramas.

The first element involves what I call "grounding practices"—activities that help you connect with your own physical presence, emotional state, and sense of inner calm before engaging with external demands. These practices might include meditation, deep breathing exercises, gentle stretching or movement, or simply sitting quietly with a cup of coffee while paying attention to your own experience.

The key to grounding practices is that they focus your attention inward rather than outward, helping you establish a sense of your own center before you begin responding to others' needs and requests. Even five or ten minutes of intentional grounding can create a significant difference in how you approach the rest of your day.

Jennifer developed a grounding practice that involved ten minutes of morning meditation followed by journaling about her intentions for the day. "This practice helped me start each day with clarity about my own priorities and values rather than immediately jumping into problem-solving mode for everyone else," she said. "When I skipped this routine, I found myself much more likely to get pulled into others' dramas and lose sight of my own goals."

The second element involves "intention setting"—consciously choosing how you want to show up in your relationships and responsibilities rather than operating on autopilot or simply reacting to whatever situations arise. This intention setting helps you approach your day from a place of choice and purpose rather than obligation and reactivity.

Intention setting might involve reflecting on your values and how you want to embody them throughout the day, considering specific situations you'll encounter and how you want to handle them, or simply choosing a word or phrase that captures how you want to approach your interactions with others.

The power of intention setting lies in its ability to create conscious choice points throughout your day. When you've set clear intentions for how you want to show up, you're more likely to recognize moments when you're being pulled away from those intentions and make conscious choices to realign with your values.

David developed an intention-setting practice that involved reviewing his calendar and considering how he wanted to approach each meeting and interaction. "I would ask myself: 'How do I want to show up in this situation? What kind of energy do I want to bring? How can I be helpful without taking over?'" he said. "This practice helped me stay conscious and intentional throughout the day rather than just automatically falling into old patterns."

The third element involves "boundary affirmation"—reminding yourself of the healthy limits you've established and your commitment to maintaining them despite pressure or convenience. This affirmation helps strengthen your resolve and prepare you to maintain your boundaries when they're tested during the day.

Boundary affirmation might involve reviewing specific boundaries you've established in different relationships, reminding yourself why these boundaries are important for your wellbeing and others' growth, or simply affirming your right to have limits and your commitment to maintaining them with love and firmness.

This affirmation practice is particularly important during periods when you're facing increased pressure to abandon your boundaries or when you're dealing with family crises that trigger your old rescue impulses. Having a regular practice of affirming your boundaries helps you maintain them consistently rather than making exceptions that gradually erode your limits.

Sarah developed a boundary affirmation practice that involved writing three specific boundaries she would maintain that day and the reasons they were important. "This practice helped me stay conscious of my limits throughout the day and gave me language for maintaining them when others pushed back," she said. "When I wrote down my boundaries each morning, I was much less likely to abandon them when faced with guilt trips or pressure."

The fourth element involves "self-care planning"—identifying specific ways you'll nurture your own wellbeing throughout the day rather than waiting until you're depleted or overwhelmed to attend to your own needs. This planning helps ensure that self-care becomes a proactive priority rather than a crisis intervention.

Self-care planning might involve scheduling specific activities that energize you, identifying moments throughout the day when you'll check in with your own emotional state, or simply ensuring that you have adequate time for rest, nutrition, and activities that bring you joy.

The key to effective self-care planning is making it specific and realistic rather than vague or overly ambitious. Small, consistent practices that you can maintain even on busy days are more valuable than elaborate self-care plans that you abandon when life becomes demanding.

Morning routines that reinforce freedom don't need to be lengthy or complicated to be effective. Even fifteen or twenty minutes of intentional morning practices can create a significant foundation for maintaining your transformation throughout the day. The key is consistency and intention rather than duration or complexity.

Daily Check-Ins: Am I Managing or Am I Living?

One of the most powerful tools for maintaining your freedom from over-management patterns involves developing regular check-in practices throughout the day that help you assess whether you're operating from choice and autonomy or slipping back into reactive management mode. These check-ins serve as course corrections that help you realign with your values and intentions when you notice yourself getting pulled off track.

The fundamental question underlying these check-ins—"Am I managing or am I living?"—helps distinguish between two very different ways of moving through the world. Managing mode involves constantly scanning for problems to solve, needs to meet, and crises to prevent. Living mode involves staying connected to your own experience, values, and goals while responding appropriately to genuine needs and opportunities.

This distinction is crucial because managing mode often feels productive and caring, but it actually prevents you from being fully present to your own life and often undermines others' development of independence and capability. Living mode allows you to be genuinely helpful and supportive while maintaining your own autonomy and encouraging others' growth.

Developing effective daily check-ins requires creating simple but powerful questions that help you quickly assess your current state and make conscious choices about how to proceed. These questions should be easy to remember and use throughout the day, even during busy or stressful periods.

The first type of check-in involves what I call "energy assessment"—regularly evaluating whether your energy is flowing primarily toward your own goals and values or being consistently redirected toward others' problems and needs. This assessment helps you notice when you're giving away your energy in ways that don't serve your own growth or others' development.

Energy assessment might involve asking yourself: "Where is my attention focused right now—on my own experience and goals, or on others' problems and needs? Am I feeling energized and engaged, or drained and resentful? Am I making choices based on my own values, or reacting to others' urgency and pressure?"

These questions help you quickly identify when you're slipping into over-management mode and need to refocus on your own priorities and boundaries. They also help you distinguish between appropriate support and excessive involvement in others' lives.

Margaret developed an energy assessment practice that involved checking in with herself every few hours throughout the day. "I would pause and ask myself whether I was feeling energized by my activities or drained by constantly focusing on others' needs," she said. "When I noticed that my energy was consistently flowing toward managing others rather than living my own life, I would take steps to redirect my attention and activities."

The second type of check-in involves "choice awareness"—regularly evaluating whether your actions and responses are coming from conscious choice or automatic reactivity. This awareness helps you maintain agency and intentionality rather than simply responding to whatever seems most urgent or demanding.

Choice awareness might involve asking yourself: "Am I choosing this response, or am I reacting automatically? Am I acting from my own values and priorities, or from others' expectations and pressure? Do I have other options in this situation that I haven't considered?"

These questions help you pause and create space for conscious decision-making rather than simply responding from habitual patterns. They also help you recognize when you're being driven by guilt, obligation, or anxiety rather than making choices that align with your authentic values and goals.

The third type of check-in involves "boundary monitoring"—regularly assessing whether you're maintaining the healthy limits you've established or allowing them to be gradually eroded through small compromises and exceptions. This monitoring helps prevent the gradual boundary decay that often occurs when limits aren't consciously maintained.

Boundary monitoring might involve asking yourself: "Am I maintaining my boundaries in this situation, or am I making exceptions based on pressure or convenience? Are my limits being respected, or am I accepting treatment that violates my standards? Am I communicating my boundaries clearly, or am I hoping others will somehow know what my limits are without clear communication?"

These questions help you stay conscious of your boundaries and take action to maintain them before they become significantly compromised. They also help you distinguish between appropriate flexibility and problematic boundary erosion.

David used boundary monitoring check-ins during family gatherings where he typically felt pressure to resume his old role as family problem-solver and conflict mediator. "I would periodically ask myself whether I was maintaining my boundary about not taking responsibility for others' conflicts, or whether I was getting pulled back into managing family dynamics," he said. "These check-ins helped me catch myself before I got too deeply involved in situations that weren't mine to handle."

The fourth type of check-in involves "presence assessment"—evaluating whether you're fully present to your own experience or constantly anticipating and preparing for others' needs and potential problems. This assessment helps you stay connected to your own life rather than living primarily in service of others' comfort and convenience.

Presence assessment might involve asking yourself: "Am I present to my own experience right now, or am I mentally focused on others' situations? Am I enjoying this moment, or am I thinking about what others might need from me? Am I living my own life, or managing everyone else's?"

These questions help you return to your own experience and remember that your life deserves your full attention and presence. They also help you recognize when you're living in constant anticipation of others' needs rather than being present to your own goals and experiences.

Daily check-ins work best when they become natural, integrated parts of your routine rather than additional tasks you have to remember to complete. This integration might involve linking check-ins to existing habits like meals, transitions between activities, or natural pauses in your day.

Micro-Practices for Staying Centered Throughout the Day

Maintaining your freedom and autonomy throughout busy, demanding days requires developing what I call "micro-practices"—small, simple actions that take only a few moments but help you stay connected to your own center and maintain your boundaries even during stressful or chaotic periods.

These micro-practices serve as what psychologists call "pattern interrupts"—brief interventions that help you pause automatic reactions and make conscious choices about how to respond to various situations. They're particularly valuable for recovering over-managers because they provide tools for staying centered without requiring significant time or creating obvious disruptions to your daily activities.

The most effective micro-practices are those that can be used anywhere, anytime, without special equipment or circumstances. They should be simple enough to remember and implement even when you're feeling stressed, overwhelmed, or pressured by others' urgency and needs.

One of the most fundamental micro-practices involves conscious breathing—using your breath as an anchor to your own experience and a tool for maintaining calm and clarity during challenging moments. This practice can be as simple as taking three deep breaths before responding to a request for help, breathing deeply during difficult conversations, or using breathing patterns to center yourself when you feel pulled into others' drama.

The power of conscious breathing lies in its accessibility and immediacy. Your breath is always available to you, and focusing on it automatically brings your attention to your own present-moment experience rather than others' problems or future concerns. Even thirty seconds of conscious breathing can create significant shifts in your emotional state and clarity.

Jennifer developed a breathing micro-practice that she used whenever she felt the urge to immediately jump into problem-solving mode when others shared challenges with her. "I would take three deep breaths before responding, which gave me time to choose whether to offer solutions or simply listen supportively," she said. "This simple practice helped me stay conscious about my role in others' problems rather than automatically taking over."

Another powerful micro-practice involves what I call "grounding touches"—brief physical actions that help you reconnect with your own body and presence. These might include feeling your feet on the floor during conversations, placing your hand on your heart when you're feeling stressed, or gently pressing your fingers together to create a sense of physical connection to yourself.

Grounding touches work by engaging your nervous system's capacity for self-regulation and helping you maintain awareness of your own physical presence rather than becoming completely absorbed in others' emotional states or problems. They're particularly helpful during emotionally intense conversations or situations where you feel pressured to take on responsibilities that don't belong to you.

A third category of micro-practices involves "perspective reminders"—brief mental phrases or questions that help you maintain a realistic perspective about your role and responsibilities in various situations. These reminders help counter the tendency to automatically assume responsibility for others' problems or to react to temporary difficulties as if they were permanent crises.

Perspective reminders might include phrases like "This is not my emergency," "They are capable of handling this," "I can care without carrying," or "My job is to support, not to solve." These phrases serve as quick reality checks that help you maintain appropriate boundaries about responsibility and autonomy.

Sarah developed perspective reminders that she used when her teenage daughter would present normal adolescent challenges as if they were catastrophic crises requiring immediate parental intervention. "I would remind myself that 'adolescent drama is normal and temporary' and 'my daughter is learning to handle life's ups and downs,'" Sarah said. "These reminders helped me stay calm and supportive without jumping into rescue mode for typical teenage experiences."

Another valuable micro-practice involves "choice recognition"—briefly pausing to consciously acknowledge that you have options in how to respond to various situations rather than assuming you must react in predetermined ways. This recognition helps maintain your sense of agency and autonomy even in challenging circumstances.

Choice recognition might involve asking yourself: "What are my options here?" "How do I want to respond to this situation?" "What would serve everyone's highest good?" or simply reminding yourself "I have choices" before deciding how to proceed.

This practice is particularly powerful because it interrupts automatic response patterns and creates space for conscious decision-making. Even acknowledging that you have choices often reveals options you didn't initially recognize and helps you respond from a place of empowerment rather than obligation.

"Values anchoring" represents another important micro-practice—briefly connecting with your core values and intentions before responding to requests, pressure, or challenging situations. This anchoring helps ensure that your responses align with what matters most to you rather than simply reacting to others' urgency or emotional intensity.

Values anchoring might involve asking yourself: "What response would align with my values?" "How do I want to show up in this situation?" "What kind of person do I want to be right now?" These questions help you choose responses that reflect your authentic self rather than simply meeting others' expectations or reducing their discomfort.

The final category of micro-practices involves "appreciation moments"—brief instances of acknowledging something you're grateful for or proud of about your own growth and transformation. These moments help maintain motivation for continued growth and provide positive reinforcement for the changes you've made.

Appreciation moments might involve acknowledging times when you successfully maintained a boundary, recognizing improvements in your relationships, or simply appreciating your own courage in choosing growth over comfort. These moments help maintain perspective about your progress and encourage continued commitment to healthy patterns.

Micro-practices work best when they become automatic responses to specific triggers or situations rather than additional items on your daily to-do list. This automation might involve linking breathing practices to your phone ringing, using grounding touches when you sit down for meetings, or practicing values anchoring when you feel pressured to make immediate decisions.

The goal is to develop a toolkit of simple practices that help you stay connected to your own center and maintain your autonomy throughout even the most demanding days. When these practices become habitual, they create a foundation of inner strength and clarity that supports all aspects of your transformation.

Evening Reflection Practices for Continuous Growth

Evening reflection represents a crucial component of the daily freedom practice because it provides dedicated time for processing your experiences, learning from challenges, celebrating successes, and preparing for continued growth. These reflection practices help consolidate the insights and learning from each day while setting intentions for ongoing transformation.

For recovering over-managers, evening reflection serves several important functions. It provides an opportunity to assess how well you maintained your boundaries and lived from your own values throughout the day. It creates space for processing any guilt, anxiety, or doubt that may have arisen from choosing healthier patterns. It allows you to acknowledge progress and celebrate growth, even when that growth involves difficult choices or uncomfortable situations.

Evening reflection also provides an opportunity to learn from situations where you reverted to old patterns or struggled to maintain your boundaries. Rather than viewing these instances as failures, reflection practices help you understand what triggered old responses and develop strategies for handling similar situations more effectively in the future.

The most effective evening reflection practices typically include several elements that work together to support processing, learning, and growth. These elements can be adapted to fit your preferences and schedule, but they share the common goal of helping you integrate the day's experiences and maintain momentum toward continued transformation.

The first element involves "daily review"—systematically examining key interactions and decisions from the day to assess how well they aligned with your values and goals. This review isn't about judging yourself harshly for imperfect responses, but about honestly assessing your choices and identifying opportunities for growth and learning.

Daily review might involve reflecting on specific situations where you maintained boundaries successfully, instances where you felt pressured to abandon your limits, moments when you chose to support rather than manage others, or times when you struggled to stay centered in your own experience.

The key to effective daily review is approaching it with curiosity and compassion rather than criticism and judgment. The goal is learning and growth, not perfect performance, and maintaining a supportive internal dialogue helps sustain motivation for continued development.

Patricia developed a daily review practice that involved asking herself three questions each evening: "Where did I successfully maintain my boundaries today? Where did I feel challenged to return to old patterns? What did I learn about myself and my relationships?" She found that this systematic review helped her recognize patterns and make conscious adjustments to her approach.

The second element involves "emotional processing"—creating space to acknowledge and work through any difficult emotions that arose during the day as a result of maintaining boundaries or choosing healthier relationship patterns. This processing helps prevent the accumulation of unresolved feelings that can undermine your commitment to transformation.

Emotional processing might involve journaling about challenging interactions, talking through difficult situations with trusted friends or therapists, or simply sitting quietly with any sadness, guilt, or anxiety that arose from choosing growth over comfort.

This processing is particularly important because choosing healthier patterns often involves disappointing others or tolerating their negative reactions to your boundaries. Without adequate emotional processing, the discomfort of these experiences can gradually erode your commitment to transformation.

Margaret found that emotional processing was crucial during the period when she was establishing boundaries with her adult children around their financial independence. "I needed time each evening to process the guilt and worry I felt about not immediately solving their financial problems," she said. "When I gave myself space to feel these emotions without acting on them, I could maintain my boundaries while still caring deeply about my children's wellbeing."

The third element involves "success acknowledgment"—consciously recognizing and celebrating instances where you successfully implemented healthier patterns, maintained boundaries, or chose empowering responses rather than managing reactions. This acknowledgment helps build confidence and motivation for continued growth.

Success acknowledgment might involve noting specific moments when you resisted the urge to take over others' problems, times when you maintained boundaries despite pressure, instances when you chose to trust others' capabilities rather than managing their challenges, or simply moments when you felt aligned with your values and authentic self.

The key to effective success acknowledgment is recognizing that success often involves choosing more difficult paths in the short term that serve everyone's long-term growth and wellbeing. Celebrating these choices helps maintain motivation during challenging periods.

David developed a success acknowledgment practice that involved writing down three specific instances each day where he had chosen healthier responses rather than reverting to old management patterns. "This practice helped me recognize how much progress I was making, even on days when maintaining boundaries felt difficult," he said. "Seeing my successes in writing helped me stay motivated during challenging periods."

The fourth element involves "learning integration"—identifying specific insights or lessons from the day's experiences and considering how to apply them to future situations. This integration helps transform daily experiences into wisdom that supports continued growth and development.

Learning integration might involve recognizing patterns in your responses to certain types of situations, identifying triggers that make it difficult to maintain boundaries, understanding what types of support help you stay centered, or discovering new strategies for handling challenging relationship dynamics.

This integration process helps prevent you from repeatedly encountering the same challenges without learning from them. It also helps you develop increasingly sophisticated skills for navigating complex relationship situations while maintaining your autonomy and supporting others' growth.

The fifth element involves "intention setting"—using insights from the day's experiences to refine your intentions and goals for continued growth. This intention setting helps maintain forward momentum and ensures that your transformation continues to evolve and deepen over time.

Intention setting might involve identifying specific areas where you want to continue growing, recognizing relationship patterns you want to change, or simply clarifying how you want to show up in challenging situations you're likely to encounter.

This forward-looking aspect of evening reflection helps prevent stagnation and ensures that you continue to evolve and grow rather than simply maintaining current levels of functioning.

Jennifer used intention setting to prepare for particularly challenging situations she knew she would face. "When I knew I would be seeing family members who typically pressured me to resume old management roles, I would set specific intentions for how I wanted to handle those interactions," she said. "This preparation helped me stay centered and maintain my boundaries even in difficult situations."

Evening reflection practices work best when they become consistent routines rather than occasional activities you engage in only when you're struggling. This consistency helps create ongoing support for your transformation and ensures that you continue to learn and grow from your daily experiences.

Building Habits That Support Your Freedom Formula

Creating lasting transformation requires more than insights and good intentions—it requires building daily habits and routines that consistently support your commitment to freedom, autonomy, and healthy relationships. These habits serve as the infrastructure that sustains your transformation through challenging periods and helps your new ways of being become automatic rather than requiring constant conscious effort.

Building effective habits that support your freedom formula involves understanding how habits work and designing them in ways that align with your transformation goals. Habits are powerful because they create automatic responses that don't require willpower or decision-making in the moment, which is particularly valuable when you're facing pressure to revert to old patterns.

The most effective freedom-supporting habits typically have several characteristics. They're specific and concrete rather than vague or abstract. They're small enough to implement consistently even during busy or stressful periods. They're linked to existing routines or natural transition points in your day. They provide immediate benefits that reinforce continued practice.

One category of freedom-supporting habits involves "boundary maintenance rituals"—regular practices that help you maintain awareness of your limits and commitment to enforcing them. These rituals might include weekly reviews of your boundaries and how well you're maintaining them, monthly assessments of your relationships and whether they're operating from healthy dynamics, or seasonal evaluations of your overall life direction and priorities.

These maintenance rituals help prevent the gradual erosion of boundaries that often occurs when limits aren't consciously maintained over time. They also provide regular opportunities to adjust your boundaries based on changing circumstances and continued growth.

Sarah developed a weekly boundary maintenance ritual that involved reviewing her calendar for the upcoming week and identifying potential situations where her boundaries might be tested. "I would look ahead and think about family events, work meetings, or social situations where I typically felt pressure to take on responsibilities that didn't belong to me," she said. "This preparation helped me maintain my boundaries even in challenging situations."

Another category involves "self-advocacy practices"—regular habits that help you speak up for your own needs, preferences, and limits rather than automatically accommodating others' requests or expectations. These practices might include daily affirmations of your right to have boundaries, weekly practices of expressing your preferences in low-stakes situations, or monthly assessments of areas where you need to advocate more effectively for yourself.

Self-advocacy practices are particularly important for recovering over-managers because they help counter the conditioning that taught you to prioritize others' needs over your own. Regular practice in small situations builds the skills and confidence needed for more significant advocacy in challenging circumstances.

"Energy protection habits" represent another important category—consistent practices that help you maintain your emotional and physical energy rather than constantly giving it away to others' problems and needs. These habits might include daily practices that help you reconnect with your own experience, weekly activities that restore your energy and enthusiasm, or monthly retreats or breaks that provide deeper renewal.

These energy protection habits help prevent the depletion and burnout that often result from chronic over-functioning. They also help you maintain the inner resources needed to support others in healthy ways rather than from a place of resentment or obligation.

Margaret developed energy protection habits that included daily meditation, weekly time in nature, and monthly activities that were purely for her own enjoyment. "These habits helped me maintain the energy and enthusiasm needed to be genuinely supportive to others without feeling depleted or resentful," she said. "When I was taking care of my own energy, I could offer support from a place of abundance rather than obligation."

"Growth tracking habits" provide another valuable category—regular practices that help you monitor your progress, celebrate your successes, and identify areas where you want to continue developing. These habits might include weekly journal entries about your growth and learning, monthly conversations with trusted friends or coaches about your transformation, or annual reviews of your overall progress and future goals.

Growth tracking habits help maintain motivation during challenging periods by providing evidence of progress that might not be immediately obvious. They also help you identify patterns in your growth and development that can inform future choices and priorities.

The process of building freedom-supporting habits requires starting small and building gradually rather than trying to implement major changes all at once. Research on habit formation suggests that small, consistent practices are more likely to become automatic than ambitious routines that require significant willpower to maintain.

This gradual approach might involve starting with one small daily practice and adding additional habits only after the first one has become automatic. It might mean linking new habits to existing routines rather than trying to create entirely new time blocks in your schedule. It might involve focusing on habits that provide immediate benefits rather than only long-term rewards.

David applied this gradual approach when building his freedom-supporting habits. "I started with just five minutes of morning reflection and gradually added other practices only after the reflection had become automatic," he said. "This approach helped me build a comprehensive set of habits without feeling overwhelmed or abandoning the practices when life became demanding."

Building habits that support your freedom formula also requires patience with the process and self-compassion when you occasionally skip practices or revert to old patterns. Habit formation typically takes weeks or months rather than days, and expecting perfection often leads to abandoning efforts entirely when temporary setbacks occur.

The key is viewing habit development as a long-term investment in your transformation rather than a short-term performance goal. When freedom-supporting habits become automatic, they provide ongoing support for your growth and help maintain your transformation with much less conscious effort and willpower.

The Freedom Morning Routine

Creating a comprehensive morning routine that supports your ongoing freedom and transformation provides the foundation for maintaining your new way of being regardless of the challenges and pressures you encounter throughout the day. This routine serves as your daily opportunity to connect with your values, reinforce your boundaries, and set intentions that align with your authentic self rather than others' expectations.

The Freedom Morning Routine is designed to be both flexible enough to adapt to your schedule and lifestyle, and comprehensive enough to address the key elements that support lasting transformation. The routine typically includes components that address mental clarity, emotional regulation, physical wellbeing, and spiritual or values-based centering.

The routine begins with what I call "awakening mindfully"—taking a few moments upon waking to transition consciously from sleep to wakefulness rather than immediately jumping into reactive mode. This might involve taking several deep breaths, setting an intention for the day, or simply spending a few moments in gratitude for the opportunity to live another day aligned with your values.

This mindful awakening helps establish a foundation of choice and intentionality rather than starting the day in reactive mode. It creates a moment of connection with your own experience before engaging with external demands and expectations.

Following mindful awakening, the routine typically includes "centering practices"—activities that help you connect with your own inner wisdom, values, and sense of purpose. These practices might include meditation, prayer, journaling, reading inspirational material, or simply sitting quietly with your own thoughts and feelings.

The key to effective centering practices is that they focus your attention inward and help you remember who you are and what matters most to you. This centering provides an anchor throughout the day when you're faced with pressure to abandon your boundaries or revert to old patterns.

Patricia's centering practice involved ten minutes of meditation followed by reading a brief passage about healthy relationships or personal growth. "This practice helped me start each day connected to my deeper purpose and reminded me of the principles I wanted to live by," she said. "When challenges arose during the day, I could remember the clarity and intention I had set in the morning."

The next component involves "boundary affirmation"—consciously reinforcing your commitment to the healthy limits you've established and preparing mentally to maintain them despite any pressure you might encounter. This affirmation might involve reviewing specific boundaries that are likely to be tested during the day, reminding yourself why these boundaries are important, or simply affirming your right to have limits.

This boundary affirmation helps strengthen your resolve and prepares you to respond from a place of clarity rather than guilt or pressure when your limits are challenged. It also helps you maintain perspective about the long-term benefits of maintaining boundaries even when doing so creates temporary discomfort.

Following boundary affirmation, the routine includes "intention setting"—choosing how you want to show up in your relationships and responsibilities rather than simply reacting to whatever situations arise. This intention setting helps you approach your day from a place of choice and purpose rather than obligation and reactivity.

Intention setting might involve considering the key interactions you'll have during the day and choosing how you want to handle them, identifying specific values you want to embody, or simply choosing a word or phrase that captures how you want to approach your relationships.

David's intention setting practice involved reviewing his calendar and asking himself how he wanted to show up in each meeting or interaction. "I would consider whether I wanted to be a listener, a supporter, a collaborator, or simply present," he said. "This practice helped me stay conscious about my role rather than automatically falling into old patterns of taking over or managing situations."

The routine also includes "self-care planning"—identifying specific ways you'll nurture your own wellbeing throughout the day rather than waiting until you're depleted to attend to your own needs. This planning helps ensure that self-care becomes a proactive priority rather than a crisis intervention.

Self-care planning might involve scheduling specific activities that energize you, identifying moments when you'll check in with your own emotional state, or simply ensuring that you have adequate time for rest, nutrition, and activities that bring you joy.

The final component involves "gratitude and appreciation"—acknowledging things you're grateful for and celebrating progress you've made in your transformation. This appreciation helps maintain motivation and provides positive reinforcement for continued growth.

This gratitude practice might involve acknowledging relationships that support your growth, recognizing progress you've made in maintaining boundaries, or simply appreciating your own courage in choosing transformation over comfort.

The Freedom Morning Routine works best when it's adapted to fit your schedule and preferences rather than following a rigid formula. Some people prefer longer, more elaborate routines, while others need shorter practices that fit into busy schedules. The key is consistency and intention rather than duration or complexity.

Jennifer adapted her Freedom Morning Routine to fit her demanding schedule by creating a fifteen-minute practice that included five minutes of breathing and centering, five minutes of intention setting and boundary affirmation, and five minutes of planning self-care for the day. "This short routine was manageable even on busy days, but it provided enough centering to help me maintain my transformation throughout the day," she said.

The routine also serves as a daily recommitment to your transformation, helping you maintain momentum during challenging periods and preventing gradual erosion of the progress you've made. When the Freedom Morning Routine becomes a consistent habit, it provides ongoing support for living from your authentic self rather than from others' expectations and demands.

Creating a Sustainable Daily Framework

The ultimate goal of the daily practice of freedom is creating a sustainable framework that supports your ongoing transformation without requiring enormous amounts of time, energy, or willpower. This framework should enhance rather than burden your daily life, providing structure and support that makes it easier to maintain healthy boundaries and empowering relationships.

Creating a sustainable framework requires balancing several important considerations. The practices need to be simple enough to maintain during busy or stressful periods, but comprehensive enough to address the key elements that support transformation. They need to provide immediate benefits that reinforce continued practice, while also supporting long-term growth and development.

The framework should also be flexible enough to adapt to changing circumstances, life transitions, and evolving needs, while maintaining enough consistency to create real habits and lasting change. This balance between structure and flexibility is crucial for creating practices that support rather than constrain your growth and development.

The sustainable daily framework typically includes four main components that work together to support ongoing transformation. These components can be customized to fit your preferences, schedule, and lifestyle, but they address the core elements needed to maintain freedom from over-management patterns.

The first component involves "daily anchoring practices"—consistent activities that help you start and end each day connected to your own values and intentions rather than others' urgency and demands. These anchoring practices create bookends for your day that help you maintain perspective and choice regardless of what challenges arise.

Morning anchoring practices might include brief meditation, intention setting, boundary affirmation, or simply taking a few conscious breaths before engaging with external demands. Evening anchoring practices might include reflection on the day's experiences, gratitude for progress made, or setting intentions for continued growth.

The key to effective anchoring practices is consistency rather than duration. Even five minutes of morning and evening anchoring can create significant stability and support for your transformation when practiced regularly.

The second component involves "intermittent check-ins"—brief moments throughout the day when you pause to assess whether you're operating from choice or reactivity, maintaining your boundaries or allowing them to be eroded, and staying connected to your own experience or getting lost in others' problems.

These check-ins might be linked to natural transition points in your day, such as before meals, between meetings, or when moving from one activity to another. They might involve simple questions like "Am I choosing this response?" "Am I maintaining my boundaries?" or "Am I present to my own experience?"

The power of intermittent check-ins lies in their ability to create course corrections throughout the day, helping you realign with your values and intentions when you notice yourself drifting into old patterns.

The third component involves "weekly integration practices"—regular activities that help you process the week's experiences, celebrate successes, learn from challenges, and prepare for continued growth. These practices provide deeper reflection and planning than daily check-ins allow, while maintaining the momentum of transformation.

Weekly integration might include longer reflection periods, conversations with trusted friends or coaches about your growth, review of your boundaries and how well you're maintaining them, or planning for specific challenges you anticipate in the coming week.

The fourth component involves "monthly and seasonal reviews"—broader assessments of your overall progress, relationship patterns, and life direction that help ensure your transformation continues to evolve and deepen over time. These reviews help prevent stagnation and ensure that your growth remains aligned with your authentic values and goals.

These broader reviews might include assessment of your overall relationship satisfaction, evaluation of whether your boundaries are serving your current needs, consideration of new areas for growth and development, or adjustment of your daily and weekly practices based on what you've learned.

Margaret created a sustainable framework that included ten minutes of morning centering, brief check-ins before meals, weekly reflection on Saturday mornings, and monthly assessment conversations with a trusted friend. "This framework provided enough structure to support my transformation without feeling overwhelming or burdensome," she said. "I could maintain these practices even during busy periods because they were simple and directly beneficial."

Creating a sustainable framework also requires what I call "practice evolution"—allowing your daily practices to grow and change as you develop and your needs evolve. What supports you during the early stages of transformation may need to be adjusted as you become more skilled at maintaining boundaries and empowering relationships.

This evolution might involve adding new elements to your practices as you identify additional areas for growth, simplifying practices that have become automatic and no longer require conscious attention, or modifying practices based on changes in your life circumstances or priorities.

The key to practice evolution is maintaining the core intention of supporting your freedom and transformation while allowing the specific practices to adapt to your changing needs and development.

Sustainability also requires what I call "imperfection acceptance"—recognizing that you won't implement your practices perfectly every day, and that temporary lapses don't mean abandoning your framework entirely. This acceptance helps prevent the all-or-nothing thinking that often leads to completely abandoning beneficial practices when life becomes challenging.

Instead of aiming for perfect consistency, aim for "good enough" consistency that maintains the overall momentum of your transformation while allowing for the natural fluctuations of daily life. This approach makes your practices more sustainable and reduces the pressure that can make them feel burdensome rather than supportive.

David learned the importance of imperfection acceptance when he initially tried to implement elaborate daily practices that he couldn't maintain during busy work periods. "I realized that having simple practices I could do most days was much more valuable than having complex practices I would abandon whenever life became demanding," he said. "When I accepted that my practices would vary in intensity and consistency, I was able to maintain them much more sustainably."

The sustainable daily framework should ultimately feel supportive rather than demanding, enhancing your life rather than adding burden to it. When your daily practices become integrated into your natural rhythms and provide genuine benefits, they support your transformation effortlessly rather than requiring constant willpower and discipline.

This integration creates what I call "effortless maintenance"—a state where living from your authentic self and maintaining healthy boundaries becomes your natural way of being rather than a constant struggle against old patterns. The daily practice of freedom gradually becomes simply the practice of living authentically, with the structure and support that makes this authentic living sustainable over time.

The Daily Liberation Review

The Daily Liberation Review represents the culmination of your daily freedom practice—a brief but powerful evening reflection that helps you process the day's experiences, celebrate your growth, learn from challenges, and prepare for continued transformation. This review serves as both a completion of each day's practice and a preparation for ongoing development.

The review is designed to be completed in ten to fifteen minutes, making it sustainable even during busy periods while providing enough depth to support meaningful reflection and learning. The structure of the review follows a specific sequence that helps you process your experiences comprehensively and constructively.

The review begins with "experience acknowledgment"—simply recognizing what happened during the day without immediately judging whether experiences were good or bad, successful or unsuccessful. This acknowledgment helps you approach reflection from a place of curiosity and learning rather than criticism and judgment.

Experience acknowledgment might involve noting key interactions you had, decisions you made, challenges you encountered, or moments when you felt particularly aligned or misaligned with your values. The goal is simply to create awareness of your actual experiences rather than the experiences you think you should have had.

Following experience acknowledgment, the review includes "boundary assessment"—evaluating how well you maintained your limits and honored your own needs throughout the day. This assessment helps you recognize progress in maintaining boundaries while identifying areas where you might need additional attention or support.

Boundary assessment might involve noting times when you successfully maintained limits despite pressure, situations where you felt challenged to abandon boundaries, moments when you honored your own needs and preferences, or instances where you felt you compromised your limits more than was appropriate.

The key to effective boundary assessment is approaching it with compassion and curiosity rather than harsh self-judgment. The goal is learning and growth, not perfect performance, and maintaining a supportive internal dialogue helps sustain motivation for continued development.

The review continues with "empowerment recognition"—identifying specific instances where you chose to empower rather than manage others, where you trusted their capabilities rather than taking over their responsibilities, or where you offered support without enabling dependency.

This recognition helps reinforce empowering relationship patterns and builds confidence in your ability to love others without losing yourself. It also helps you recognize progress that might not be immediately obvious, particularly the subtle shifts in how you relate to others that characterize healthy transformation.

Jennifer found empowerment recognition particularly valuable during the period when she was learning to step back from managing her adult children's lives. "I would note times when I listened supportively rather than immediately offering solutions, when I expressed confidence in their abilities rather than anxiety about their choices, or when I maintained boundaries about what I would and wouldn't help with," she said. "Recognizing these moments helped me see how much my relationship style was actually changing."

The review also includes "learning integration"—identifying specific insights or lessons from the day's experiences and considering how to apply them to future situations. This integration helps transform daily experiences into wisdom that supports continued growth and development.

Learning integration might involve recognizing patterns in your responses to certain types of situations, understanding what triggers make it difficult to maintain boundaries, identifying what types of support help you stay centered, or discovering new strategies for handling challenging relationship dynamics.

Following learning integration, the review includes "growth celebration"—acknowledging progress you made during the day, even if that progress involved difficult choices or uncomfortable situations. This celebration helps maintain motivation and provides positive reinforcement for continued transformation.

Growth celebration might involve acknowledging courage you showed in maintaining boundaries, progress you made in trusting others' capabilities, moments when you chose your own wellbeing over others' convenience, or simply recognition of your commitment to ongoing growth and development.

The review concludes with "tomorrow's intention"—using insights from the day's experiences to set intentions for how you want to show up on the following day. This forward-looking component helps maintain momentum and ensures that each day's learning contributes to ongoing transformation.

Tomorrow's intention might involve identifying specific situations where you want to apply what you've learned, choosing how you want to handle anticipated challenges, or simply setting an overall intention for how you want to embody your values in the coming day.

Patricia found that setting tomorrow's intention helped her approach each new day with purpose and clarity rather than simply reacting to whatever situations arose. "When I ended each day by setting intentions for the next day, I started each morning with direction rather than just hoping things would go well," she said.

The Daily Liberation Review works best when it becomes a consistent routine rather than an occasional activity you engage in only when you're struggling. This consistency helps create ongoing support for your transformation and ensures that you continue to learn and grow from your daily experiences.

The review can be completed through journaling, mental reflection, or conversation with trusted friends or partners. The key is creating a regular opportunity to process your experiences consciously and maintain momentum toward continued growth and development.

When the Daily Liberation Review becomes a natural part of your evening routine, it provides closure for each day while creating preparation for continued transformation. It helps you maintain perspective about your progress, learn from both successes and challenges, and approach each new day with intention and purpose rather than simply hoping to survive whatever comes your way.

The ultimate goal of the daily practice of freedom is creating a way of living that supports your authentic self while maintaining loving, empowering relationships with others. When your daily practices become integrated into your natural rhythms, when your boundaries become automatic rather than effortful, when your empowering communication becomes your natural way of relating to others, you discover that freedom isn't something you have to constantly strive for—it becomes simply the way you live.

This integration represents the true success of your transformation: not just changing how you behave in relationships, but changing who you are in a way that naturally creates healthy, empowering patterns in all areas of your life. The daily practice of freedom ultimately becomes simply the practice of being your authentic self, with the support and structure that makes this authenticity sustainable and joyful rather than burdensome or isolated.

When you've established this foundation of daily practices that support your freedom, you discover that you can love others deeply without losing yourself, that you can offer genuine support without enabling dependency, and that you can maintain caring relationships while honoring your own boundaries and autonomy. This is the daily experience of freedom: living from your own center while remaining open and connected to the people you love most.

CHAPTER 15

Advanced Freedom Strategies

The call came at 2:47 AM on a Saturday night. Jennifer's phone buzzed insistently until she fumbled for it in the dark, her heart immediately racing with the familiar combination of concern and dread that had characterized her relationship with crisis calls for decades. The caller ID showed her sister's name, and Jennifer's mind immediately began generating the possible scenarios: a medical emergency, a relationship crisis, a financial disaster, or perhaps just another dramatic late-night emotional breakdown.

But this time, instead of immediately answering and launching into crisis management mode, Jennifer paused. She took three deep breaths, connected with her own sense of center, and asked herself a crucial question: "Is this my emergency to handle, or is this an opportunity for my sister to develop her own crisis management skills?"

After five rings, Jennifer made a conscious choice that would have been unthinkable eighteen months earlier: she declined the call and sent a text message. "I see you called. I'm not available for emergencies that aren't genuine health or safety issues. I'm confident you can handle whatever this is, and we can talk at a reasonable hour if you'd like my perspective."

This response represented what I call "advanced freedom"—the ability to maintain loving boundaries and empowering responses even during high-stakes situations that trigger your deepest rescue impulses. It demonstrated mastery not just of basic boundary-setting skills, but of sophisticated strategies for handling complex situations while maintaining both compassion and autonomy.

Jennifer's sister, it turned out, had been calling because she was upset about an argument with her boyfriend and wanted Jennifer to mediate the conflict by calling him and "explaining her side." By morning, the couple had worked through their disagreement themselves, and Jennifer's sister actually thanked her for not getting involved in what she realized was their issue to resolve.

This situation illustrates the evolution that occurs as you develop advanced freedom strategies. You move beyond basic boundary-setting to sophisticated approaches that can handle complex, emotionally charged situations while maintaining your commitment to empowering rather than enabling others. You develop what I call "crisis immunity"—the ability to remain centered and make conscious choices even when others present their problems as emergencies requiring your immediate intervention.

Advanced freedom strategies represent the culmination of your transformation from over-manager to empowering partner in relationships. These strategies require integration of everything you've learned about boundaries, communication, emotional regulation, and healthy relationship dynamics, but they take your skills to a level that allows you to handle even the most challenging situations with grace and effectiveness.

Handling Crisis Situations Without Reverting to Old Patterns

Crisis situations represent the ultimate test of your transformation because they trigger the deepest psychological and emotional patterns that drove your original over-management behaviors. When someone you love is in genuine distress, when family emergencies arise, when workplace crises demand immediate attention, or when health issues create urgent needs, your automatic impulse may be to abandon all boundaries and return to familiar patterns of taking over and managing everything.

Advanced freedom strategies for crisis management involve developing what I call "crisis discernment"—the ability to quickly and accurately assess whether a situation represents a genuine emergency requiring immediate intervention or a manufactured crisis designed to override your boundaries and pull you back into management mode.

This discernment requires understanding that true emergencies involving immediate threats to health, safety, or wellbeing are actually quite rare. Most situations that are presented as crises are actually urgent problems, uncomfortable situations, or normal life challenges that feel overwhelming to people who haven't developed adequate problem-solving skills or emotional regulation abilities.

The key distinction lies not in the emotional intensity surrounding the situation, but in whether immediate intervention is genuinely necessary to prevent serious harm. A true emergency might involve someone having a heart attack, a child being in physical danger, or a situation where delay could result in irreversible negative consequences.

A manufactured crisis, by contrast, might involve someone being upset about a work conflict and demanding immediate advice, a family member creating drama about holiday plans and insisting on immediate resolution, or an adult child presenting poor planning as an emergency requiring parental rescue.

Dr. Harriet Lerner, whose research on family systems has influenced thousands of therapists, explains: "People often escalate the emotional intensity around normal problems to create a sense of urgency that bypasses others' rational decision-making. Learning to respond to the actual situation rather than the emotional drama surrounding it is crucial for maintaining healthy boundaries during difficult periods."

Developing crisis discernment requires creating what I call "emergency criteria"—clear standards for determining when situations warrant abandoning your normal boundaries and when they require maintaining limits while offering appropriate support. These criteria help you respond consistently rather than making reactive decisions based on emotional pressure or guilt.

Emergency criteria might include: Is someone's physical health or safety at immediate risk? Are there legal consequences that could be irreversible if not addressed immediately? Is this situation beyond the person's current capacity to handle with available resources? Would delaying response create significantly worse outcomes than the discomfort of immediate action?

Sarah developed emergency criteria when her elderly father began presenting increasingly frequent "crises" that required her immediate attention and intervention. "I had to distinguish between situations like him falling and needing medical attention, which was a genuine emergency, and situations like him being upset about his cable bill and demanding that I call the company immediately to resolve it," she said. "Having clear criteria helped me respond appropriately rather than treating every upset as a crisis."

When genuine emergencies do arise, advanced freedom strategies involve what I call "emergency response with integrity"—providing necessary help while maintaining as much of your empowering approach as possible and planning for how to transition back to normal boundaries once the crisis has passed.

This might involve providing immediate practical assistance while expressing confidence in the person's ability to handle the broader situation, offering emergency support while connecting the person with ongoing resources that don't depend on you, or stepping in temporarily while creating clear expectations for how and when you'll step back out.

The key to emergency response with integrity is treating crisis intervention as a temporary departure from normal patterns rather than evidence that your boundaries were inappropriate or that the person genuinely needs ongoing management. This approach allows you to respond compassionately to genuine emergencies while preventing crisis situations from becoming permanent returns to over-management patterns.

Marcus applied this approach when his adult daughter was hospitalized unexpectedly and needed immediate practical support with childcare and work coordination. "I stepped in fully to handle the immediate logistics, but I also had conversations with her about how we would transition these responsibilities back to her or to other support systems as she recovered," he said. "I wanted to be helpful during the crisis without creating expectations that I would permanently manage these areas of her life."

Advanced crisis management also involves developing what I call "crisis prevention awareness"—recognizing when your over-management has been preventing others from developing the crisis management skills they need, and gradually creating opportunities for them to build these capabilities before emergencies arise.

This prevention awareness helps you understand that some of the "crises" you've been managing weren't actually beyond others' capabilities, but rather situations where your immediate intervention prevented them from developing their own emergency response skills. Creating space for others to handle manageable difficulties helps them build confidence and competence for dealing with more significant challenges.

Advanced Emotional Regulation Techniques

As you develop more sophisticated freedom strategies, you need increasingly advanced emotional regulation techniques that can help you maintain your center even during highly charged situations that trigger intense emotions in yourself and others. These techniques go beyond basic boundary-setting to address the complex emotional dynamics that arise in intimate relationships and high-stakes situations.

Advanced emotional regulation begins with what I call "emotional anticipation"—developing the ability to predict your own emotional responses to challenging situations and prepare strategies for managing those responses effectively. This anticipation allows you to maintain your boundaries and values even when situations trigger intense feelings of guilt, anxiety, fear, or anger.

Emotional anticipation involves identifying the specific situations, people, or dynamics that are most likely to trigger your rescue impulses or cause you to abandon your boundaries. It also involves understanding the particular emotional states that make you most vulnerable to reverting to old patterns of over-management.

For many recovering over-managers, the most challenging emotional triggers involve others' expressions of disappointment, anger, or distress about your boundaries. Learning to tolerate these emotions in others without immediately taking action to relieve them represents a crucial advanced skill.

This tolerance requires developing what psychologists call "distress tolerance"—the ability to experience uncomfortable emotions without immediately acting to make them go away. For people who have been conditioned to manage others' emotional states, sitting with others' upset without trying to fix it can feel almost physically painful.

Patricia developed distress tolerance skills when her teenage daughter would have emotional outbursts about Patricia's refusal to solve typical adolescent problems. "I had to learn to stay calm and compassionate while my daughter was upset, without immediately jumping in to fix whatever was bothering her," she said. "This required developing the ability to tolerate my own anxiety about her distress without taking action to relieve it."

Advanced emotional regulation also involves what I call "emotional differentiation"—the sophisticated ability to distinguish between your own authentic emotional responses and emotions you're absorbing from others, even in highly charged situations where these boundaries become blurred.

This differentiation becomes particularly important in family systems or close relationships where emotional fusion has been the norm. Learning to maintain your own emotional center while remaining empathetically connected to others requires high levels of self-awareness and emotional sophistication.

The technique involves regularly checking in with yourself during emotionally intense interactions: "What am I feeling right now that belongs to my own experience? What emotions might I be taking on that belong to the other person? How can I remain compassionate without absorbing their emotional state?"

Advanced emotional regulation techniques also include what I call "values-based responding"—the ability to choose responses based on your deeply held values and long-term relationship goals rather than on immediate emotional impulses or pressure from others.

This values-based responding requires developing clarity about what you most want to create in your relationships and using that clarity to guide your choices even when those choices feel emotionally difficult in the moment. It means choosing responses that serve everyone's long-term growth and wellbeing rather than responses that simply reduce immediate emotional discomfort.

Jennifer used values-based responding when her adult son pressured her to cosign a loan for a purchase she thought was financially irresponsible. "My immediate emotional impulse was to help him avoid disappointment by agreeing to cosign, but my deeper values involved supporting his financial independence and responsibility," she said. "I chose to respond from my values rather than from my emotions, even though it meant tolerating his temporary anger and disappointment."

Another advanced technique involves "meta-emotional awareness"—the ability to observe and understand your emotional responses without being overwhelmed by them. This awareness creates space between experiencing emotions and acting on them, allowing for more conscious and intentional responses.

Meta-emotional awareness involves developing what mindfulness teachers call "the observer self"—the part of your consciousness that can witness your emotional experiences with some objectivity and perspective. This observer self helps you maintain choice about how to respond to emotions rather than being automatically driven by them.

The practice involves regular check-ins during challenging situations: "I notice that I'm feeling anxious about this person's problem. I can feel the urge to jump in and fix it. I'm choosing to breathe and stay present with my own experience while supporting them in handling their own situation."

David developed meta-emotional awareness skills that helped him stay centered during family gatherings where he typically felt pressured to resume his old role as family problem-solver and conflict mediator. "I learned to notice the anxiety and guilt that arose when family members had conflicts, but to observe those feelings rather than immediately acting on them," he said. "This awareness helped me choose supportive responses rather than automatically taking over family dynamics."

Advanced emotional regulation also involves developing what I call "emotional resilience"—the ability to recover quickly from emotionally challenging interactions and return to your own center rather than carrying others' emotions or relationship drama for extended periods.

This resilience includes specific practices for releasing emotions that don't belong to you, processing your own authentic emotional responses to challenging situations, and restoring your emotional equilibrium after difficult interactions. It also involves developing the capacity to maintain perspective about temporary relationship difficulties without catastrophizing or losing faith in your overall transformation.

Building Influence Without Control

One of the most sophisticated aspects of advanced freedom involves learning to create positive influence in your relationships and environments without reverting to control and management strategies. This influence is based on modeling, inspiration, and authentic leadership rather than on over-functioning and taking responsibility for others' choices and outcomes.

Building influence without control requires understanding the fundamental difference between these two approaches to creating change. Control-based influence involves trying to get others to do what you want them to do through pressure, manipulation, consequences, or taking over their responsibilities. This approach often produces compliance in the short term but creates resentment and dependency over time.

Influence without control, by contrast, involves inspiring others to make positive choices by modeling healthy behavior, creating environments that support good decisions, offering resources and perspective when requested, and trusting others' capacity for growth and positive change.

This type of influence is more sustainable and effective because it respects others' autonomy while encouraging their development. It also allows you to maintain your own integrity and authenticity rather than constantly trying to manage others' responses and behaviors.

The foundation of influence without control is what I call "modeling mastery"—becoming so skilled at living according to your own values and maintaining healthy boundaries that others naturally want to learn from your example rather than feeling pressured to comply with your expectations.

This modeling involves demonstrating what healthy relationships look like through your own behavior rather than trying to teach or convince others to change their patterns. It means showing rather than telling others what's possible when someone lives authentically and maintains appropriate boundaries.

Margaret discovered the power of modeling when she stopped trying to convince her adult children to be more financially responsible and instead focused on demonstrating healthy financial practices in her own life. "Instead of lecturing them about budgeting and savings, I simply lived according to my own financial values and was available to share my perspective when they asked," she said. "Over time, they became curious about my approach and started asking for guidance rather than resisting my advice."

Building influence without control also involves what I call "environmental influence"—creating conditions and contexts that naturally support positive choices rather than trying to control others' decision-making directly. This might involve changing family traditions that supported unhealthy dynamics, establishing new social patterns that encourage growth, or simply removing yourself from situations that enable others' problematic behaviors.

Environmental influence recognizes that people's choices are significantly affected by their surroundings and circumstances. By consciously creating environments that support healthy choices, you can have positive influence without directly trying to control others' behavior.

This approach might involve declining to participate in family dynamics that depend on your over-functioning, creating social activities that encourage healthy interaction patterns, or establishing household routines that support everyone's independence and responsibility.

Sarah used environmental influence when she stopped participating in family gatherings that consistently devolved into drama and conflict because family members expected her to mediate and manage everyone's relationships. "Instead of trying to fix the family dynamics, I started hosting different types of gatherings that had structure and activities that naturally encouraged positive interaction," she said. "I found that changing the environment was much more effective than trying to change people's behavior directly."

Another aspect of building influence without control involves what I call "resource provision"—offering tools, information, and support that help others make positive choices while leaving the responsibility for using those resources with them. This approach provides genuine help without taking over others' decision-making or problem-solving processes.

Resource provision might involve sharing books or articles that offer useful perspectives, connecting others with professionals who can provide specialized help, offering to brainstorm options without imposing your preferred solutions, or simply being available to listen and provide emotional support when requested.

The key to effective resource provision is offering resources without attachment to whether others use them and without making others' utilization of resources a condition of your continued relationship or support. The goal is providing tools that might be helpful while maintaining respect for others' autonomy to choose their own path.

David used resource provision when his adult son was struggling with career direction. Instead of trying to solve his son's career problems or pressure him to make specific choices, David shared information about career counseling services, offered to help him network with professionals in fields that interested him, and remained available for conversation when his son wanted to talk through his thinking.

"I focused on providing resources and support for his own decision-making process rather than trying to direct his choices," David said. "This approach helped him develop confidence in his own judgment while still feeling supported and cared for."

Advanced influence without control also involves what I call "systems thinking"—understanding how relationship dynamics and family systems work and making strategic changes to your own participation in those systems rather than trying to change others' behavior directly.

This systems approach recognizes that relationships are interconnected webs where changes in one person's behavior naturally create changes throughout the entire system. By changing your own participation in unhealthy dynamics, you can create positive influence throughout the entire relationship system without directly trying to control others.

Systems thinking might involve identifying your role in problematic family dynamics and changing your participation in those patterns, understanding how your over-functioning enables others' under-functioning and gradually shifting toward more balanced participation, or recognizing how your anxiety about others' choices affects the entire family system and working to manage your own anxiety rather than trying to control outcomes.

This approach requires patience because systems changes often take time to stabilize, and other people may initially resist changes to familiar patterns. However, systems-level changes tend to be more sustainable and comprehensive than attempts to control specific behaviors or outcomes.

Creating Positive Change Through Modeling Rather Than Managing

The most powerful and sustainable way to create positive change in your relationships and environments involves becoming a living example of the principles and values you want to see rather than trying to convince, pressure, or manage others into adopting different behaviors. This modeling approach respects others' autonomy while demonstrating what's possible when someone lives authentically and maintains healthy boundaries.

Modeling differs from managing in several crucial ways. Managing involves trying to control others' choices and behaviors through intervention, advice-giving, consequences, or taking over their responsibilities. Modeling involves living according to your own values so consistently and authentically that others become curious about your approach and want to learn from your example.

The power of modeling lies in its ability to inspire rather than pressure others toward positive change. When people see the benefits of healthy boundaries, authentic living, and empowering relationships demonstrated through your example, they often become motivated to make similar changes in their own lives. This motivation comes from their own desire for the peace, satisfaction, and authentic relationships they observe in your life rather than from external pressure to comply with your expectations.

Effective modeling requires what I call "authentic consistency"—living according to your values and maintaining your boundaries not for the purpose of influencing others, but because these patterns genuinely serve your own wellbeing and growth. When your healthy behavior is authentic rather than performative, it has a much more powerful influence on others.

This authenticity means maintaining your boundaries and values even when others don't notice or appreciate them, continuing to live according to your principles even when others resist or criticize your choices, and focusing on your own growth and development rather than on whether others are learning from your example.

Patricia discovered the power of authentic modeling when she stopped trying to convince her family members to develop better communication skills and instead focused on communicating authentically and respectfully in all her interactions. "I stopped giving advice about communication and started simply demonstrating what respectful communication looked like through my own behavior," she said. "Over time, family members began adopting similar communication patterns without my ever suggesting that they should."

Modeling also involves what I call "transparent authenticity"—being open about your own growth process, challenges, and learning rather than trying to appear perfect or having all the answers. This transparency makes your example more accessible and inspiring because others can see that positive change is possible for imperfect people working on their own development.

Transparent authenticity might involve sharing your own struggles with maintaining boundaries when others express interest in your approach, acknowledging mistakes you've made in your transformation process and what you've learned from them, or simply being honest about the ongoing nature of personal growth rather than presenting yourself as having arrived at some final destination.

This transparency helps others understand that developing healthy relationship patterns is a process rather than a perfect state, and that they can begin making positive changes even if they're not ready to transform everything at once.

Jennifer practiced transparent authenticity when family members began asking about the changes they observed in her relationships and stress levels. "Instead of giving advice about what they should do, I shared my own experience of learning to set boundaries and develop healthier relationships," she said. "I was honest about how difficult it had been and how much I was still learning, which made the process seem more accessible to them."

Advanced modeling also involves what I call "boundary demonstration"—consistently maintaining your limits in ways that show others what healthy boundaries look like without lecturing or explaining why boundaries are important. This demonstration is often more effective than any amount of advice or persuasion about the value of limits.

Boundary demonstration might involve consistently declining requests that violate your limits regardless of others' reactions, maintaining your self-care practices even when family members suggest you're being selfish, or calmly redirecting responsibility back to appropriate people without extensive explanations about why you're not taking over.

The key to effective boundary demonstration is maintaining your limits with calm confidence rather than defensive explanations or apologetic justifications. When others see that boundaries can be maintained with love and respect rather than anger or withdrawal, they often become more open to developing their own healthy limits.

Another aspect of advanced modeling involves what I call "empowerment demonstration"—consistently treating others as capable and competent while offering appropriate support, thereby showing them what empowering relationships look like rather than trying to convince them to stop accepting or seeking enabling help from others.

Empowerment demonstration might involve expressing confidence in others' abilities even when they're struggling, asking thoughtful questions that help others access their own wisdom rather than immediately offering solutions, or providing support that builds their capabilities rather than replacing their efforts.

This demonstration helps others experience what it feels like to be treated as capable and autonomous, which often motivates them to seek more empowering relationships and to treat others with similar respect and confidence.

David used empowerment demonstration when his adult children were accustomed to having their problems solved by family members rather than developing their own problem-solving skills. "Instead of criticizing the family pattern or trying to convince them that they were too dependent, I simply consistently treated them as capable people who could handle their own challenges," he said. "Over time, they started coming to me less for solutions and more for perspective and encouragement, which helped them develop more confidence in their own abilities."

The Ripple Effect of Your Transformation

When you successfully implement advanced freedom strategies and live consistently from a place of healthy boundaries and empowering relationships, your transformation creates ripple effects that extend far beyond your immediate circle. These ripple effects represent the broader impact of your personal growth on your family system, workplace culture, social networks, and community relationships.

Understanding these ripple effects helps you recognize the full significance of your transformation and maintain motivation for continued growth even during challenging periods. Your personal commitment to freedom and healthy relationships doesn't just benefit you—it models possibilities for others and creates positive changes throughout your entire relational ecosystem.

The first level of ripple effects occurs within your immediate family system. When you stop over-functioning and enable others to take more responsibility for their own lives, the entire family system must reorganize around healthier patterns of interaction and responsibility. This reorganization often leads to increased competence and confidence in family members who have become dependent on your management.

These family system changes can be particularly profound because they affect multiple generations. Children who grow up seeing healthy boundaries modeled learn these patterns as normal rather than having to unlearn problematic patterns as adults. Spouses who experience empowering rather than managing relationships often become more confident and autonomous in all areas of their lives.

Margaret observed this family system transformation when her adult children began adopting healthier relationship patterns in their own marriages and friendships after experiencing more empowering dynamics with her. "My children started setting their own boundaries and treating their partners as capable rather than managing their relationships," she said. "They had learned from experiencing empowering relationships that this approach actually created stronger connections."

The second level of ripple effects occurs in your workplace and professional relationships. When you maintain appropriate boundaries at work, refuse to consistently over-function, and treat colleagues as capable rather than managing their responsibilities, you contribute to healthier organizational culture and more sustainable work practices.

These workplace changes can be particularly significant because they model alternatives to the burnout culture that characterizes many professional environments. Your example of maintaining work-life boundaries while remaining productive and collaborative shows others that it's possible to be successful without sacrificing personal wellbeing.

Sarah experienced this workplace ripple effect when her modeling of healthy boundaries encouraged colleagues to establish their own limits around overtime, email availability, and taking on responsibilities outside their job descriptions. "Several people told me that seeing me maintain boundaries while still being effective at my job gave them permission to establish their own limits," she said. "The whole team culture gradually became more sustainable and respectful of people's personal time."

The third level of ripple effects occurs in your broader social networks and community relationships. When you consistently demonstrate what healthy relationships look like, you attract others who are interested in similar patterns while naturally creating distance from those who prefer more dysfunctional dynamics.

This social network transformation often leads to deeper, more satisfying friendships based on mutual respect and support rather than one-sided caretaking or drama. It also creates opportunities to influence community culture toward healthier relationship norms.

The ripple effects of your transformation also include what I call "permission giving"—showing others through your example that it's possible to live authentically, maintain boundaries, and prioritize your own wellbeing without being selfish or uncaring. This permission is particularly powerful for others who have been trapped in similar over-management patterns.

When others see you successfully maintaining boundaries while keeping loving relationships, pursuing your own goals while remaining supportive of others, and living authentically while maintaining community connections, they often feel empowered to make similar changes in their own lives.

Jennifer discovered this permission-giving effect when friends and family members began asking for guidance about establishing their own boundaries and reducing their own over-management patterns. "People started saying things like 'I see how much happier you are since you stopped managing everyone else's problems, and I want to learn how to do that too,'" she said. "My transformation gave them permission to consider that they could make similar changes."

The ripple effects of advanced freedom strategies also include what I call "standard elevation"—raising the bar for what constitutes healthy relationship dynamics in your various environments. When you consistently demonstrate respect, empowerment, and healthy boundaries, you make it more difficult for others to maintain obviously dysfunctional patterns.

This standard elevation doesn't involve criticizing or confronting others about their relationship patterns, but rather making healthy dynamics so consistently visible that problematic patterns become more obviously problematic by comparison.

The long-term ripple effects of your transformation can extend to future generations as healthy relationship patterns become established in your family and social systems. Children who grow up experiencing empowering relationships are more likely to create healthy relationships in their own adult lives, breaking cycles of codependency and over-management that may have persisted for generations.

These generational effects represent perhaps the most significant impact of your transformation. By learning to love others without losing yourself, to support without enabling, and to care without controlling, you contribute to healing relationship patterns that may have been problematic in your family system for decades or longer.

David recognized this generational impact when he observed his adult children developing much healthier relationship patterns than he had modeled in his own marriage and parenting during their childhood. "Seeing them create relationships based on mutual respect and empowerment rather than management and control helped me understand that my transformation wasn't just about my own happiness," he said. "It was about healing patterns that could affect my family for generations."

Advanced Resilience and Integration

The culmination of advanced freedom strategies involves developing what I call "integrated resilience"—the ability to maintain your transformation consistently across all areas of your life and all types of challenging situations. This resilience represents the deep integration of healthy relationship patterns into your core identity and automatic responses rather than requiring constant conscious effort to maintain.

Integrated resilience means that healthy boundaries, empowering communication, and authentic self-expression become your natural way of being rather than practices you have to remember to implement. It means that your transformation is robust enough to withstand stress, crisis, relationship pressure, and life transitions without reverting to old patterns of over-management.

This integration occurs gradually as new patterns become deeply habituated and as you develop confidence in the effectiveness of healthy relationship dynamics. The more you experience the benefits of living authentically and maintaining appropriate boundaries, the more natural these patterns become and the less vulnerable you are to pressure to abandon them.

Building integrated resilience requires what I call "stress testing"—consciously maintaining your healthy patterns during increasingly challenging situations to build confidence in their sustainability. This stress testing helps you discover that your boundaries and empowering approach can withstand much more pressure than you initially believed.

Stress testing might involve maintaining your limits during family crises, keeping your boundaries intact during workplace pressures, or staying true to your values during relationship conflicts. Each successful navigation of challenging situations while maintaining your transformation builds resilience and confidence.

Integrated resilience also involves developing what I call "identity evolution"—shifting your core sense of self from someone who gains worth through being needed and managing others to someone who contributes to others' lives through empowerment and authentic modeling. This identity evolution makes your transformation more sustainable because it's supported by deep internal changes rather than just behavioral modifications.

This identity evolution often involves grieving the loss of your old identity as the family rescuer, workplace hero, or relationship manager, while embracing a new identity as someone who trusts others' capabilities and focuses on living authentically. This grief process is important because it acknowledges the real losses involved in transformation while making space for the benefits of your new way of being.

The final aspect of integrated resilience involves what I call "wisdom cultivation"—developing the sophisticated judgment needed to navigate complex relationship situations while maintaining your commitment to healthy patterns. This wisdom includes knowing when flexibility is appropriate and when firmness is required, when to offer support and when to step back, when to engage and when to disengage.

This wisdom develops through experience and reflection rather than through following rigid rules or formulas. It represents the art of living authentically in relationship with others while maintaining your own integrity and supporting their growth and development.

When you have developed integrated resilience, your transformation becomes a stable foundation for all aspects of your life rather than a fragile achievement that requires constant protection. You discover that you can handle whatever challenges arise while maintaining your commitment to healthy, empowering relationships and authentic living.

This integrated resilience ultimately allows you to love others deeply without losing yourself, to be genuinely helpful without being controlling, and to create positive change in your world through the power of your example rather than through management and intervention. It represents the full flowering of your freedom formula—a way of living that honors both your own autonomy and your genuine care for others while creating ripple effects of health and empowerment throughout all your relationships and communities.

CHAPTER 16

Living Your Freedom Formula

The morning sun streamed through the windows of Sarah's home office as she reviewed her calendar for the day ahead. Two years ago, this same time of morning would have found her frantically checking messages to see what crises had emerged overnight, making mental lists of everyone else's problems she needed to solve, and feeling the familiar knot of anxiety about whether she could manage all the demands on her time and energy.

Today, however, Sarah felt a deep sense of peace and purposefulness as she approached her day. Her calendar reflected a life organized around her own values and priorities: a client meeting for her growing coaching practice, lunch with a friend who energized rather than drained her, time blocked for working on a creative project that brought her joy, and an evening family dinner where she would be present as a loving partner and parent rather than as a crisis manager and problem-solver.

The most remarkable thing about Sarah's transformation wasn't the absence of challenges in her life—her teenagers still faced typical adolescent struggles, her husband still dealt with work stress, and her elderly parents still navigated the complexities of aging. The difference was that Sarah now related to these challenges from a place of supportive partnership rather than anxious management, trusting in others' capabilities while maintaining her own emotional equilibrium and life direction.

This shift represented what I call "living your freedom formula"—the integration of everything you've learned about healthy boundaries, empowering relationships, and authentic living into a natural way of being that enhances every aspect of your life. It's the difference between practicing freedom as a set of techniques you remember to implement and embodying freedom as your fundamental approach to life and relationships.

Living your freedom formula means that healthy patterns have become so integrated into your identity and automatic responses that they no longer require conscious effort to maintain. You naturally respond to others' problems with empowering support rather than taking over. You automatically maintain boundaries that honor both your own well-being and others' growth. You instinctively communicate in ways that build rather than diminish others' confidence and capability.

This integration represents the culmination of your transformation journey—not an end point where growth stops, but a stable foundation from which you can continue evolving while maintaining your commitment to healthy, empowering relationships and authentic living.

Celebrating Your Progress and Transformation

One of the most important aspects of living your freedom formula involves regularly acknowledging and celebrating the profound changes you've made in how you relate to yourself and others. This celebration isn't about congratulating yourself on reaching perfection, but about recognizing the courage, persistence, and growth that brought you from patterns of over-management to authentic empowerment.

For many recovering over-managers, celebrating personal progress feels uncomfortable or selfish because they've been conditioned to focus on others' achievements rather than their own. Learning to acknowledge your own growth and transformation is itself an important part of living authentically and modeling healthy self-regard for others.

This celebration involves recognizing both the dramatic changes and the subtle shifts that characterize your transformation. The dramatic changes might include major life decisions you've made based on your own values rather than others' expectations, significant boundaries you've established despite intense pressure, or career transitions that align with your authentic interests rather than family obligations.

The subtle shifts might include moments when you naturally responded with empowering questions rather than immediate advice, times when you automatically trusted someone's capability rather than jumping in to help, or conversations where you stayed present to your own experience while supporting others without absorbing their emotional states.

Patricia found that acknowledging subtle shifts was just as important as celebrating major milestones in her transformation. "I started noticing small moments when I would pause before offering to solve someone's problem, or when I would express confidence in someone's judgment rather than anxiety about their choices," she said. "These small changes were evidence that my transformation was becoming integrated into my automatic responses rather than requiring constant conscious effort."

Celebrating your progress also involves recognizing the courage it took to change patterns that were familiar and rewarded by others, even when those patterns were ultimately harmful to everyone involved. Breaking free from over-management requires facing others' disappointment, tolerating uncertainty about outcomes you can't control, and choosing growth over comfort repeatedly in small and large decisions.

This courage often goes unrecognized because over-management patterns are typically praised and reinforced by others who benefit from them. Choosing to stop over-functioning despite social pressure to continue requires significant strength and commitment to your own values and others' long-term wellbeing.

Jennifer reflected on the courage required for her transformation: "I had to risk disappointing my children by refusing to solve their problems, face my husband's initial resistance to me pursuing my own goals, and tolerate my own anxiety about not being needed in the same way. Each choice to maintain my boundaries despite pressure felt scary, but together they created a completely different life."

The celebration process also involves acknowledging the benefits your transformation has created not just for you, but for the people you love. While others may have initially resisted your changes, most relationships ultimately become stronger and more respectful when they're based on mutual empowerment rather than dependency and management.

This broader impact recognition helps you understand that your personal transformation wasn't selfish, but rather a gift to everyone in your life. When you model authentic living and healthy boundaries, when you trust others' capabilities and support their growth, when you love without losing yourself, you create possibilities for healthier relationships throughout your entire relational network.

Margaret discovered this broader impact when her adult children began commenting on how much more confident and capable they felt after she stopped managing aspects of their lives. "They told me that learning to handle their own challenges had made them feel stronger and more self-reliant," she said. "I realized that my transformation hadn't just freed me from over-management—it had given them the gift of discovering their own competence."

Celebrating your progress also involves acknowledging the ongoing nature of transformation and recognizing that living your freedom formula doesn't mean you'll never face challenges or moments of doubt. The difference is that these challenges now arise from a foundation of self-knowledge, healthy boundaries, and empowering relationships rather than from chronic patterns of self-sacrifice and over-functioning.

This recognition helps you approach ongoing challenges with confidence rather than despair, knowing that you have the tools and awareness needed to navigate difficulties while maintaining your commitment to authentic living and healthy relationships.

Maintaining Your Gains Over Time

Living your freedom formula successfully requires developing strategies for maintaining your transformation over time, through life transitions, changing circumstances, and the inevitable pressures that can tempt you to revert to old patterns of over-management. This maintenance isn't about rigidly holding onto specific behaviors, but about preserving the core principles and awareness that support healthy relationships and authentic living.

One of the most important aspects of maintenance involves what I call "transformation anchoring"—regularly reconnecting with the insights, values, and experiences that motivated your original changes and continue to support your commitment to growth. These anchors help you maintain perspective during challenging periods and resist pressure to abandon the progress you've made.

Transformation anchors might include journaling about your growth and the benefits you've experienced, regularly reviewing the costs of your old patterns and the advantages of your new approach, maintaining connections with people who support and encourage your transformation, or simply taking time to appreciate the peace and authenticity that characterize your current way of living.

These anchoring practices help prevent what psychologists call "change drift"—the gradual erosion of positive changes that can occur when you lose touch with why those changes were important and beneficial. Regular anchoring keeps your transformation conscious and intentional rather than allowing it to fade into unconscious habits that can be easily disrupted.

David developed transformation anchoring practices that included monthly reflection on his growth, quarterly conversations with a trusted friend about his ongoing development, and annual assessment of how his relationships and life satisfaction had evolved. "These practices helped me stay conscious of the benefits of my transformation and motivated to maintain the patterns that supported my wellbeing," he said.

Maintaining your gains also requires developing what I call "pressure resilience"—the ability to maintain your transformation even when facing intense pressure to revert to old patterns. This pressure might come from family crises that trigger your rescue impulses, workplace demands that push you toward over-functioning, or relationship conflicts that tempt you to abandon boundaries in favor of temporary peace.

Building pressure resilience involves anticipating the types of situations that are most likely to challenge your transformation and developing specific strategies for maintaining your healthy patterns during these challenging periods. This preparation helps you respond from intention rather than react from old conditioning when difficult situations arise.

Pressure resilience also involves developing what I call "values clarity"—such a deep understanding of what matters most to you that you can maintain your commitment to those values even when maintaining them is difficult or unpopular. This clarity provides a foundation for decision-making that doesn't depend on others' approval or temporary circumstances.

Sarah built pressure resilience by identifying family situations that typically triggered her over-management impulses and developing specific strategies for handling those situations while maintaining her boundaries. "I knew that family emergencies and holiday gatherings were times when I felt most pressure to resume my old role as family manager," she said. "Having clear strategies for these situations helped me maintain my transformation even during stressful periods."

Another crucial aspect of maintenance involves "relationship evolution"—recognizing that your relationships will continue to change and develop as you maintain your transformation, and being prepared to navigate these changes with flexibility while maintaining your core commitments to healthy patterns.

Some relationships may become deeper and more satisfying as they evolve toward greater mutual respect and empowerment. Others may become more distant or even end if they were primarily based on your over-functioning and the other person's under-functioning. Still others may require ongoing negotiation and adjustment as both parties learn to relate in healthier ways.

This relationship evolution requires patience and faith that healthier relationship patterns will ultimately create more satisfying connections, even when the transition period involves some loss or discomfort. It also requires maintaining your boundaries consistently while remaining open to growth and change in how those boundaries are expressed.

Maintaining your transformation also involves developing what I call "adaptation skills"—the ability to apply your core principles and awareness to new situations and life stages rather than following rigid rules that may not fit changing circumstances. This adaptation ensures that your transformation remains relevant and effective throughout different phases of your life.

These adaptation skills involve understanding the underlying principles that support healthy relationships and authentic living, rather than just memorizing specific behaviors or responses. When you understand principles like mutual respect, appropriate responsibility, emotional autonomy, and empowering support, you can apply these principles creatively to new situations rather than feeling lost when circumstances change.

Jennifer applied adaptation skills when her role as a parent evolved as her children became adults and started families of their own. "The specific boundaries and communication patterns that worked when my children were teenagers needed to be adjusted as they became independent adults," she said. "But the underlying principles of trusting their capabilities and maintaining my own autonomy remained the same."

Handling Setbacks and Relapses with Self-Compassion

Living your freedom formula successfully requires understanding that setbacks and temporary returns to old patterns are normal parts of the growth process rather than evidence of failure or reasons to abandon your transformation efforts. Learning to handle these setbacks with self-compassion while quickly returning to healthy patterns is crucial for long-term success.

Setbacks in transformation typically occur during periods of high stress, major life transitions, or when you encounter situations that strongly trigger old conditioning. These might include family crises that activate your rescue impulses, workplace pressures that push you toward over-functioning, relationship conflicts that tempt you to abandon boundaries, or simply periods of fatigue when maintaining new patterns requires more energy than you have available.

Understanding setbacks as temporary lapses rather than permanent failures helps you respond to them constructively rather than with self-criticism and despair. This understanding is particularly important for recovering over-managers, who often have perfectionist tendencies that make them harshly self-critical when they don't maintain their new patterns perfectly.

Dr. Kristin Neff, whose research on self-compassion has influenced thousands of people working on personal change, explains: "Self-compassion during setbacks involves treating yourself with the same kindness you would offer a good friend who was struggling. It means recognizing that imperfection and temporary failures are part of the human experience, and that these experiences don't define your worth or your ability to grow."

Developing self-compassion for setbacks involves several key elements. The first is what I call "setback normalization"—recognizing that everyone who makes significant personal changes experiences periods of reverting to old patterns, and that these experiences are evidence of the human learning process rather than personal inadequacy.

This normalization helps prevent the shame spiral that often follows setbacks, where people become so discouraged by their temporary return to old patterns that they abandon their transformation efforts entirely. Understanding setbacks as normal and temporary helps you maintain perspective and motivation for getting back on track.

The second element involves "learning extraction"—approaching setbacks with curiosity about what triggered the old patterns and what you can learn from the experience to prevent similar setbacks in the future. This learning approach transforms setbacks from failures into valuable information about your ongoing growth and development.

Learning extraction might involve examining what circumstances contributed to the setback, what emotions or pressures triggered old responses, what warning signs you might have missed, or what additional support or strategies might help you handle similar situations more effectively in the future.

Patricia used learning extraction when she found herself reverting to old patterns of over-managing during a family crisis involving her elderly father's hospitalization. "Instead of berating myself for falling back into old habits, I examined what had triggered my automatic responses and what I could do differently if a similar situation arose," she said. "I learned that medical crises were a particular vulnerability for me and developed specific strategies for maintaining my boundaries during health emergencies."

The third element involves "rapid recovery"—developing the ability to recognize setbacks quickly and return to healthy patterns without extensive self-criticism or elaborate processes for getting back on track. This rapid recovery prevents temporary setbacks from becoming extended periods of reverting to old patterns.

Rapid recovery often involves having simple practices or reminders that help you reconnect with your values and commitments after recognizing that you've slipped into old patterns. This might involve revisiting your reasons for transformation, reconnecting with supportive people who understand your growth process, or simply taking a few deep breaths and choosing to respond differently in the next interaction.

The fourth element involves "setback planning"—anticipating the types of situations that are most likely to trigger old patterns and developing specific strategies for maintaining your transformation during these challenging periods. This planning helps prevent setbacks when possible and minimizes their impact when they do occur.

Setback planning might involve identifying your particular vulnerabilities to old patterns, developing specific strategies for high-risk situations, creating support systems that can help you maintain perspective during difficult periods, or simply having reminders available that help you stay connected to your values and commitments.

David developed setback planning strategies for family gatherings where he typically felt pressure to resume his old role as family problem-solver and conflict mediator. "I would prepare specific responses for common scenarios, remind myself of my boundaries before attending events, and have plans for taking breaks or leaving early if the pressure became overwhelming," he said. "This preparation helped me maintain my transformation during situations that had previously triggered old patterns."

Handling setbacks with self-compassion also involves recognizing the difference between temporary lapses and fundamental abandonment of your transformation. Temporary lapses involve specific situations where you revert to old patterns but quickly recognize what's happening and choose to respond differently. Fundamental abandonment involves giving up on your transformation entirely and returning to chronic patterns of over-management.

This distinction is important because it helps you maintain perspective about the significance of setbacks and respond appropriately to different levels of challenge to your transformation. Most setbacks are temporary lapses that require gentle course correction rather than major intervention or complete reevaluation of your approach.

Teaching Others the Freedom Formula Without Managing Their Journey

One of the most advanced applications of living your freedom formula involves sharing what you've learned with others who are interested in similar transformation while maintaining appropriate boundaries about their growth process. This teaching requires applying the same principles of empowerment and respect for autonomy that characterize your other relationships, even when you're in a position of having knowledge or experience that others want to access.

The temptation when others ask about your transformation is often to slip back into management mode—trying to solve their relationship problems, directing their growth process, or taking responsibility for their success in implementing healthier patterns. However, teaching others effectively requires modeling the same trust in their capabilities and respect for their autonomy that you've developed in your other relationships.

Effective teaching of the freedom formula begins with what I call "experience sharing"—talking about your own journey, challenges, and learning rather than giving advice about what others should do or how they should approach their own transformation. This sharing provides information and inspiration while leaving others free to apply or ignore your experience based on their own judgment and circumstances.

Experience sharing might involve describing specific situations where you learned to maintain boundaries, challenges you faced in changing old patterns, benefits you've experienced from your transformation, or ongoing areas where you continue to grow and develop. The key is sharing your experience without implying that others should follow the same path or make the same choices.

Margaret found that experience sharing was much more effective than giving advice when friends and family members asked about the changes they observed in her life. "When I shared stories about my own journey rather than telling them what they should do, people seemed much more receptive and interested," she said. "They could take what resonated with them and leave what didn't fit their situation."

Teaching others also involves what I call "resource provision"—offering tools, information, and support that might be helpful while leaving others free to use or ignore these resources based on their own preferences and readiness. This provision respects others' autonomy while making useful information available to those who want it.

Resource provision might involve recommending books that were helpful in your own transformation, sharing information about therapists or coaches who understand boundary-setting processes, connecting others with support groups or communities focused on healthy relationship patterns, or simply being available to answer questions when others are ready to hear perspectives.

The key to effective resource provision is offering resources without attachment to whether others use them and without making others' utilization of resources a condition of your continued relationship or support. The goal is providing tools that might be helpful while maintaining respect for others' right to choose their own path and timing for growth.

Jennifer used resource provision when her sister expressed interest in developing better boundaries with their elderly parents. "Instead of trying to coach her through the process or solve her boundary problems for her, I shared some books that had been helpful to me and offered to listen if she wanted to talk about what she was learning," Jennifer said. "I let her know I was available for support but made it clear that her growth process was hers to direct."

Teaching others the freedom formula also involves what I call "modeling consistency"—continuing to demonstrate healthy relationship patterns in your interactions with people who are learning from your example, rather than reverting to old patterns of managing and directing when you're in a teaching role.

This consistency means applying the same empowering communication, boundary maintenance, and trust in others' capabilities to your teaching relationships that you apply to your other relationships. It means asking empowering questions rather than giving directive advice, expressing confidence in others' ability to figure out their own approach rather than anxiety about whether they're doing things correctly.

Modeling consistency is particularly important because people often learn more from observing how you treat them than from listening to what you say about healthy relationships. When you demonstrate respect for their autonomy and capability while sharing information about transformation, you provide a powerful example of what empowering relationships actually look like.

The most important aspect of teaching others without managing their journey involves maintaining what I call "outcome detachment"—caring about others' wellbeing and growth while not being attached to whether they successfully implement the changes you've found beneficial. This detachment allows you to be genuinely helpful without becoming invested in others' transformation in ways that recreate old patterns of over-responsibility.

Outcome detachment recognizes that others' growth process belongs to them, that they may choose different approaches or timelines than you would recommend, and that their success or failure in transformation doesn't reflect on your worth or the validity of your own changes. This detachment actually makes you more helpful because it allows you to support others' growth without the anxiety and pressure that often undermine effective teaching.

David learned the importance of outcome detachment when several colleagues expressed interest in the work-life balance strategies he had developed. "I had to resist the urge to monitor their progress or feel responsible for whether they successfully implemented healthier patterns," he said. "When I focused on sharing my experience without attachment to what they did with it, I could be much more helpful and supportive of whatever approach they chose."

Your Ongoing Evolution as a Free Person

Living your freedom formula is not a destination where growth stops, but rather a foundation for ongoing evolution and development throughout your life. This evolution involves continuing to deepen your understanding of healthy relationships, expanding your capacity for authentic living, and applying your principles to new challenges and opportunities as they arise.

Understanding transformation as an ongoing process rather than a completed achievement helps you maintain openness to continued learning and growth while appreciating the stability and progress you've already created. This perspective prevents both complacency about your current level of development and discouragement about areas where you continue to face challenges.

Ongoing evolution involves what I call "mastery deepening"—continuing to refine and sophisticate your skills in boundary-setting, empowering communication, emotional regulation, and authentic living even after these patterns have become relatively natural and automatic. This deepening involves applying your principles to increasingly complex situations and relationships.

Mastery deepening might involve learning to maintain your transformation during major life transitions like career changes or family restructuring, developing more nuanced skills for handling difficult people or situations, expanding your capacity to influence positive change in larger systems like organizations or communities, or simply continuing to grow in wisdom and perspective about human relationships and personal development.

Sarah experienced mastery deepening as she applied her transformation principles to new roles like becoming a grandmother and caring for aging parents. "The specific situations were different from what I had faced when my children were young, but the underlying principles of trusting others' capabilities and maintaining my own boundaries remained relevant," she said. "I found that I could apply what I had learned to new challenges while continuing to grow and develop."

Ongoing evolution also involves what I call "influence expansion"—gradually expanding the scope of your positive influence from your immediate relationships to broader circles of family, work, community, and social connection. This expansion occurs naturally as your transformation becomes more stable and you gain confidence in your ability to model healthy patterns in various contexts.

Influence expansion might involve taking leadership roles that allow you to model healthy organizational culture, becoming involved in community activities that promote empowering relationship dynamics, mentoring others who are interested in similar transformation, or simply continuing to demonstrate what authentic living looks like in an expanding range of relationships and situations.

This influence expansion is not about trying to change others or manage their growth, but about being so consistent in your authentic way of being that you naturally contribute to positive change in whatever environments you participate in. It represents the natural outcome of living your freedom formula consistently over time.

Another aspect of ongoing evolution involves what I call "wisdom integration"—using your experience and growth to develop an increasingly sophisticated understanding of human nature, relationship dynamics, and the conditions that support individual and collective flourishing. This wisdom allows you to navigate complex situations with greater ease and effectiveness while maintaining your commitment to healthy patterns.

Wisdom integration often involves understanding the deeper principles underlying specific techniques and strategies, developing intuitive sense about when different approaches are appropriate, and gaining perspective about the larger patterns and purposes that guide human growth and development.

Margaret described her experience of wisdom integration: "Over time, I stopped thinking so much about specific boundary techniques or communication strategies and started operating more from an intuitive understanding of what serves everyone's highest good in different situations. The principles had become so integrated into my way of being that I could trust my instincts about how to respond in new or complex situations."

Ongoing evolution also involves what I call "service expression"—finding ways to use your transformation and growing wisdom in service of others' wellbeing and growth, while maintaining appropriate boundaries about responsibility and outcome. This service represents the natural fruition of personal transformation—using what you've learned to contribute to positive change in the world.

Service expression might involve formal roles like coaching, teaching, or counseling, but it more often involves informal ways of contributing to others' growth through your presence, example, and availability for support when requested. It represents the natural overflow of your own fullness and authenticity rather than obligation or effort to fix others' problems.

The ultimate goal of ongoing evolution is what I call "integrated authenticity"—a way of being where your transformation principles are so deeply embodied that they require no conscious effort to maintain, where healthy boundaries and empowering relationships are simply your natural way of being, and where you contribute to others' growth and wellbeing through the power of your authentic presence rather than through management or intervention.

This integrated authenticity represents the full flowering of your freedom formula—not a perfect state without challenges, but a stable foundation of self-knowledge, healthy relationships, and authentic living from which you can continue growing and contributing throughout your life.

The Continuous Freedom Evolution Plan

Creating a framework for ongoing growth and development ensures that your transformation continues to evolve and deepen rather than becoming static or stagnant. The Continuous Freedom Evolution Plan provides structure for lifelong learning and development while maintaining the flexibility to adapt to changing circumstances and emerging opportunities for growth.

The plan begins with what I call "growth area identification"—regularly assessing areas where you want to continue developing your skills, understanding, or application of freedom principles. This assessment helps ensure that your growth remains intentional and directed rather than random or reactive to whatever challenges happen to arise.

Growth area identification might involve reflecting on relationships or situations where you still feel challenged to maintain your transformation, considering new applications of your principles to different areas of your life, identifying skills or knowledge that would enhance your ability to live authentically and maintain healthy relationships, or simply recognizing areas where you feel called to deeper development.

This identification process helps prevent stagnation by keeping you actively engaged in your own development while building on the foundation of stability and growth you've already created. It also helps ensure that your continued growth serves your authentic interests rather than just addressing external pressures or expectations.

The plan also includes "learning integration strategies"—systematic approaches for incorporating new insights, experiences, and knowledge into your ongoing practice of living authentically. These strategies help ensure that learning leads to meaningful change rather than just intellectual understanding without practical application.

Learning integration might involve regular reflection on new experiences and what they teach you about yourself and relationships, experimentation with new approaches or techniques that align with your growth goals, seeking out mentors or teachers who can support your continued development, or simply maintaining practices that help you stay open to learning and growth.

Patricia developed learning integration strategies that included quarterly reflection on her growth, annual goal-setting for areas she wanted to develop, and ongoing participation in communities focused on personal development and healthy relationships. "These strategies helped me continue growing in intentional ways rather than just hoping I would somehow keep developing," she said.

The plan includes "impact assessment"—regular evaluation of how your transformation is affecting not just your own life, but the lives of others and the broader systems you participate in. This assessment helps you understand the fuller significance of your growth and maintain motivation for continued development.

Impact assessment might involve noting changes in your relationships and how others respond to your transformed way of being, observing how your example influences family, workplace, or community dynamics, considering how your growth contributes to positive change in larger systems, or simply appreciating the ripple effects of living authentically and maintaining healthy boundaries.

This assessment helps you recognize that your personal transformation has significance beyond your own wellbeing and happiness—that it contributes to healing and positive change in ways that extend far beyond your immediate experience.

The evolution plan also includes "service integration"—finding ways to use your growing wisdom and experience in service of others' wellbeing while maintaining appropriate boundaries about responsibility and outcome. This integration represents the natural expression of your transformation as a contribution to collective growth and healing.

Service integration might involve formal volunteering or professional activities that utilize your skills and knowledge, informal mentoring or support of others who are interested in similar growth, participation in community or organizational leadership that models healthy relationship dynamics, or simply being available as a resource for others while maintaining clear boundaries about what you will and won't take responsibility for.

The final component involves "legacy consciousness"—developing awareness of how your transformation contributes to positive change that will outlast your own life and influence future generations. This consciousness provides perspective and motivation for continued growth while connecting your personal development to larger purposes and meanings.

Legacy consciousness might involve considering how your transformed way of being affects your children and their future relationships, thinking about how your example influences others to make positive changes in their own lives, recognizing how your contributions to healthy organizational or community culture will continue beyond your direct involvement, or simply appreciating how living authentically contributes to the overall healing and development of human consciousness.

David developed legacy consciousness through reflecting on how his transformation was affecting his children's approach to relationships and responsibility. "I began to see that learning to live authentically and maintain healthy boundaries wasn't just about my own happiness—it was about modeling possibilities for my children and contributing to healing patterns that had been problematic in my family for generations," he said.

Living your freedom formula ultimately means embodying the principles and practices you've learned so completely that they become your natural way of being rather than techniques you have to remember to apply. It means trusting yourself so deeply that you can navigate any situation while maintaining your integrity and authenticity. It means loving others so genuinely that your very presence contributes to their growth and wellbeing without any effort to manage or control their experience.

This embodiment represents not an end point, but a beginning—the foundation from which you can continue growing, contributing, and evolving throughout your life while maintaining the healthy boundaries and empowering relationships that make authentic living possible. It's the difference between practicing freedom and being free, between managing relationships and loving authentically, between trying to live well and naturally embodying wisdom and compassion in all your interactions.

When you're living your freedom formula, you discover that the greatest gift you can offer others is your own authentic presence—not your management of their problems, not your solutions to their challenges, not your worry about their choices, but simply your own embodiment of what's possible when someone chooses to live from their deepest truth while maintaining loving connection with others. This presence becomes a beacon of possibility that lights the way for others to discover their own freedom while honoring the interconnected nature of human life and relationship.

www.ingramcontent.com/pod-product-compliance
Lightning Source LLC
Chambersburg PA
CBHW020339010526
44119CB00048B/532